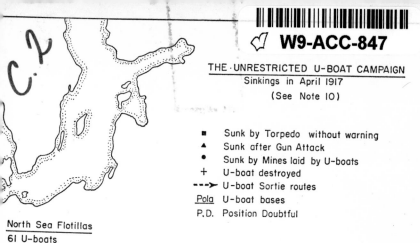

THE UNRESTRICTED U-BOAT CAMPAIGN
Sinkings in April 1917
(See Note 10)

- ■ Sunk by Torpedo without warning
- ▲ Sunk after Gun Attack
- ● Sunk by Mines laid by U-boats
- + U-boat destroyed
- ---> U-boat Sortie routes
- <u>Pola</u> U-boat bases
- P.D. Position Doubtful

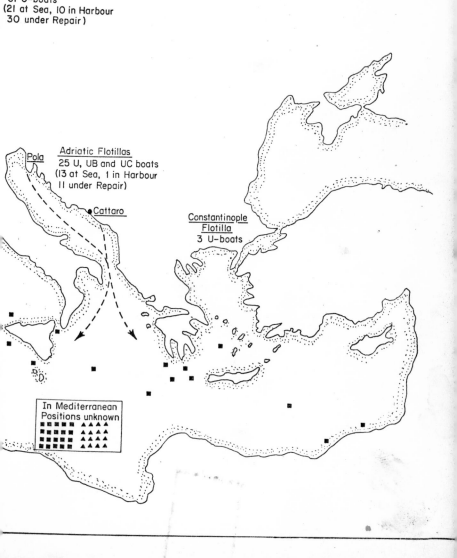

North Sea Flotillas
61 U-boats
(21 at Sea, 10 in Harbour
30 under Repair)

Adriatic Flotillas
25 U, UB and UC boats
(13 at Sea, 1 in Harbour
11 under Repair)

<u>Pola</u>

● Cattaro

Constantinople Flotilla
3 U-boats

In Mediterranean Positions unknown

THE SUB
AND
SEA POWER

THE SUBMARINE
AND
SEA POWER

Vice Admiral Sir Arthur Hezlet
K.B.E., C.B., D.S.O., D.S.C.

STEIN AND DAY/*Publishers*/New York

Printed in Great Britain
Stein and Day/*Publishers*/7 East 48 Street,
New York, N.Y. 10017

CONTENTS

ILLUSTRATIONS

Preface

Since the Second World War, the importance of the submarine as a warship has increased immeasurably and its future influence is of exceptional interest. Although most of this book deals with the past, it is believed that it is from such a study that a clearer picture of the future can be obtained. The book is an attempt to trace the evolution and history of the submarine to show what its effect has been on the command of the sea and on war generally. This is a large subject and in the space available it is not possible to deal with more than the broader issues. It is therefore a book about submarine campaigns rather than exploits and submarine 'aces' who expect to see their names in print will be disappointed; to avoid being invidious no individual submarine captain's names are mentioned at all. The history cannot be complete in this one volume and not every action in which submarines have taken part can be mentioned. The book deals with naval policies and strategies: why and for what purposes submarines were and are being built and an analysis of their problems, successes, failures and possibilities.

Most of the material is taken from published sources and no very new facts will come to light. It is hoped, however, that the presentation of the facts and the comment upon them will be new as well as the inclusion in one volume of the whole history on an international scale.

My thanks are due to the publishers who commissioned this book and without whose prompting I doubt if the thoughts behind it would have appeared in print. My thanks are also due to Dr J. S. N. Sewell, who has criticized and commented upon the drafts and who has greatly improved them. The staffs of the Admiralty Library and the Library of the Royal United Services Institution have invariably been most courteous and helpful and have my gratitude.

Bovagh House, Aghadowey,
Co. Londonderry, Northern Ireland.
31 March 1966.

I

The Evolution of the
Submarine as a Ship of War

It has been recognized from the earliest times that, by diving beneath the surface of the sea, a warship can become invisible. It is this advantage above all that has spurred on inventors, to whom the physical principles of submersion have been available since Archimedes laid them down in the third century B.C. Indeed, even before Archimedes made his experiments, Alexander the Great is reputed to have used some form of submersible vessel during the siege of Tyre in 332 B.C.

It was not however until the sixteenth century that actual details of inventions for descending into the sea began to be recorded. By this time the gun had become the arbiter of sea power, and submersion offered the added advantage that it could provide a complete protection against it. In the two hundred years from 1578 to 1763 there are records of no less than seventeen submarine inventions. Some of these, it is true, were intended for peaceable uses, such as recovering goods from shipwrecks, but over half had some military purpose. However these vessels had not the slightest influence on or indeed use in naval warfare, mainly because they did not work and were of more danger to their crews than to the enemy. The technical problems to be solved were far too great for the means at the inventors' disposal. To try to compete with the immense pressure of the sea with wood, greased leather and hand power was asking a great deal too much. The most successful inventor was probably Cornelius van Drebbel who built several submersible boats between 1620 and 1630. Although nominally he navigated submerged in the Thames, propelled by twelve rowers, it is doubtful if he did more than wallow between the surface and a few feet below it whilst drifting with the tide. James I is believed to have encouraged van Drebbel, but there is no indication that he did this with any military purpose in mind but rather to further what he thought was an interesting scientific experiment.

1

In 1775, a young American engineer named Bushnell made some practical experiments in which he proved that gunpowder could be exploded under water and would cause considerable damage to a ship's bottom. He can therefore claim to be the father of the underwater weapon which gave to the submarine for the first time a ship-killing armament. He then produced his famous submarine, the *Turtle*, which was the first to be built with a metal hull (see p. 6; fig. 1). This seems to have been shaped rather like a modern navigational buoy with a crew of one man who was able to see out through glass scuttles round the top. With these glass scuttles just above the surface he could manœuvre the craft with propellers alongside a ship and then by flooding a tank submerge it under her bottom. A heavy charge of gunpowder would then be attached by screwing it into the wooden hull and firing it with a time fuse. The craft could remain submerged only for half an hour or so or the operator would be suffocated and, as it was propelled by hand, it could go only a few hundred yards before he was exhausted. Bushnell, as well as having the inclination to design submarines, had an incentive. His country was being blockaded by the British during the War of American Independence, which was causing some hardship. The *Turtle* seemed to offer a way to attack the blockading ships, which were so bold as to anchor in their enemy's harbours. On a night in July 1776, she attacked H.M.S. *Eagle*, a 64-gun ship of the line, lying at anchor off Staten Island in New York harbour. The *Turtle* had to be towed to a position up tide of the *Eagle* by two rowing boats. Although she manœuvred successfully into position, the attack failed because the ship was coppered and the screw which was to attach the charge would not penetrate it. The *Turtle*, however, escaped and was used on two other occasions in the Hudson River, but also without success. All Bushnell's attempts therefore failed and, although he deserves the credit for the first use of a submarine in war, he certainly did not break the blockade. The most that can be claimed is that he inconvenienced the blockading ships by forcing them to keep a better lookout and to lie farther out to sea.

Some twenty years elapsed before another American, the famous engineer Fulton, designed another submarine. America was not at war at the time and had no need of it. He therefore attempted to sell his design in a number of European countries. In 1800 he was granted a sum of money by Napoleon which enabled him to build the *Nautilus* in Paris (see Figure 1). The *Nautilus* was very much more mobile than the *Turtle* and had a crew of three. The hull was cigar-shaped, propelled by hand when submerged but using a small collapsible mast and sail on the surface. The trials of the *Nautilus* in 1801 were very successful and Fulton succeeded in blowing up a hulk put at his disposal by the French government. The *Nautilus* had a longer endurance than the *Turtle* and on one occasion her crew remained submerged in her for no less than five hours. She would undoubtedly have been able to sortie from a port in good weather and attack the ships of a blockading fleet in the offing. When it came to the point, however, the French lost their nerve and refused to embark on such a method of warfare which they considered dishonourable. The stumbling-block in their agreement with Fulton was his status as a combatant, without which he feared he would be hanged as a pirate if he fell into the hands of the British.

In 1804 Fulton brought his ideas to England. Here his inventions were examined by a committee of which Pitt was a member. The most interesting part of this visit lies in the famous policy statement made by Earl St. Vincent, then First Lord of the Admiralty. He said: 'Pitt is the greatest fool that ever existed to encourage a mode of war which those who command the sea do not want and which if successful will deprive them of it'. This statement was to be the basis of British policy for nearly a hundred years.

Fulton's submarine was never put to the test in war. His claims that it could raise the blockade of France and, in its turn, blockade the Thames and cut off the trade of London were nothing less than fantastic. If built in quantity and well handled they would no doubt have sunk a few ships and made the maintenance of a close blockade dangerous. The blockade, which was in any case not a very close one, would still have been effective and it is very doubtful whether they would have made any difference to the main strategy of the war.

During the next fifty years French and American inventors produced a steady stream of submarine designs. The purpose of these vessels was generally military but some were for salvage or other civil activity such as building a breakwater. None of them proved to be of any particular merit and, while testing, a number of the inventors were drowned. Only the French government sustained an interest, although in America there was another operation by a submarine of the Bushnell type in the war of 1812, when an unsuccessful attack is recorded upon H.M.S. *Ramillies* off New London, Connecticut.

In 1850 in the war between Germany and Denmark, the superior Danish Navy was able to blockade the north German ports. A corporal called Bauer in the German Army designed a submarine which was built at Kiel out of army funds. The submarine was similar to the *Nautilus* in that it had a metal hull, was propelled by hand and armed with a mine to be fixed to a ship's bottom. It was not a great success and made only one short sortie. This was nevertheless enough to force the Danish blockading ships out into a more distant position although, as before, it could not claim to have broken the blockade. The *Plongeur Marin*, as this submarine was called, was subsequently lost by accident and Wilhelm Bauer received no further encouragement from his countrymen.

Bauer, like Fulton, went abroad with his designs, one of which he built and sold to the Russian government. Although he made several improvements in submarine design, his vessels were not in fact a very great advance over those of Bushnell or Fulton. Bauer also made a trip to England and was encouraged by Scott Russell, the designer of the famous ironclad *Warrior*. Subsequently, during the Crimean War, Scott Russell used Bauer's ideas to design a submersible vessel to help in the attack on Sebastopol. A sum of £7,000 was allowed by the government on Lord Palmerston's advice, but the project was a complete failure and an expensive one in money and lives. Perhaps this sole departure during the century from the policy of Lord St. Vincent can be excused because of its extremely limited object, which was to assist in an attack on a fortress and not to contest the general command of the sea.

The submarine's greatest limitation up to this time was that it was still propelled by hand when submerged. A submarine, if it was to dive at all, had to be heavy and to propel it with the few men that could be got inside it was hard work and used up the available air very quickly. The crew were invariably exhausted after a few miles. By the middle of the century, the advance in engineering began to offer to inventors a hope of mechanical propulsion. Steam was by now well developed but no way could be seen to use it submerged. Electricity was still in too early a stage for practical application. A remarkable submarine, *Le Plongeur*, of 420 tons propelled by compressed air was built at Rochefort in 1863. However on trials its endurance was found to be only a few miles at slow speed and, as it also had great difficulty with its longitudinal stability and control, it proved a failure.

The other weakness of the submarine was its armament. The invention of the spar torpedo, which was simply a large bomb run out ahead of the ship on a spar, held out the hope that the submarine could be developed to attack ships on the move. Theory was however still ahead of practice and, in spite of the advance of science and the encouragement of the French and American governments, no inventor produced a practicable submarine before the outbreak of the American Civil War.

In the American Civil War the familiar pattern of a superior fleet blockading a weaker belligerent at sea was repeated. The need for the Southern States to find some way to break the blockade was as great as ever. The Confederates therefore set to work to design some weapon for this purpose. The need for some kind of underwater vessel was strengthened by the advent of the ironclad. Ironclads were able to sink any wooden ship with ease and, for a short space until the invention of the armour-piercing gun, reigned supreme. Some method to compete with the ironclad was a very great necessity and attacking it 'below the belt' was an attractive solution. The vessels (see Note 1) that were evolved by the South to meet these needs were not really submarines in the strict sense of the word. They were submersibles which steamed along just under the surface of the water with the upper part of them awash. They were all armed with the spar torpedo which, although very effective against the enemy, was often suicidal.

In all, four attacks were made on ships of the Federal blockading squadrons, the first being against the ironclad *Ironsides* off Charleston on 5 October 1863. In this attack a steam-propelled submersible managed to explode its torpedo close alongside but it was set too shallow and probably not quite in contact and so only damaged the ship (see p. 6; fig. 1). A second attack four

5

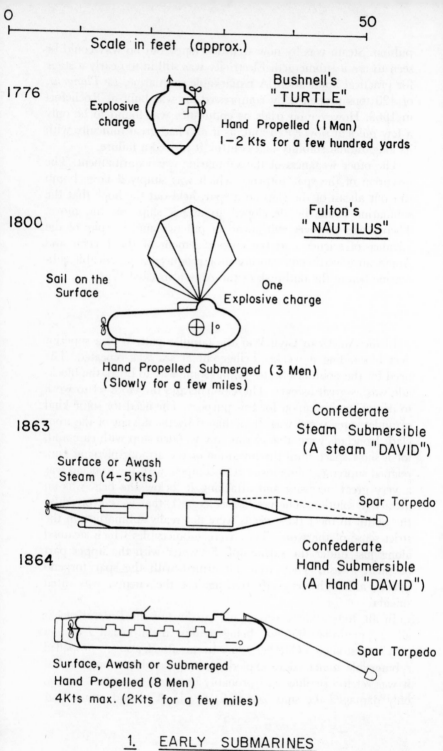

0   50

Scale in feet (approx.)

1776

Bushnell's
"TURTLE"

Explosive charge

Hand Propelled (1 Man)
1—2 Kts for a few hundred yards

1800

Fulton's
"NAUTILUS"

Sail on the Surface

One Explosive charge

⊕ 1°

Hand Propelled Submerged (3 Men)
(Slowly for a few miles)

1863

Confederate
Steam Submersible
(A steam "DAVID")

Surface or Awash
Steam (4-5 Kts)

Spar Torpedo

1864

Confederate
Hand Submersible
(A Hand "DAVID")

Spar Torpedo

Surface, Awash or Submerged
Hand Propelled (8 Men)
4Kts max. (2Kts for a few miles)

1.   EARLY SUBMARINES

months later was more successful. This was by one of the hand-propelled submersibles with a crew of eight men and a coxswain. This particular vessel had sunk four times on trials, drowning several crews. Although it was capable of submerging completely, the crew preferred to run awash with the hatches open when they were able with great exertions to reach 4 knots. On the night of 17 February 1864 they attacked the new screw-sloop *Housatonic* of 13 guns which was anchored just outside the bar. Although sighted during their approach, they were too close for any effective counter measures and the spar torpedo was exploded in the *Housatonic's* engine room. Both ships sank with the loss of the whole crew of the submersible.

Submarine warfare had now taken a firm step forward : it had sunk a surface warship, although we must add in parenthesis that it had committed suicide in doing so. Out of four attacks during the war, the 'bag' was one new steam wooden sloop sunk and an ironclad and another steamer damaged for the loss of one submersible. These attacks were all made at night against ships at anchor whose crews were alert to the danger and ready to take counter measures. The total number of submersibles built is not recorded but nine were found at Charleston alone on its capture. However we are forced to admit that the general strategic effect was little greater than that achieved by Bushnell. These submersibles, even the steam variety, could not go very far and had poor sea-keeping qualities. They stood little chance unless the target ship was stopped or at anchor. They failed therefore to break the blockade although, as Bushnell had done before them, they inconvenienced and endangered the blockading ships. Nevertheless these operations of the Civil War are of great interest and are the first application of the submarine in numbers by a belligerent. Bushnell, Fulton and Bauer were individuals who produced their 'inventions' by private enterprise. The Confederates were the first government to build up a force of submersible torpedo boats as an act of naval policy.

In the decade following the American Civil War, inventors continued to design submarines, some very ingenious but mostly impracticable and failures. But by far the most important development for the submarine in this period was the Whitehead locomotive torpedo. Although not designed specifically as an armament for submarines, it gave them the weapon which was to lead to their ultimate success as warships. Although the Whitehead was still very slow and of short range, it gave the submarine the power to attack ships at sea and without the risk of suicide. Oddly enough it was not until 1879, ten years after the torpedo had become a practicable proposition, that it was actually included as the armament in the design of a submarine.

From 1875 onwards a number of competent inventors with sufficient resources to persevere set to work to design submarines. Holland in America, Drzweicki in Russia and Garrett in England produced a series of designs which, although at first little superior to Fulton's *Nautilus*, steadily improved with each succeeding type. Government interest continued in America, France and Russia but discouragement remained the policy in Great Britain. In 1872 the United States Government had actually accepted a submarine known as the 'Intelligent Whale' but it was lost on trials. In 1879, the Russian government ordered no less than fifty of Drzweicki's submarines for coast defence although they were so small that they could not have been expected to go far outside the harbour entrances. No doubt the memory of the Crimean War, in which the British and French fleets had complete command of the sea and had operated in the immediate vicinity of the Russian ports, prompted this policy. This was the first large-scale investment by a government in the submarine in peacetime but, although many were built, the project seems to have faded within a few years.

In parallel with the advent of the Whitehead torpedo, inventors' hopes for power for submerged propulsion now began to be realized. Electric accumulators and motors of sufficient reliability to propel a submarine became available. This system, being independent of the atmosphere and a far more compact way to store energy than compressed air, offered the submarine submerged mobility fifty times greater than could be achieved by hand power. Garratt produced an alternative by using steam both on the surface and submerged. With the relatively high steam pressures then available, he found it possible to extinguish the furnaces and dive with a full head of steam in the boiler which he used to propel the submarine for a surprising distance submerged (see Note 2). Although this did not give such a good performance as electric propulsion, it had the merit that the same set of engines could do much better on the surface.

Submarine design was at this time being approached from two directions. There were the successors of Bushnell, Fulton and Bauer who were trying to produce a vessel to operate totally and continuously submerged. They realized that the prime need was invisibility and stealth and so produced fish-shaped hulls and preferred electric propulsion so as to obtain the best submerged performance. The rival school stemmed from the submersible torpedo boats of the American Civil War and were more interested in submersion as a protection against the enemy's gunfire. They wanted a surface performance under steam as good as a surface torpedo boat, and were satisfied with a short endurance submerged which they needed only to make the final attack. Both schools recognized that the Whitehead torpedo was the best armament but these differing concepts led to somewhat different designs.

The decade of the 1880s was a prolific one for submarine designs: there are records of no less than forty-two separate projects, fifteen of which actually led to the construction of a submarine. In spite of the official policy of discouraging the submarine, the British in fact led the world during this period. Garratt lost his boat, the *Resurgam*, off the Welsh coast but his designs were a considerable achievement and he led the submersible torpedo boat school. Supported by the Swedish industrialist Nordenfelt, he designed and built four more submersibles, the first of which was built in Sweden and was sold to the Greek government in 1886. It was by no means perfect and had the greatest difficulty in controlling itself submerged: so much so that it seems to have been used mainly as a surface torpedo boat. The Turks promptly ordered two slightly larger vessels of the same type which were built at Chertsey and delivered to them in 1887 (see p. 14; fig. 2). They were also difficult to control and the Turkish Navy was unable to maintain or operate them efficiently. Nevertheless they remained on their Navy List until 1910. In 1886 Campbell and Ash completed their 50-ton *Nautilus,* which was the first large electrically-powered submarine, in which they hoped to make 6 knots for eighty miles or so. This submarine had many faults and in its early trials Sir William White, the Director of Naval Construction, was stuck in it at the bottom of the London docks for an anxious period, which did nothing to alter the prejudice of the Admiralty against the submarine. In Parliament and Press this boat was ridiculed and we hear no more of it, although it seems in fact to have been better than anything being produced in

9

any other country. Also in England, Waddington built his *Porpoise*, another electrically-propelled submarine which claimed a higher speed and longer range. It was however a much smaller vessel intended to be carried on board larger ships; although moderately successful it did not find a market. With the sale of Garratt's last submarine, the *Nordenfelt*, to Russia in1889, British enterprise dried up. There seemed no hope whatever of selling submarines to the Royal Navy. The British policy of discouragement, although short-sighted, is easy to understand. They already had the largest navy in the world and were at this time rebuilding it, under the Naval Defence Acts, to ensure that they could command the sea against all comers. They needed no assistance from the submarine to do this and had very much to fear from it. They believed that there was still a good chance, provided they stuck to their policy, that the submarine would never develop into an effective warship.

In France the attitude was very different : strategically her position has always been a difficult one. France's need to be a major land power has always clashed with her interests at sea. To keep an army large enough to secure her frontiers as well as a navy able to compete with any maritime threat has generally been beyond her means. After the war of 1870 with Germany, it was natural that the army should take first place and the navy should suffer. Although the French accepted the need for a small battlefleet for fighting second or third class sea powers such as Germany, Austria or Italy, they realized that they had not a hope of building one large enough to compete with Great Britain. It was therefore very important they they should try to find some other way to wage war at sea which was cheaper than building up a large rival battlefleet. The strategy of the *guerre de course* (see Note 3) had therefore been devised in which fast cruisers were to prey upon British trade and the French fleet was not to seek action with the British but remain 'in being'. It would then at least prevent the British battlefleet from being dispersed to protect commerce. There was, however, a gap in this strategy. If the British could maintain a close blockade of the coastline of France, they could land troops or bombard it at will and probably make it very difficult for the cruisers to sortie and attack trade. An

10

inferior French battlefleet could not prevent such counter moves without risk of defeat in a general action.

Admiral Aube, the French Minister of Marine in 1886, therefore decided to develop the submarine and in this he was opposed by all his experts. In this way he hoped to produce a defence which would prevent a close blockade or an attack on the coast. He ordered a small submarine of about 5 tons from M. Goubet, and shortly afterwards another of 30 tons to the design of M. Gustave Zédé. Both were driven by electric batteries and armed with the Whitehead torpedo. The Goubet boat did not meet its specification and was rejected. The other, the *Gymnote*, was a success and showed for the first time that it was possible to run submerged at a steady depth. A much larger boat, the *Gustave Zédé* (see p. 14; fig. 2) of 260 tons, was at once ordered, but it was recognized that the jump in tonnage was somewhat ambitious, so an intermediate vessel, the *Morse*, was also put in hand. The *Gustave Zédé* was at first a dismal failure, being unable to keep her depth and suffering more than one battery explosion. But by perseverance over a number of years, she was made into a very satisfactory submarine. To the French, therefore, goes the credit for being the first country to put the resources of the state into the systematic development of the submarine to meet a definite strategic need.

In Spain the electric battery type of submarine armed with the Whitehead torpedo was developed simultaneously and quite independently of the French to the design of M. Peral. The *Peral* was launched in 1887 and was proclaimed a success at her trials. Although she proved to be of extremely short endurance and not too steady at keeping her depth, she succeeded in torpedoing and blowing up a hulk at the end of her trial period. Iberian lethargy and want of funds prevented further development and the *Peral* remained the only submarine in the Spanish Navy for well over a decade. Throughout the Hispano-American War of 1898, she remained in Cadiz and had no influence whatever on the conflict. If the Spaniards had developed submarines and built them in quantity, which they had the technical ability and means to do, there is no doubt that the war would have gone differently. Admiral Dewey was later to give his views about the effect that submarines might have had on the defence of Manila. Certainly Admiral Sampson could not have blockaded Cervera at Santiago, lying stopped with fires banked just off the harbour entrance.

11

In America, the true home of the submarine, a number of private designers persevered throughout the eighties. Baker's and Tuck's submarines were only partly successful but Holland began to make real progress. At the end of this period, Mr Whitney, the Secretary for the Navy, organized a competition for the design of a submarine torpedo boat. His reason for doing so was tactical. He believed the quick-firing gun had become so effective that attacks by surface torpedo boats were no longer possible. As it was out of the question to armour torpedo boats, the only way to compete with the quick-firing gun seemed to be to submerge. The principal entrants for the competition were Holland, Baker and Nordenfelt. In America the electrically-propelled submarine was thought to be of too limited endurance for practical purposes, but Holland's early experiments with a gasoline engine using compressed air to run it submerged gave no better results. In America, therefore, it was considered necessary to have two complete propulsion systems in the submarine, steam for the surface and electricity when submerged. This idea was not new; it had been suggested in a submarine design produced in America as early as 1863. Although it combined the good points of both the Nordenfelt submersibles and the French battery-driven submarines, the need to divide the available weight and space between two propulsion systems meant that both would have an inferior performance. But as the steam plant could now be used to recharge the electric battery at sea, its smaller size was more than compensated for. It was the Holland design, propelled by a steam-electric system and armed with the Whitehead torpedo, which was finally accepted for the American Navy. Various delays meant that their first submarine, the *Plunger*, was not in fact laid down until 1897.

The Germans built two vessels of the Nordenfelt type in 1890. They were not at all satisfied with their performance when they took part in the manœuvres of 1892. Their failure and the coming to power of Admiral von Tirpitz held back any further submarine design in Germany, except for one or two private ventures, for a period of over ten years. The reason given by Tirpitz is that he did not wish to supply anything for the German Navy that was not fully developed and proved, and the submarine was certainly not yet in this category. At the same time he emphasized that the geography of the German coast with its shallow water meant that submarines were not suitable for its defence. The real reason was however probably more profound. Tirpitz was trying at this time to build up the German fleet into an ocean-going navy with a powerful battlefleet, and clearly he wanted no rivals to this policy. A submarine force would be much cheaper and, if it could be shown to be capable of defending the homeland, might well have been preferred by the Reichstag. In these circumstances it is understandable that Tirpitz played down submarine development in Germany.

In 1896 the French Minister of Marine organized a competition for much the same reasons as Mr Whitney had done in America. He required a submersible which could operate on the surface as a second-class torpedo boat but be able to complete its attack submerged. No less than 29 designs were sent in, many of considerable merit, the competition being won by M. Laubeuf with his design for the *Narval* (see p. 14; fig. 2). The *Narval*, which was immediately put in hand, had, like the *Plunger*, a dual propulsion system using steam and electricity. She had a complete double hull, the inner being of submarine shape and the outer similar to that of a torpedo boat. Her endurance was far greater than that of the *Gustave Zédé* and enabled her to operate anywhere in the Channel, but she had the great disadvantage that she took twenty minutes to dive and was almost uninhabitable submerged because of the heat of the boiler.

The *Gustave Zédé* had meanwhile, in 1898, proved in manœuvres that she could torpedo battleships both in harbour and at sea. In these trials the *Gustave Zédé* used the battleship *Magenta* as target. She had no periscope and had to break surface from time to time to allow the captain to look out of the conning-tower scuttles. The conning-tower was clearly seen from the battleship but it was generally agreed that it was visible for so short a time and was so small that it was unlikely to be hit by quick-firing guns. The *Gustave Zédé* had also demonstrated her mobility by making the voyage under her own power from Toulon to Marseilles, a distance of forty-one miles. Her battery endurance was enough to patrol all day within a radius of thirty miles from a port and this type of submarine would clearly be extremely valuable for defence. These trials caused a wave of enthusiasm in France. The French were now sure that they had in the submarine a practicable and useful warship and started to order both the *Narval*, or submersible type, and the *Gustave Zédé*, or sousmarin type, in quantity.

In America, however, Mr Holland lost faith in his design for

13

0   50   100

Scale in feet

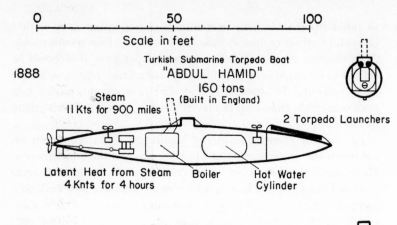

Turkish Submarine Torpedo Boat

1888   "ABDUL HAMID"
        160 tons
       (Built in England)

Steam
11 Kts for 900 miles

2 Torpedo Launchers

Latent Heat from Steam Boiler Hot Water
4 Knts for 4 hours   Cylinder

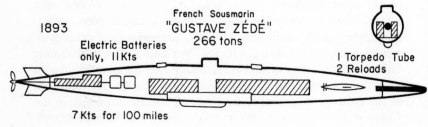

French Sousmarin

1893   "GUSTAVE ZÉDÉ"
      266 tons

Electric Batteries
only, 11 Kts

1 Torpedo Tube
2 Reloads

7 Kts for 100 miles

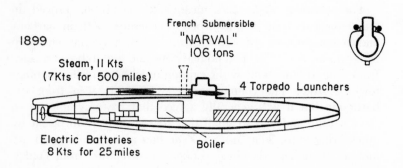

French Submersible

1899   "NARVAL"
     106 tons

Steam, 11 Kts
(7 Kts for 500 miles)

4 Torpedo Launchers

Electric Batteries
8 Kts for 25 miles Boiler

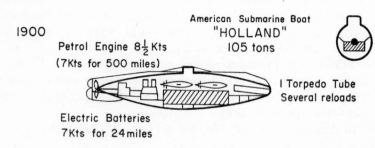

American Submarine Boat

1900   "HOLLAND"
     105 tons

Petrol Engine 8½ Kts
(7 Kts for 500 miles)

1 Torpedo Tube
Several reloads

Electric Batteries
7 Kts for 24 miles

2. SUBMARINES AT THE TURN OF THE CENTURY

the *Plunger*, mainly because of the heat generated by the steam plant after diving, and she was never completed. With the agreement of the U.S. Navy he substituted at his own expense the *Holland*, a new design which was undoubtedly the most successful submarine that had yet been produced (see Figure 2). She had a dual propulsion system but instead of steam for use on the surface, she had a gasoline internal-combustion engine. She was not finally accepted by the navy until after the Hispano-American war was over and so missed the chance to prove herself on active service.

By 1900 six navies owned a total of ten submarines with another eleven under construction. France was well in the lead with a total of fourteen built and building. The U.S.A. had two, one of which was probably the most advanced submarine in the world. Italy, Spain and Portugal had one experimental vessel each and Turkey still kept her two old Nordenfelt boats. The combination of a metal hull, to withstand the great pressure of the sea, with an electric propulsion system which was independent of the atmosphere for use submerged, had made submarine navigation possible. Being armed with the Whitehead torpedo, which it could carry unobserved to effective range, made a submarine capable of sinking even a battleship. Steam power or, better still, internal-combustion engines, promised a seagoing endurance. By the turn of the century, therefore, the submarine after over a hundred years of development was accepted as a warship with a future.

II

The Development of the
Submarine up to the First World War

The turn of the century saw a great increase in submarine construction among the major naval powers. In 1899 the French produced a plan for rebuilding their fleet, and this included thirty-eight submarines as an integral part of it. In the 1901 estimates, therefore, they made provision for the twenty-three submarines required to build up to this number from the fourteen or so which they already possessed. These were all of the short range but reliable sousmarin type as opposed to the experimental submersibles.

In the 1901 manœuvres, the sousmarin *Gustave Zédé* made her famous attack on the French Mediterranean fleet leaving Ajaccio and 'torpedoed' the battleship *Charles Martel*. The *Gustave Zédé* had come from Toulon under her own power and the attack was a complete surprise. The problem of defence against submarines was now seen in a new light. The issue was not whether quick-firing guns could hit a porpoising conning-tower but whether a ship would know that she was being attacked at all. The *Gustave Zédé* had operated at the extreme limit of her range with a tug standing by, but this distance would have been well within the endurance of a submersible of the *Narval* type.

During the war of 1898 with Spain the U.S. Navy had been handicapped by the demands of the populace for defence round the coasts. Many old monitors from the scrap list had to be commissioned to satisfy public opinion and the movements of the main fleet were inhibited. The submarine now seemed to offer a cheap and effective way to provide a coast defence which would free the battlefleet for proper maritime operations. A case was made to Congress for twenty submarines for the defence of New York, Long Island Sound, the Delaware and Chesapeake Bays, San Francisco and other places, and as a first instalment, six improved Holland submarines were ordered in 1900.

Throughout the nineties all commercial building of submarines

16

in Great Britain had ceased, but the Admiralty had watched their development in France and America with anxiety and fervently hoped that they would be found impracticable. They were at pains to explain to Press and Parliament that the submarine was of use only to weaker naval powers and that it was anti-submarine measures which were important to stronger naval powers. The submarine moreover was not a counter to the submarine so there was little point in building them. In 1901 the British were somewhat shaken by the size of the French submarine construction programme and it was clear to them that the policy of St. Vincent had failed. The submarine had become an effective warship in spite of British discouragement and the time had come for a change of policy. The Admiralty soon found that they could not devise effective counter measures unless they knew more about submarines than they could gain from intelligence. In other words they realized that they could not counter the submarine unless they had submarines themselves and so the decision was made to acquire a few of them. The Admiralty's discouragement of the submarine now meant that there were no British designs available and they had to go abroad to obtain them. Fortunately for them the U.S. Government permitted Mr Holland to supply his latest drawings and five boats were laid down, using American patents, in Great Britain.

In Germany, Admiral von Tirpitz still refused to believe that the submarine was a practicable weapon of war. In particular the German Navy objected to the use of steam or petrol for propulsion and their objections had some substance. Nevertheless they saw that if submarines could be developed for use offensively they would be of considerable value especially against Great Britain. They therefore put in hand experiments with heavy-oil engines which they rightly saw were the key to the future development of the submarine.

From 1903 onwards, after the trials of the new submersible *Aigrette* against the experimental sousmarin *Z*, the French decided to go entirely for submersibles in the future. The submersible was gradually enlarged to give it greater speed, seakeeping capacity, habitability and endurance. Their early attempts to propel submersibles with internal-combustion engines were, however, a failure and they had to revert to steam for the majority of their boats.

Although the French had always stressed that the submersible

17

could be used offensively, this was really only a relative term. It certainly had a much greater radius of action than the sousmarin type which was tied to within thirty miles of its base. It is clear from the manœuvres in the early years of the century, however, that the French use for their submersibles was defensive in a strategic sense. Their role was to defend the coast in co-operation with other forces including their battlefleet and torpedo boat flotillas. In other words, submersibles extended submarine defence from the vicinity of ports to the whole coast line. Both submersibles and sousmarins were soon fitted with periscopes with the result that they were seldom seen and their attacks came as a complete surprise. Successes in manœuvres became more frequent and in 1906 French submarines scored a major 'victory' in the Mediterranean by 'torpedoing' twenty-one ships whilst defending Toulon, Marseilles and Bizerta. By now the French had established submarine flotillas for the defence of Rochefort and Dunkirk, as well as Toulon and Cherbourg, and several boats had been transported to Bizerta and Saigon. The French were now reasonably confident that the purpose for which they had developed the submarine had been achieved. They believed that they would make it impossible for enemy battleships to approach their coasts or for transports to land troops.

Once the British had decided to add submarines to their navy, they spared no expense in their development. The Admiralty, although still not enamoured of them, allowed the Inspecting Captain of Submarine Boats a free hand. This officer set to work to improve and enlarge the Holland type, and to give it better seakeeping qualities. All the essentials of the Holland design, however, remained unchanged, except its size, and when the *B.1* was launched she was already larger than most of the French submersibles (see p. 22; fig. 3).

The arrival of Sir John Fisher as First Sea Lord in 1904 brought about a second and important change in British policy. He saw that the submarine was not only the weapon of the weaker power but could be of value to the stronger power too. He decided straight away that it could replace all the controlled minefields at naval ports and provide an extended defence well beyond the range of the shore batteries. With the increase in the size of the submarine it also became possible, in the same way as for the French, to link up the port defences and defend considerable sea areas. A co-ordinated plan was produced for surface

18

torpedo boats to continue to defend these areas by night and sub-marines, which promised to be much more effective, to take over by day. By 1907 the war plans gave to the smaller submarines of the Holland and A classes the duty of defending the home ports whilst the larger B class were to be stationed at Dover with the more important role of defending the Straits. An average of ten submarines a year was built in Great Britain and flotillas were formed at Devonport, Harwich and Dundee, as well as at Ports-mouth. A plan was produced to use them in the North Sea as a defence all the way down the east coast. British policy had now therefore been extended from the possession of submarines as an aid to the development of counter measures, to a requirement for them for base and coast defence.

The technical development of the submarine soon made more extensive operation possible. In the British C class the ultimate development of the original Holland type seemed to have been reached and, if any further progress was to be made in endurance, seakeeping qualities and habitability, some radical redesign was essential. The D class was the result; its size was increased to 500 tons and it was given twin screws driven on the surface by the new diesel engines (see p. 22; fig. 3). It had a new hull-form with external main ballast tanks to give it a high buoyancy like the French submersibles. *D.1*, the first of this class, was technically a considerable success, indeed this basic type was to last for forty years and fight two world wars. Not only was her endurance double that of the C class but the elimination of petrol made her safer and the twin screws more reliable. Furthermore she had the battery capacity to remain submerged for the whole of daylight hours. It was clear that these characteristics made offensive opera-tions possible. Although she was not specifically designed for this purpose, such a role had never been far from Sir John Fisher's thoughts. Indeed in the 1907 war orders, one plan visualized a British battlefleet entering the Baltic : the B class were to go with it and operate offensively against Kiel from the Danish Islands.

As a result of manœuvres in France as well as in Great Britain it was evident by 1908 that the submarine was now for the first time to have a significant effect on the conduct of naval warfare. Its ability to extend the defence of bases well beyond the range of shore batteries and to deny whole coastal areas to an enemy battlefleet finally made the old-fashioned close blockade impossible. For Great Britain this was strategically a disadvantage: it would be harder to command the sea if she were not able to impose a close blockade on an enemy. There were many, however, who saw that an offensive use of submarines could do much to replace a close blockade and that this function was more important to Great Britain than to use submarines for defence. In *D.1* they had the means to implement this policy. She was not only able to reach the enemy coasts but could operate in the face of opposition by remaining submerged by day, only surfacing at night to recharge her batteries. Her capabilities were well demonstrated in the 1910 manœuvres. In these she was attached, not to the defensive submarine force of the weaker side, but as an offensive submarine belonging to the stronger fleet. She went on her own from Portsmouth to the west coast of Scotland and there 'torpedoed' two of the opposing cruisers (see Note 4). This exploit made a great impression at the time and convinced many former doubters of the offensive possibilities of the submarine. From now on Great Britain built the 'overseas' or offensive type of submarine similar to *D.1* in preference to the smaller coastal or defensive type.

In Germany the Korting heavy-oil engine had been developed by 1905 and the Imperial Navy now had no technical objection to the submarine. The Germans built their first boat during 1906; it was actually smaller than the British C boats and was not an unqualified success. Their second submarine was not completed until 1908 but from 1907 onwards they embarked on a programme of large 'overseas' submarines similar to the British *D.1*. In 1912 they carried out secret trials in the North Sea which confirmed that they could patrol for a worthwhile period off the English coasts. Altogether they ordered forty-two 'overseas' type submarines between 1908 and 1914, of which twenty-nine had been completed before war broke out. This meant that they then had twice as many 'overseas' submarines built or building as the British. Tirpitz had therefore waited until he was sure that submarines were an effective offensive weapon and had then built them in quantity for the express purpose of using them against Great Britain.

In spite of the French assertion that the submersible could be used offensively, they do not seem to have had any plan for

20

deploying them off an enemy coast. Indeed this is understandable as few of their submersibles were really capable of operating unsupported against opposition. The French had had great difficulty in making their internal-combustion engines reliable and so had had to revert to steam engines in many of their submersibles and they consequently took a long time to dive. The modern French submersibles, although as large as the British and German 'overseas' types, were not really in the same category and were of use only for defence.

In America, submarine construction continued at less than half the rate of the British or French. Both the Holland and Lake types were small and of use only for the defence of the coasts. Although second to the French at the turn of the century, the American submarine fleet had fallen in importance to fourth place by 1914.

Advanced submarine thinkers had always visualized their taking part in a fleet action in close co-operation with battleships, cruisers and destroyers. Interest in this role for the submarine was stimulated in Great Britain by the French manœuvres in which they seemed to be trying to achieve co-operation between their submersibles and the battlefleet. In the British 1912 manœuvres four submarines were attached to one fleet and succeeded in 'torpedoing' a battleship belonging to the other side. In order to make this exercise possible the speed of the fleet, which had the submarines with it, had to be reduced to allow them to keep up. It was obvious that if submarines were to operate as part of a fleet, their surface speed would have to be substantially increased and no further progress could be made until this had been done. As a result two new submarines of greater surface speed were authorized for the Royal Navy and to achieve this they had to be considerably larger and have experimental power plants (see p. 22; fig. 3).

In the fifteen years following the attack by the *Gustave Zédé* on the *Magenta* in 1898, submarines had become established as an important part of many of the navies of the world. They had

21

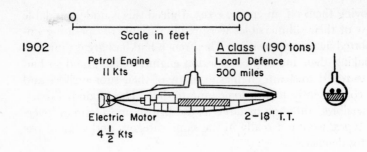

1902

Petrol Engine
11 Kts

<u>A class</u> (190 tons)
Local Defence
500 miles

Electric Motor
4½ Kts

2–18" T.T.

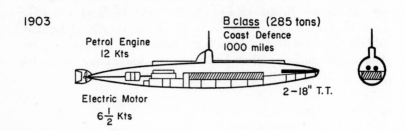

1903

Petrol Engine
12 Kts

<u>B class</u> (285 tons)
Coast Defence
1000 miles

Electric Motor
6½ Kts

2–18" T.T.

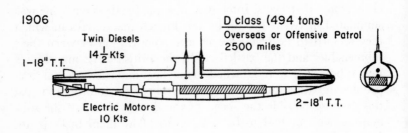

1906

1–18" T.T.

Twin Diesels
14½ Kts

<u>D class</u> (494 tons)
Overseas or Offensive Patrol
2500 miles

Electric Motors
10 Kts

2–18" T.T.

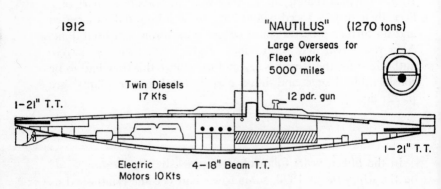

1912

1–21" T.T.

Twin Diesels
17 Kts

<u>"NAUTILUS"</u> (1270 tons)
Large Overseas for
Fleet work
5000 miles

12 pdr. gun

1–21" T.T.

Electric
Motors 10 Kts

4–18" Beam T.T.

<u>3. BRITISH SUBMARINE DEVELOPMENT 1902–1912</u>
(See note 5)

C7, a 'Coastal' submarine

E11, a 'Patrol' submarine

K6, a 'Fleet' submarine

The standard 'Mittel U' type

The very small UB type

The later and larger UBIII type

The large U-Cruiser type

Imperial War Museum photographs

developed from small coastal vessels of some 200 tons into sea-going vessels of over 500 tons. From being propelled on the surface either by dangerous petrol engines or unhandy steam plants, they now used diesel engines which were safe and had almost doubled their endurance.

In these fifteen years the number of submarines had grown from a dozen or so to over 400 in sixteen of the world's navies. Half of these belonged to Great Britain and France and were still predominantly of the coastal type, although the British had an expanding force of 'overseas' submarines. In total numbers the Americans and Germans came next but, whilst the American submarine force was a coastal one, the German was composed entirely of large 'overseas' boats and already constituted the most powerful submarine fleet of the day.

The role of the submarine had grown from base to coast defence and from this to an offensive task in enemy waters. It was already visualized that it would before long form part of a fleet in action. In Great Britain submarines were still auxiliary to the traditional method of commanding the sea and in tonnage and manpower they only represented $1\frac{1}{2}$ per cent of the Royal Navy. In France the proportion was higher and they depended upon them to make up for their inferior battlefleet. Although, in those days of vast fleets of Dreadnoughts, the submarine could not yet claim a decisive influence, its advent had made a close blockade by any power impossible and so had affected the fundamental strategy of the sea power.

III

The Submarine as a
Warship in the First World War
(August 1914–June 1916)

At the outbreak of war in 1914, the British Navy's command of
the sea was very nearly absolute. It had been able to transfer the
British Expeditionary Force to France without loss and to concentrate the Imperial Forces from all over the Empire in Europe.
Whilst protecting British commerce against the German cruisers
with negligible losses, it had swept German trade from the seas.
The key to the whole of this success was the Grand Fleet which
from its bases at the northern entrance to the North Sea was able
to control that passage and prevent the egress of the German
High Seas Fleet. It was also so positioned that if the High Seas
Fleet attacked the coast or through the Straits of Dover, it could
come south and force it to action, if not before the attack then
most certainly afterwards. The Grand Fleet covered all the subsidiary operations necessary to exercise command of the sea. These
included the patrol forces which defended the east coast against
raids : the defences of the Straits of Dover : the northern patrol
which blockaded Germany; and all the distant cruiser squadrons
on the oceans which formed the main protection for trade. The
part of the British submarines in this great system was auxiliary
and comparatively minor. The majority of them were disposed
among the patrol flotillas in a defensive posture to protect the
east coast and a few were allocated to the local defence of the
naval home ports. Seventeen of the best and largest submarines of
the 'overseas' type were based at Harwich to form a striking force
to work offensively towards the German coasts (see p. 32; fig. 4).

The Grand Fleet was superior in Dreadnoughts to the Germans
by three to two and this was enough to make victory practically
certain if it could bring the High Seas Fleet to action. The German policy at the outset was therefore to avoid battle at all costs.
They believed that the British would make an attack on the
German coast and probably try to seize Borkum or Sylt. The

24

German strategy was thus defensive from the beginning. Although the German submarine force was composed entirely of 'overseas' boats designed for offence, they were attached to the Scouting Force and disposed round Heligoland as part of this defensive system. It was the British 'overseas' boats from Harwich which first penetrated into enemy waters and it is understandable that the German submarine officers bridled under their restricted role as 'mobile sentry boxes'. When the expected attack by the British Fleet did not materialize they got permission to operate more offensively. German policy now became one of attrition. The High Seas Fleet was to remain 'in being' whilst they prosecuted a vigorous minor offensive with light craft, mines and submarines to try to reduce the superiority of the Grand Fleet to a point where action could be contemplated. Early in the war, therefore, the German submarines assumed an important role in their general strategy.

In 1914 there was no method of detecting submarines submerged and, unless they showed their periscopes or conning-towers or disturbed the surface by firing a torpedo, they were safe. The main danger to a submarine in those days was to be caught on the surface where it could be rammed or engaged with gunfire. Its survival depended on a good lookout to sight the enemy first, followed by a 'crash' dive. If, when submerged, it allowed its periscope to be sighted, it could still be rammed, or sunk by an explosive sweep, unless it was able to dive deep rapidly. Submarines were of course vulnerable to mines in the same way as any other ship.

The submarine had a comparatively weak armament. Torpedoes were normally fired singly and were generally of the smaller type, 18″ in diameter, which had a short range. The chance of success outside half a mile was small and the single hit, if achieved, was not enough to sink Dreadnoughts which were the principal units of sea power of the day. Submarines were capable, however, of sinking armoured cruisers and even pre-Dreadnought battleships as well as other types of ship, including their own kind. Shallow-draught ships were however safe, as the torpedoes would run under them, and small ships were difficult to hit.

Submarines normally spent much time on the surface so as to gain the mobility conferred by their diesel engines, only diving to make an attack or avoid being seen. Once submerged they became practically fixed on the map and could only make one short dash at 8 knots or so. They were capable of staying submerged at very slow speed on their electric batteries all day and so could still maintain a patrol where enemy anti-submarine craft were in evidence. They would then have to surface for some hours after dark to recharge their batteries. On completion of the charge they could either rest on the bottom until dawn or patrol on the surface, keeping a sharp lookout. Submerged attacks at night were not generally possible as the light transmission of periscopes was not good enough to see anything, but torpedoes could still be fired from the surface.

The British 'overseas' boats were at first operated rather like ships. Groups of them made thrusts or offensive reconnaissances into the Bight, penetrating to Heligoland and the mouths of the German rivers. Here they would stay for a few days and then return. These operations were later extended to the Skagerrak and often coincided with some other operation by British surface ships when the chance of German ships presenting themselves as targets was increased. The aim of these sorties was partly reconnaissance but mainly to do as much damage to the enemy as possible. Information could be brought back by the submarine only when it returned to its base, as its wireless signals could not be received in England from the Bight. Attempts were also made by Commodore Keyes, who commanded the British submarines, to form patrol lines to intercept the enemy during fleet operations. This was done by a destroyer leading a group of submarines and placing them in lines where the tactical situation seemed best for them to intercept the enemy. In the Dogger Bank action and the German raid on the Yorkshire coast, it was soon found that submarines were too slow to counter the moves of fast ships and, there being no method of communicating with them once they had dived, it was difficult to redispose them. Although it proved effective to preposition submarines in patrol lines when an offensive operation was planned, as in the Heligoland Bight action, patrol lines when the enemy had the initiative were of little use.

Up to the end of 1914, the successes of British submarines in the North Sea, which were all achieved in enemy waters, were the sinking of the German light cruiser *Hela* and a destroyer for the loss of three British submarines (see p. 32; fig. 4). They would have sunk a second cruiser if it had not been for a torpedo failure. The sinking of the *Hela* caused all exercising by German ships to be transferred to the Baltic. The submarines brought back a great deal of information about enemy patrols, swept channels and minefields and indeed the operations which led to the Heligoland Bight action were planned on submarine intelligence.

The defensive submarines on the east coast were kept in readiness in harbour to be used as a striking force in the event of a raid. In the Dover area, however, these submarines maintained a patrol line across the Straits. At the end of 1914 the Gorleston and Scarborough raids by the German battle-cruisers took place and were not intercepted or attacked by the defending submarines. In the raid on Hartlepool and Scarborough there were four submarines in the Humber, six in the Tyne and one in Hartlepool itself. All were surprised in harbour and by the time they had got to sea the raid was over. The 'overseas' submarines which were already formed on a patrol line off Terschelling were too far south and were moved at once into the Heligoland Bight. *E11* attacked a heavy unit of the German Fleet without success as they returned.

The first German offensive submarine operation was by ten U-boats in August and took the form of a sweep up the North Sea to try to find the Grand Fleet. The Grand Fleet was at the time in a covering position between Scotland and Norway during the passage of the British Expeditionary Force to France. *U15* sighted one of the battle squadrons, fired a torpedo at the *Monarch* and missed, and was later rammed and sunk by the cruiser *Birmingham*.

In September, *U21* sank H.M.S. *Pathfinder* off St. Abbs Head, and this being, in fact, earlier than any of the British results, was the first success by a submarine in action since the sinking of the *Housatonic* during the American Civil War. This was soon followed by the famous exploit of *U9* in sinking the armoured cruisers *Cressy*, *Hogue* and *Aboukir* off the Dutch coast. *U9* was not one of the most modern German U-boats. She had four torpedo tubes, two in the bow which also had reloads, and two in the stern, making six torpedoes in all. She sailed on 20 September for the Flanders Bight to try to prevent British landings on the Belgian coast during the Battle of the Marne. She had trouble with her gyro compass during the voyage south and found herself off the Dutch coast some fifty miles from her patrol position. Here she encountered a heavy gale and had to remain submerged at fifty feet all night.

The British armoured cruisers *Cressy*, *Hogue* and *Aboukir*

27

were on patrol in the southern North Sea in support of the Harwich destroyer flotillas. The gale had, however, driven the destroyers into harbour and the cruisers were left on their own. At dawn on 22 September the weather had moderated and *U9* surfaced to charge her batteries. Visibility was good and she soon sighted the masts of the cruisers to the southward. Her Korting heavy-oil engines were making a lot of smoke and so she dived at once. The cruisers approached on a steady course at 10 knots in line abreast two miles apart. *U9* took them to be light cruisers of the Birmingham class and at 6.20 fired one bow torpedo at a range of 500 yards at the *Aboukir*, hitting her on the starboard side. The *Aboukir* stopped and her captain, believing that he had run into a line of mines, signalled to the other two ships to close but keep ahead of him.

U9 had dived deep after the first shot to reload her torpedo tube and now returned to periscope depth. She saw the *Aboukir* sinking and the other two ships standing by. This time she correctly identified the targets as armoured cruisers. At 6.55 she fired both bow tubes at a range of 300 yards at the *Hogue* which was stopped with her boats away picking up survivors. Both torpedoes hit and *U9* was so close that she had to go astern on one propeller to avoid collision. She broke surface and the *Hogue* opened fire but failed to secure a hit before she sank ten minutes later. *U9*'s battery was now almost completely exhausted but she had already reloaded her last spare torpedo forward and still had the torpedoes in her stern tubes. The *Cressy* also had all her boats away rescuing survivors and was busy making wireless signals for assistance. *U9* turned for a stern shot but, just before firing, the *Cressy* saw her periscope on the port quarter. She went full speed ahead but one of the two torpedoes hit and stopped her dead in the water. *U9* turned yet again for a bow shot and fired her last torpedo which hit and sank her.

U9 then disengaged to the north and surfaced to recharge her depleted batteries as soon as she was clear of the wreckage. Steering a northerly course close in to the Dutch coast, she was not seen by the British destroyers sent to Terschelling to cut her off and she returned to Germany without further incident. The British could not believe at first that they had been attacked by a single submarine and attributed the disaster to a whole flotilla. The defeat was greater than in the Battle of Coronel although in fact the three cruisers were obsolete, and not a very great loss. Nevertheless it was a startling illustration of the power of the submarine and emphasized in no uncertain terms the precautions that must be taken against it.

Confidence in the ability of the U-boats to operate in enemy waters rose rapidly and they extended their patrols. *U18* and *U20* penetrated the Straits of Dover into the Channel to attack the transports to France. *U20*, not relishing the idea of returning the way she had come, circumnavigated the British Isles and arrived back in Germany after eighteen days at sea. In October an attempt was made against the Grand Fleet in Scapa Flow but failed: another attempt was made in November but the Grand Fleet was away at sea and *U18* was sunk by the patrols. The sinking of the cruiser *Hawke* of the northern patrol forced the British blockade line to move out of the North Sea to the longer and stormier gap between Iceland and Scotland. By November the German Army had arrived on the Belgian coast and advanced submarine bases were established at Zeebrugge and Bruges. On 1 January 1915, *U24* sank the old battleship *Formidable* in the Channel and this attack completed the first phase of U-boat operations which had been directed entirely against the warships of the Royal Navy.

In spite of these successes, the policy of attrition with its aim of wearing down the size of the Grand Fleet had not really achieved very much. All the ships sunk were old: one pre-Dreadnought battleship out of a fleet of forty of them, and four armoured cruisers out of thirty-four cannot be said to have depleted the British Fleet significantly. They had not succeeded in hitting a single Dreadnought of the Grand Fleet which was what really mattered. Nevertheless they had forced the fleet when at sea to move at high speed and to zigzag, with a consequent decrease in its endurance and increase in wear and tear of machinery. Destroyer screens were now necessary at all times, so reducing the endurance and seakeeping qualities of the fleet to that of its destroyers. Large warships could no longer stop to examine merchant ships or render assistance to colleagues in distress.

Strategically the U-boats forced the Grand Fleet to the westwards to seek refuge in bases on the west coast of Scotland and even in Ireland at a time when it should have been in a covering position in the North Sea. Had the High Seas Fleet realized this and wished to raid the Channel, the Grand Fleet could not have forced it to action before it got back to its base. The purpose of the western move of the Grand Fleet lay partly in seeking new and unknown bases whilst the anti-submarine protection of the old ones was being strengthened, and partly in the belief that they could outrange the U-boats. In fact the endurance of the U-boats was ample to attack them anywhere in the vicinity of the British Isles as the voyage of *U20* had already demonstrated.

All these results were achieved by a force of twenty-five U-boats, which represented an effort less than that required to keep two Dreadnoughts. In February the main German U-boat effort was turned against trade, nevertheless it continued to exert the same restrictions on naval operations as if it had still been directed against them.

The British counter measures to the U-boat although far from effective were rapid and widespread. They consisted in general of the arming of 500 trawlers and yachts to try to keep the whole of the waters adjoining the British Isles under continuous observation. The trawlers were armed with a gun which was, of course, of use only if the U-boat came to the surface. It was hoped that if the trawlers attacked the U-boats whenever they saw them, they would drive them out of the area. The trawlers also had an explosive sweep, which was simply a bomb towed underwater astern of the ship which could be exploded electrically as she passed over the submarine. But the use of this weapon depended on sighting the periscope or some other evidence of the presence of a submerged submarine. The first device for detecting a submerged submarine which could not be seen was still under development. It was a light indicator net which would show the position of a submerged submarine if it ran into it.

One of the best ways to sink submarines at this time was to use a decoy to lure them to the surface where they could be destroyed in a surprise attack. Fishing vessels and colliers were secretly armed so that when they were attacked by a submarine using its gun they could unmask their armament and open a heavy fire at point-blank range. C class submarines were also towed by disguised trawlers and in 1915 they succeeded in torpedoing two U-boats. Other anti-submarine measures of those early days were the laying of a large minefield north of the Dover Straits and the bombardment of Zeebrugge. All these measures only brought about the destruction of five U-boats in this phase, whereas ten new U-boats of the pre-war construction programme were commissioned.

Up to the end of 1914 Germany ordered another fifty-two U-boats and took over six more building in Germany for foreign governments. Thirty-two of the new boats were very small and were to be completed quickly for the southern North Sea and Adriatic. They were designed to be transported overland in sections for assembly and it was hoped that their rapid construction would allow them to be completed before the end of the war, which was still expected to be a very short one!

On the outbreak of war the British had thirty-two submarines under construction. In November 1914 an Emergency War Programme of sixty-five boats, twenty of which were to be built in Canada and the United States, was put in hand. Seven new submarines joined the fleet in 1914 against the three that had been lost.

In the Mediterranean the French Fleet blockaded the Austrians in the Adriatic by patrolling the Straits of Otranto. The blockading forces were soon attacked by the small Austrian submarines and after the cruiser *Waldeck Rousseau* had been missed in October, the new Dreadnought *Jean Bart* was hit and badly damaged. The battleships of the blockading force were at once withdrawn to Malta and Bizerta and the blockade left to cruisers and lighter vessels. In April the armoured cruiser *Gambetta* was sunk and then the blockade was reduced to destroyers in the Straits of Otranto and submarines acting offensively off the Austrian base at Cattaro. The pre-war prediction that a close blockade would no longer be possible was therefore soon fully confirmed.

After the Dogger Bank action in January 1915 and the relief of Commodore Keyes, the British 'overseas' submarines in the North Sea settled down to a routine of patrols in the Heligoland Bight and the Skagerrak and on occasions off the Norwegian coast. These operations continued to take the form of thrusts or sorties into enemy waters by varying numbers of submarines and the patrols were not yet continuous. Normally they were synchronized with surface operations or with expected enemy movements. They were directed against U-boats and German surface minelayers as well as the High Seas Fleet and in September 1915 they even tried to shoot down Zeppelins. A large proportion of the 'overseas' submarines were, however, kept in harbour ready to put to sea at the first sign that the High Seas Fleet was moving. The High Seas Fleet in fact came out seven times during 1915 after the Dogger Bank action, but on only two of these occasions were British sub-

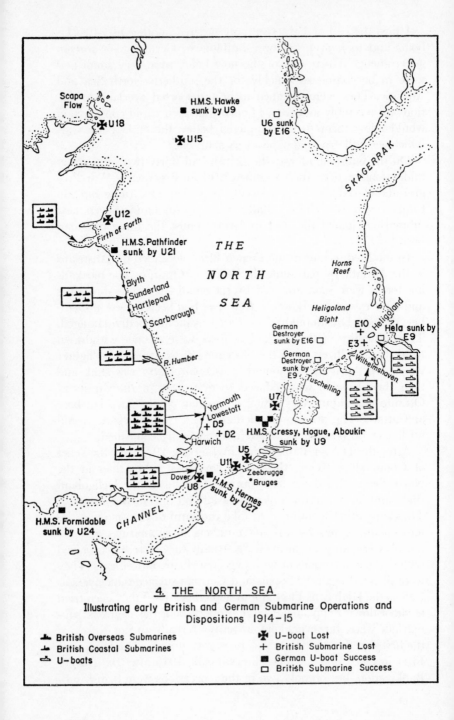

Scapa Flow

✠ U18

✠ U15

H.M.S. Hawke
sunk by U9

U6 sunk
by E16

U12
Firth of Forth

H.M.S. Pathfinder
sunk by U21

THE

NORTH

SEA

SKAGERRAK

Blyth
Sunderland
Hartlepool
Scarborough

R. Humber

Horns
Reef

Heligoland
Bight

E10
+

E3 +

Heligoland

Hela sunk by
E9

German
Destroyer
sunk by E16

German
Destroyer
sunk by
E9

Wilhelmshaven

Tuschelling

Yarmouth
Lowestoft
+ D5
+ D2
Harwich

U7

H.M.S. Cressy, Hogue, Aboukir
sunk by U9

U5

U11

Dover

U8

Zeebrugge
Bruges

H.M.S. Hermes
sunk by U27

H.M.S. Formidable
sunk by U24

CHANNEL

4. THE NORTH SEA

Illustrating early British and German Submarine Operations and
Dispositions 1914–15

⚓ British Overseas Submarines
⚓ British Coastal Submarines
⚓ U–boats

✠ U–boat Lost
+ British Submarine Lost
■ German U-boat Success
□ British Submarine Success

marines on patrol in the Heligoland Bight. *E6* sighted and attacked on both occasions but missed the battle-cruiser *Moltke* in May and the light cruiser *Rostock* in October. Although a force of submarines was sailed as soon as the enemy were known to be at sea, it was always too late to intercept. The results in the North Sea during 1915 were consequently meagre, only one destroyer, a U-boat and a naval auxiliary being sunk. Six British submarines were lost in the North Sea during the year, but thirty-one were commissioned so that, in spite of fourteen being detached to the Baltic and the Dardanelles, strength rose steadily.

The Grand Fleet could not command the sea in the Baltic. The great danger from mines in the narrow entrances and the lack of bases made it impracticable for them to operate there at all. Furthermore the strategic position of the Kiel canal would have allowed the High Seas Fleet a free hand in the North Sea whilst the Grand Fleet was in the Baltic. As the Russian Fleet was markedly inferior, the Germans had complete control. The High Seas Fleet made good use of the Baltic for exercises and for the trials of new ships and, in October 1914, the British decided to send in submarines to see if they could attack it (see p. 34; fig. 5). Three submarines were selected: *E1* and *E9* penetrated the shallow waters of the Sound in spite of the German patrols but *E11* had to turn back. *E1* and *E9* did not find the main High Seas Fleet although they had many encounters with ships of the local German Baltic Fleet. It had been decided that the submarines should go on to Russia and on arrival they were placed under the command of the Russian Commander-in-Chief. Thereafter their operations were directed against the German warships on the flank of the Russian army rather than against the High Seas Fleet itself. The Russian Fleet was old and much cramped by political and military restrictions on its movements, so that *E1* and *E9* became the most active force in the Baltic. They damaged the pre-Dreadnought battleship *Pommern* and sank a destroyer and three naval auxiliaries. The Germans paid them the compliment of saying that they considered it was as important to sink a British submarine as a Russian armoured cruiser.

In July 1915 the Germans began an offensive by land on the eastern front which included an amphibious operation on the

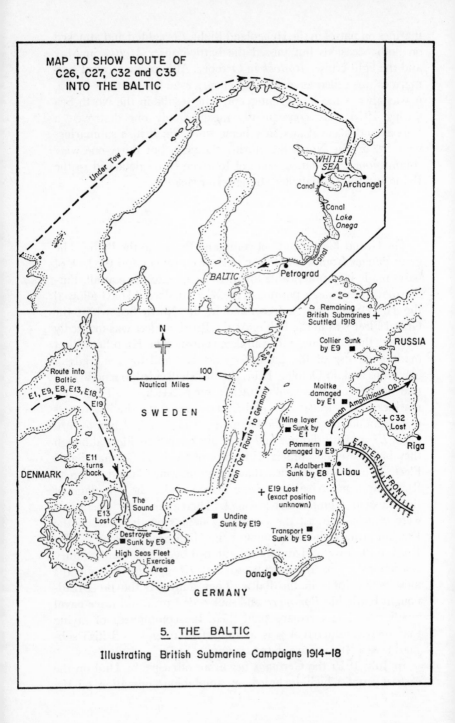

MAP TO SHOW ROUTE OF
C26, C27, C32 and C35
INTO THE BALTIC

Under Tow

WHITE
SEA

Canal

Archangel

Canal
Lake
Onega

Canal

BALTIC

Petrograd

Remaining
British Submarines
Scuttled 1918

Collier Sunk
by E9

RUSSIA

Route into
Baltic
E1, E9, E8, E13, E18,
E19

Moltke
damaged
by E1

N

0   100

Nautical Miles

SWEDEN

Mine layer
Sunk by
E1

German Amphibious Op.

C32
Lost

Riga

E11
turns
back

Pommern
damaged by E9

P. Adalbert
Sunk by E8

Libau

EASTERN FRONT

DENMARK

The
Sound

E19 Lost
(exact position
unknown)

E13
Lost

Undine
Sunk by E19

Transport
Sunk by E9

Destroyer
Sunk by E9

High Seas Fleet
Exercise
Area

Danzig

GERMANY

Iron Ore Route to Germany

5. THE BALTIC

Illustrating British Submarine Campaigns 1914-18

Baltic flank. To support the landing they brought in the battle-cruisers from the High Seas Fleet. The Russians asked Great Britain for more help and in the autumn of 1915 four more E class submarines were sent in to the Baltic, *E13* being lost on the way. Four small C class submarines, being unable to penetrate the Sound on their own, were towed to Archangel and sent through the canal system to the Baltic in barges. *E1* damaged the battle-cruiser *Moltke* during the operations in the Gulf of Riga and this was the only success against a unit of the High Seas Fleet itself. This attack prompted the Germans to abandon their landing which had in any case failed. *E8* scored another success by sinking the German armoured cruiser *Prinz Adalbert* and *E19* sank the light cruiser *Undine*. Thereafter there was a lull in the military operations and the submarines were turned against the iron ore traffic from Sweden to Germany.

Operations had to stop during the winter because of ice but the campaign continued in 1916 and 1917 with gradually decreasing effect. Two submarines were lost on operations for the sole success of a transport sunk. The submarines suffered from lack of spares and refitting facilities and from the events leading up to the Russian revolution. Nevertheless it is of interest that in the Treaty of Brest-Litovsk the Germans insisted that all British submarines in the Baltic be surrendered. However the surviving submarines were scuttled early in 1918 and the crews evacuated overland.

Although the eleven British submarines which were expended in the Baltic did not encounter the High Seas Fleet itself as originally intended, they undoubtedly restricted its movements. They greatly assisted the Russians in disputing command of the sea and did far more damage than the much larger submarine force in the North Sea. On a smaller scale they inconvenienced the Germans much as the U-boats inconvenienced the British.

Although their numbers were small, the influence of submarines on both sides during the Dardanelles campaign was immense (see p. 39; fig. 6). Early in the war the British had moved up their coast defence submarines from Malta and the French had sent a flotilla to help blockade the *Goeben* and *Breslau* after their flight to Turkey. In December *B11*, one of these small coast defence sub-

35

marines, dived under the minefields and sank the Turkish armoured ship *Messoudieh* halfway up the Straits.

When the decision to land at Gallipoli had been taken it was obviously of great importance to prevent the peninsula from being reinforced especially in the early stages. There were two supply lines for the Turkish army in Gallipoli. The main one was by sea from Constantinople through the Sea of Marmora to small ports on the Gallipoli peninsula and this route was of ample capacity and by far the quicker. The other route was by road and rail to the head of the Bulair isthmus and thence by road. As the Turks had no motor transport, the supplies had to go by camel, pack mule or ox cart, taking seven days to cover 100 miles. Moreover the road along the isthmus was open to attack from the sea for its whole length. The capacity of this route was insufficient to maintain the Turkish Army in the peninsula and the sea route was not only more convenient, but was essential. The exploit of *B11* indicated that a modern 'overseas' submarine with a larger battery would be able to pass through the Straits and enter the Sea of Marmora. It would then be possible to cut the sea communications between Constantinople and Gallipoli. Admiral Carden therefore asked for modern submarines to be sent out for this important task.

E15, the first boat to attempt the passage, ran aground on the way up and was lost. The Australian *AE2* successfully entered the sea of Marmora but was sunk by a torpedo boat without doing very much damage. The first aim, of preventing the reinforcement of the peninsula during the landings, therefore failed. But when the campaign settled down to be a long one, instead of the swift success that had been hoped for, the submarine attack on communications was obviously worth persevering with. *E14*, the third submarine, not only successfully negotiated the passage but did a considerable amount of damage to Turkish shipping. Furthermore she came out again and was relieved by *E11* with even better results. From then on, except for a short period of three days, there was always a submarine in the Marmora and often there were two, while for a time in October there were four.

The campaign lasted nine months, from April to December 1915. Nine British and four French submarines took part and they succeeded in making fifteen patrols between them in the Sea of Marmora. The most notable patrol was by *E11* in August, and lasted twenty-nine days. She sank the Turkish battleship

Barbarousse Haireddine, a gunboat, seven transports and twenty-three sailing vessels. In the first few patrols, British submarines had no gun and were unable to deal satisfactorily with the many craft which were too small to torpedo. Six-pounder and later twelve-pounder and four-inch guns were soon fitted which enabled them to deal with this traffic as well as to bombard shore targets.

The passage up through the Straits and down again was a very considerable feat and was as dangerous as trying to force the entrance to a defended naval base. They had to compete with mines, nets, patrols, shore batteries and torpedo tubes as well as with the tortuous passage and strong current. Altogether four submarines were lost on the way up the Straits and one coming down. Of these the French submarine *Joule* was mined, the *Mariotte* and *E7* were caught in the nets, whilst *E15* and the *Turquoise* ran aground under the shore batteries. Two submarines were lost in the Sea of Marmora itself: *AE2*, as already told, by a torpedo boat and *E20* by the German U-boat *UB14*. The casualties in this campaign were therefore over 50 per cent of the force engaged.

The total number of ships sunk was one battleship, a destroyer and five gunboats, eleven transports, forty-four steamers and one hundred and forty-eight sailing vessels. In addition, troops marching along the road were shelled, the railway was bombarded and a bridge blown up by a landing party. The submarines also assisted the army by preventing Turkish warships from giving fire support to their army over the peninsula from the Sea of Marmora. The *Goeben* and *Breslau*, the best ships for this purpose, never once ventured down the Straits. By the end of the campaign there were very few steamers left and throughout the struggle the supply of the Turkish army was a great anxiety to them. At one time it was reduced to 160 rounds of rifle ammunition per man and the transport of troops by sea was stopped altogether from July onwards. Nevertheless the sea route was never entirely severed: small craft moving at night managed to bring in just sufficient supplies to prevent disaster. At the same time the railway was extended to the Gulf of Xeros and supplies were brought down the Asiatic side and across the Dardanelles by ferry under cover of the shore batteries.

It is always difficult to assess the effect on a campaign when its supply lines are throttled, but there is no doubt that the part played by the Allied submarines was out of all proportion to the effort expended. The submarines penetrated into waters where our own surface ships could not command the sea and here they were able to disrupt the enemy's communications. But for them the Turkish Army in the peninsula would have been much stronger and better able to take the offensive which, in that finely balanced campaign, might have ended in disaster for the Allies.

The Turks asked the Germans for naval assistance at the Dardanelles quite early in the campaign. The Germans were already sending small submarines of the UB and UC types to the Adriatic in sections for assembly at Pola. They now decided to send a larger U-boat direct from Germany to the Mediterranean. *U21* left Kiel on 25 April and, rounding the north of Scotland, attempted to fuel from a German supply ship off Cape Finisterre. The fuel proved useless but she was just able to reach Pola. After a week's rest she pressed on to the Dardanelles. The British army at Gallipoli depended a great deal on fire support from ships of the fleet and there were normally four or five old battleships either stopped or at anchor off the beaches. At the same time a mass of transports and supply ships was anchored off the open beaches, unloading troops and supplies. *U21* had been seen by a torpedo boat passing through the Straits of Gibraltar and the British naval forces at the Dardanelles were well aware that she was coming. They did their best with all the known anti-submarine measures : ships zigzagged on passage with destroyer screens and the battleships off the beaches kept their torpedo nets down and had destroyers patrolling round them. On arrival on 25 May *U21* missed both the *Swiftsure* and the *Vengeance* but later in the day sank the pre-Dreadnought battleship *Triumph* and two days later the *Majestic* as well. This remarkable feat set a new standard in submarine warfare and certainly emphasized that the submarine was no longer a short-range weapon.

The effect on the Dardanelles campaign was far-reaching. The battleships had to withdraw to Mudros to lie behind the anti-submarine boom and the army was deprived of almost all naval fire support–furthermore their departure tended to lower morale. All troops and stores had to be transhipped in Mudros to smaller vessels for onward transport to the beaches and this interfered with the supply of the army. Although later in the campaign the fire support was restored to a certain extent by the use of monitors and bulged cruisers, the arrival of *U21* was a very great military success for the Germans and largely offset the good the British

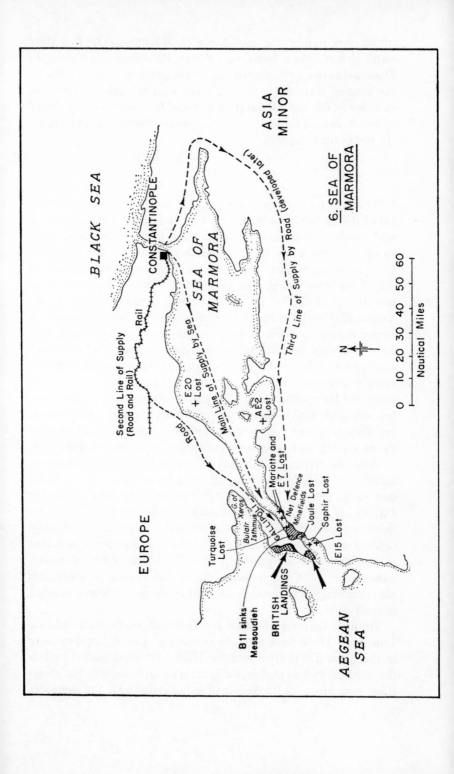

6. SEA OF MARMORA

submarines were doing in the Sea of Marmora. The first three small U-boats to complete assembly at Pola were also sent to the Dardanelles but were used mainly in the Black Sea. In fact, during the ensuing months German U-boats were scarcely off the Dardanelles at all, but the full effect of *U21*'s appearance continued to be felt and all the restrictions she imposed remained in force for the rest of the campaign.

Although most of the results in 1915 were achieved by a handful of British submarines in the Baltic and at the Dardanelles, the main body of them remained stationed in the North Sea, ready to counter any move by the High Seas Fleet. By the middle of 1916 there were thirty-eight 'overseas' or patrol submarines, as they were now called, operating from bases at Harwich, Yarmouth and Blyth. With these increased numbers, patrols in the Terschelling and Horns Reef areas became more frequent and of longer duration; as the danger from mines was considerable they were still only ordered when thought necessary and were not continuous. A few of the new submarines were minelayers which entered service in March and were used to lay small minefields inside the Heligoland Bight. The patrol submarines now had wireless sets with which they could report back direct to the shore, but these were not very reliable and the submarines had to come to the surface and hoist large collapsible masts to transmit.

With the arrival of Admiral Scheer in January 1916 to command it, the High Seas Fleet began a more active career. In its first sortie, some of its ships were seen by the British submarine *D3*, which was making a reconnaissance in the Bight, but four more boats, which sailed at once, arrived too late. The Admiralty ordered a continuous patrol before the next operation and four submarines were in position. The High Seas Fleet, however, passed over them when they were on the bottom at night and also returned safely through the submarine line in heavy weather next day.

Towards the end of April the Germans made their raid on Lowestoft. There were three submarines on patrol, but they were in the Lister Deep area, and the High Seas Fleet passed well to the south of them. Intelligence had, however, indicated that something was afoot and a group of submarines with the destroyer

Melampus was at once sent from Harwich to a position in the middle of the southern North Sea. This group was to form a patrol line over which it was hoped the Harwich destroyers might be able to lead the enemy if they made contact. The enemy, however, passed well to the north of this line. There were now no local defence submarines stationed between Dover and the Humber, so the Admiralty ordered six of the patrol submarines to be put at gun range off Yarmouth. These submarines were not placed exactly where the Admiralty intended and only *H5* sighted the German ships. She was seen by the enemy and was not able to get in an attack but is credited with having saved Yarmouth from being subjected to a bombardment. The *Melampus* group in the middle of the North Sea was then moved northwards at full speed to try to intercept the enemy on their way back. The northern boat *E55* just sighted them at long range but without result. Although the patrol submarines which were deployed defensively might have done better if they had been in the right place, the use of a patrol line was again shown to be unsuccessful. After this raid a flotilla of small coastal submarines from the Firth of Forth was moved down to Yarmouth to strengthen defence in the area.

In May political objections to the U-boat war on commerce became so strong that Admiral Scheer withdrew them from west of the British Isles and they became available again for military purposes. Instead, however, of employing them as weapons of attrition, as in the early part of the war, he intended to place them off British bases and entice the Grand Fleet over them by carrying out an operation with the High Seas Fleet. In a plan he laid to bombard Sunderland he intended to use sixteen U-boats, ten of which were to make a preliminary sweep in the North Sea and then take up positions off the Grand Fleet bases. Three submarine minelayers were to lay new minefields off the Firth of Forth, Cromarty and Scapa Flow and the other three U-boats were disposed to secure the flank of the High Seas Fleet off Terschelling.

The plan to bombard Sunderland had to be changed by Admiral Scheer at the last moment and a sweep towards the Skagerrak was substituted, which led to the Battle of Jutland. The U-boat dispositions had, however, already been made and remained unaltered. Several unsuccessful attacks were executed by the U-boats on minor units as the Grand Fleet put to sea, and Admiral Beatty with his battle-cruisers passed right through the concentration off the Firth of Forth unscathed. *U66* sighted the Second Battle Squadron but her attack was foiled by the destroyer screen. The submarine trap for the Grand Fleet therefore failed completely. The U-boats were no more successful for reconnaissance and did not give Admiral Scheer a clear picture of what was happening, with the result that he found himself in the presence of the whole Grand Fleet without any warning.

After the main action strenuous attempts were made by the U-boats to finish off damaged ships as they returned. The *Marlborough* was attacked by *U46* and the *Warspite* by *U51* but all their torpedoes missed. The *Warspite* also frustrated an attack by *U63* by turning to ram and forcing her to dive deep.

The part of the British submarines in the Battle of Jutland was even less successful. Again there were no submarines on patrol to detect the German fleet emerging from the Bight, and although three submarines were well placed to intercept the enemy on their way home, they had been ordered to lie on the bottom and wait for an operation which never materialized and the High Seas Fleet passed over them in safety. Submarines on both sides therefore failed dismally to achieve anything in the biggest naval battle of the war and it was obvious to both sides that they were not using them to the best advantage.

IV

The Submarine as a Commerce Raider in the First World War 1914-16

Contrary to popular belief, the Germans had no plans to use their U-boats to attack commerce before the Great War began in 1914. They had indeed hoped to use them offensively against Great Britain but did not know enough about their capabilities to judge whether they would be effective in an attack on trade. Germany had not intended to become involved in a war on two fronts or a long struggle of attrition : a U-boat attack on trade would need time to take effect and so did not fit in with their concept of war. The deadlock on the western front came as a surprise and meant that the war was going to be a much longer one than they expected. The paralysing of Germany's ocean commerce by the British blockade had already led to considerable shortages in Germany by the beginning of 1915, and they realized that the longer the war the greater these shortages would become. Furthermore it was beginning to be clear that the attrition policy was unlikely to lead to the ultimate defeat of the Grand Fleet and so to the breaking of the blockade.

At the same time the German cruiser attack on British commerce had already failed. Notwithstanding the great successes achieved by the *Emden* and the *Karlsruhe*, in a period of five months the cruiser forces as a whole had sunk only fifty-two merchant vessels for the loss of nine of their number. Not only had the raiders been driven from the seas but they had only achieved an 'exchange rate' (see Note 6) of six merchant ships for every cruiser sunk. With the overwhelming strength and strategic position of the Grand Fleet there seemed little hope of renewing, let alone extending, an attack by surface raiders.

The U-boats, on the other hand, had exceeded all expectations. In spite of the great superiority of the British Fleet they were able to cruise at will and had shown themselves capable of operating not only off the English North Sea coast but to the west of the British Isles as well. Already a few U-boats on their own initiative had shown the possibilities by sinking merchant ships in accordance with the Prize Regulations. The first definite proposal to use the U-boats against commerce, however, came from the Commander-in-Chief of the German High Seas Fleet in November 1914, but there is little doubt that the suggestion emanated from the submarine command itself.

No one doubted the ability of a submarine to sink a merchant ship and its potential as a commerce raider seemed greater than that of the cruisers, as it could operate close off the British Isles where the traffic converged from all over the world. The snag was that it was difficult to comply with international law whilst doing so. The sinking of ships in a surprise attack without warning was certainly illegal. To apply the full procedure of visit and search required by law was not easy and, with the geographical position of the United Kingdom astride the routes to Germany, it was obviously impossible to send ships in to a Prize court. Certainly there was no room on board a submarine to accommodate the crews of sunken ships as in a surface raider.

During the last months of 1914 and into January 1915, there was a lively debate within the German government on whether to use the U-boat against commerce or not. The protagonists pointed out that this was the only way to retaliate against the British blockade, whilst the opponents thought that the inevitable breaches of international law might be so unfavourably received by neutrals as to be in the long run to Germany's disadvantage. Admiral von Tirpitz was keen to use the submarine against commerce eventually and he had in fact already given an interview to American journalists to try to sound out the attitude of neutrals. He did not however wish to start so soon, as he believed German U-boat strength at the end of 1914 to be quite inadequate to be effective. The extreme protagonists of a U-boat war on commerce, headed by Admiral von Pohl, the naval Chief of Staff, believed that by a ruthless attack on neutrals they could frighten them away from trading with the United Kingdom. This would be a serious blow as nearly one third of the imports into the country were carried in neutral bottoms.

In the end Admiral von Pohl won the day and approval was given to a U-boat war on commerce to start in February. The German High Command fully understood the difficulties of operating with submarines against commerce and the problems of international law, and met them by declaring a war zone. This war zone which was declared on 4 February to be effective from 18 February surrounded the British Isles. All ships in it including neutrals would be liable to be sunk and the warning was given that it would not always be possible to save the crews. The clear contraventions of international law were justified by alleged illegalities in the British blockade and because the British had ordered their merchant ships to use neutral colours and so it would not always be possible to distinguish them. The Germans had however seriously underestimated neutral reaction, which was so violent that before the war zone came into effect they had to undertake not to attack ships flying neutral flags unless they were definitely identified as enemy. Thus the campaign, which by the original declaration was to be virtually unrestricted, became restricted to a certain extent even before it had begun.

The first German U-boat campaign against commerce was therefore not conceived initially as a war-winning measure but as a form of retaliation for the British blockade. If the blockade could not be broken, at least the British could be made to suffer too. It was also believed that the U-boats could be used to greater effect by a direct attack on commerce than by continuing the campaign of attrition against British warships.

The U-boats could cruise against commerce on the trade routes either on the surface or submerged and could attack merchant shipping in one of two ways. They could simply dive and torpedo them without warning, in the same way as they would attack a warship, or they could surface and engage with their gun. There was no doubt that the first method was quite illegal but in the second they could comply with international law by ordering the ship to stop and carrying out visit and search. If found to be carrying contraband the ship could then legally be sunk, but the problem of saving the crew remained. In the torpedo attack which was certain to be a very effective way to sink a merchant ship it was necessary to get to close range to be sure of a hit. With its slow submerged speed a submarine would not be able to close all the ships it sighted and so some targets would escape. The U-boats carried only six or seven torpedoes and, as a hit could not be expected with every one, they would be lucky if they could sink more than four ships by the first method before they had to return to base to replenish with torpedoes. In the gun attack the destruction of the ship could be completed by gunfire but this was liable to be slow and expensive in ammunition. Alternatively,

45

explosive charges could be placed or a single well-aimed torpedo fired or the seacocks could simply be opened. Apart from its comparative legality, the gun attack had the great advantage that a submarine on a single patrol could destroy far more than four ships. Furthermore with the gun it could chase ships sighted over the horizon and, being faster when on the surface than most merchantmen, would be able to overhaul them. For commerce raiding therefore, where the majority of the targets were slow or small, the U-boat preferred to work as a gunboat on the surface. For attacking large fast ships which could outdistance a U-boat before its fire could take effect, however, it might have to resort to a submerged torpedo attack.

The first phase of the German submarine campaign lasted for seven months from January to September 1915. In May its character changed considerably and it divides itself naturally into two periods, which are best considered separately (see Note 7). On 18 February at the start of the campaign, the Germans had a total of twenty-seven operational U-boats, twenty-one of which were stationed in the North Sea and were available to attack trade: the rest were in the Baltic. Seventy-five more U-boats were in various stages of construction and as new boats were delivered during the campaign the size of the attacking force rose slightly (see p. 103; fig. 11, ii). They operated from bases in Germany throughout the war zone round the British Isles and made sporadic attacks in the Channel, Irish Sea and off the east coast of Britain as well as to the north of Scotland and the west and south coasts of Ireland. Six U-boats were normally at sea at a time, four of which were actually in their operational areas, and two of these were generally to the west of the British Isles.

In the first three months, fifty-seven torpedo attacks were made without warning, thirty-eight of which were successful, but fifteen ships were missed and four of the ships hit were able to reach port. Ninety-three attacks were made by gunfire from which no less than forty-three ships escaped. Another twenty-eight very small ships and fishing vessels which were not worth a torpedo were also sunk by gunfire. The type of attack was chosen by individual U-boats as the tactical situation required except that neutral ships were not allowed to be sunk without warning.

In these first three months the Germans lost only five U-boats. Except for the passage of the Dover Straits the U-boats were in fact little worried by any of the British anti-submarine measures.

In the same period some twenty-five new U-boats, mostly of the small UB and UC types, were delivered, making the total operational strength in the middle of May up to thirty-five.

The British anti-submarine measures in this period consisted of an auxiliary patrol, of anti-submarine barriers in narrow straits and of self-defence measures by merchant ships. The Auxiliary Patrol consisted of some five hundred trawlers and yachts stationed in twenty-one areas covering the coastal waters of the British Isles. They patrolled their areas at random and were in general easily evaded by the U-boats. They succeeded in sinking *U12* however and in rescuing one merchant ship under attack. The barriers were to try to block the Straits of Dover and the North Channel into the Irish Sea and consisted of minefields and lines of drifters working indicator nets, supported by patrol vessels armed with guns. The drifters had great difficulty in keeping in place the nets, many of which were lost in bad weather. The mines were of a type inefficient for sinking U-boats and many gave away their position by being seen on the surface at low tide. Nevertheless in April, after the sinking of *U8* in the Dover barrier and the disappearance of *U37* coupled with disagreeable experiences by *U32* and *U33* with nets and mines, the Germans abandoned the passage of the Dover Straits. In consequence the sinkings of merchant vessels in the Channel greatly decreased and the northabout route, which the U-boats were now forced to take, increased their time on passage to the operational areas west of the British Isles. The self-defence measures for merchant ships were mainly applied by tactical instructions which had been given to them at the beginning of the campaign. These were to turn towards U-boats, force them to dive and then escape by running over them and using their speed. These measures were fairly successful and thirty-eight of the forty-three ships which escaped did so by obeying these instructions. A start had also been made in equipping merchant ships with a gun as a defensive armament and five ships escaped by defending themselves with their guns.

It was realized by the British that these anti-submarine measures were not going to be enough. Of the five U-boats lost only two losses had been caused by them. Many new measures were considered, the best of which was to fit out Q ships, some of which had already started work. Q ships were merchant vessels secretly manned by the Navy with a heavy concealed gun armament with which they hoped to sink any U-boat which closed to attack them on the surface. There was also considerable discussion about a more fundamental solution to the problem by attacking the U-boat bases in Germany itself. However the ships that would be required for this purpose were sent to the Dardanelles and this plan had to be postponed.

The actual effect of the U-boat campaign in the first three months was very small. They had failed to interrupt the communications of the Allied armies in France or at the Dardanelles or to disrupt the vital terminals of the trade routes. The neutrals, although they had suffered casualties, had not been frightened away from trading with the United Kingdom. Furthermore Great Britain had been able to use the German disregard of international law to retaliate by tightening the blockade and by increasing her hold over neutral shipping, and the balance was decidedly in her favour. In fact the British casualties to the U-boats were less than fifty steamers of little over 100,000 tons (see p. 103; fig. 11, i), which was a slower rate of sinking than that by the German cruisers at their peak in the early part of the war. The sunken ships were more than replaced by new construction and with the capture of enemy merchant vessels the tonnage available to the Allies actually increased during this period.

Apart from the fact that there was an immense demand for shipping for military purposes so that even these losses could be ill afforded, there were some significant facts about the German submarine campaign. Although the rate of loss of merchant ships was less than that imposed by the cruisers, it had been achieved with an 'exchange rate' of twenty steamers for every U-boat sunk. Anti-submarine measures were not able even to impede the U-boats in the vital focal areas and the casualties were low solely because there were so few submarines operating. There were many U-boats building and greater losses seemed certain in the future.

On 30 April 1915, *U20* sailed from Wilhelmshaven and her cruise, apart from its significance, is typical of the campaign. After negotiating the swept channels out of the Heligoland Bight, *U20* set a course up the middle of the North Sea running on the surface. She passed to the north of the Orkneys and sighted some Auxiliary Patrol vessels but had no difficulty in evading them. On 4 May, after four days on passage, she arrived in her operational area south of Ireland and missed a steamer with a torpedo off the Fastnet. Next day she sank a sailing vessel by gunfire near the Old Head of Kinsale and on 6 May sank two steamers south of

Waterford in foggy weather, the first by gunfire and the second without warning by torpedo. On 7 May, as her fuel was already running low and she had only two torpedoes left, *U20* started on her return passage, the weather being still very foggy. In the afternoon the fog cleared and she sighted a large ship approaching which she hit without warning with her last two torpedoes. The target was then identified as the *Lusitania* and she sank in twenty minutes with the loss of over a thousand lives including a number of American citizens. After watching her sink, *U20* dived deep and continued on her course for Germany. Although nearly forty ships had already been torpedoed in this way, the sinking caused an uproar throughout the world. It is not intended to enlarge upon the rights and wrongs of the case here except to note that the attack was absolutely illegal by international law. Nevertheless, legality apart, it was the only way for a submarine to deal with so large and fast a ship. The *Lusitania* had a speed of over 25 knots and would be certain to escape before gunfire could take effect and two torpedo hits were necessary to make sure of even stopping her.

The next four months, from June to September 1915, were overshadowed by difficulties with America over the sinking of the *Lusitania* which had a decided influence on the submarine campaign and were the principal reason for its change of character. In June the U-boats were further restricted when the Germans, under pressure, prohibited the sinking of large passenger vessels altogether. These four months were also marked by a decrease in the number of ships torpedoed without warning and an increase in the number sunk after being stopped by gunfire. Not only did this have an air of greater legality about it, but the U-boats were actually able to sink more as a result. During this period there were seven gun attacks to every torpedo attack. Although a number of neutral ships and fishing vessels were sunk in the North Sea, the principal attack was concentrated in the south-western approaches to the British Isles and the Channel and Irish Sea were comparatively immune. At the end of June and the beginning of July *U20* and *U39* in the south-western approaches sank twenty ships between them, missing a dozen others. In August (see p. 50; fig. 7) no less than thirteen U-boats were at sea altogether, *U38*, *U27* and *U24* being all in the south-western approaches where the shipping casualties became heavier than at any time in the war to date, no less than forty-nine ships being sunk.

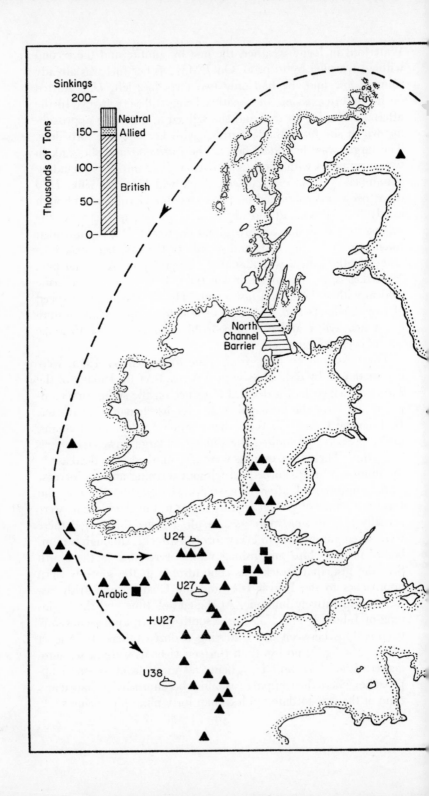

7. THE FIRST RESTRICTED CAMPAIGN BY THE U-BOATS

August 1915

■   Torpedoed without warning

▲   Attacked by gunfire and sunk by gun, torpedo or scuttled

●   Sunk by Mine laid by U-boat

+   U-boat destroyed

⌒   Typical U-boat patrol position

Bruges   U-boat bases underlined

--→   U-boat passage routes

Somewhere in North Sea

Heligoland

○ Wilhelmshaven

Emden

North Sea Flotillas

20 U-boats
(10 at Sea
2 in Harbour
8 under Repair)

+ UB4

HOLLAND

○ Zeebruge
○ Bruges
Ostend

Flanders Flotillas

15 UB and UC boats
(3 at Sea
12 in Harbour)

over rrage

UC 5

WESTERN FRONT

In June 1915 a new U-boat flotilla which consisted of very small boats of the UB and UC types started to operate from Flanders. They were based inland at Bruges, having been sent overland in sections from Germany and assembled at Antwerp. From Bruges they used the canals to Ostend and Zeebrugge to reach the open sea. These very small submarines were no bigger than the British A class which were considered by them as fit only for harbour defence. The UB type carried only two torpedoes and a machine-gun and were very slow. They nevertheless operated in the southern North Sea and even began to penetrate through the Straits of Dover again. The UC boats inaugurated a new form of attack by submarines. Instead of two torpedoes they carried twelve mines which they were able to plant in complete secrecy close in to the British coast. They laid fields in the Thames estuary, the Straits of Dover and off the East Anglian coast and claimed a number of victims.

From June to September 1915 the Germans lost in all eleven U-boats but during the same period seventeen new ones were delivered, mostly of the small UB and UC types. The Germans, during the summer of 1915, ordered the building of another seventy-two U-boats equally divided between the U, UB and UC types, raising the number under construction to over a hundred.

The Germans were becoming chary of stopping and examining ships, since seven of the eleven U-boats lost had been sunk by decoys of some kind. Three had been destroyed by Q ships, two by secretly armed fishing vessels and two by British submarines working in conjunction with disguised trawlers. On more than one occasion U-boats had escaped from the attacks of these decoys, so knowledge of them got back to Germany and U-boats were therefore ordered to take no chances. The success of the decoys was made possible by the greatly increased use of the gun by U-boats which, although it led to more merchant ships being sunk, was more dangerous for the U-boats than attacking without warning when submerged.

In September, after the sinking of the passenger ship *Arabic*, German relations with America became dangerously strained and the Imperial Chancellor informed the U.S.A. that no further ships would be sunk without warning. The campaign was still further restricted by orders that no passenger ships of any size were to be sunk at all. This meant that all ships had to be examined to see if they carried passengers. The Commander-in-Chief of the

High Seas Fleet considered these orders were quite impracticable and on 18 September 1915 called off the attack on commerce to the west of the British Isles.

Decoys were therefore the first real counter measure to the submarine as a commerce raider. The calling off of the campaign was, however, not a victory for any anti-submarine measure. That barometer, the 'exchange rate', rose in this period to twenty-three ships sunk for every U-boat destroyed, which showed that the U-boats were doing better than before. An immense effort was however put into anti-submarine measures by the British. The barriers in the Dover Straits and the North Channel were joined by a new one across the St. George's Channel. Small airships were now being used to patrol them and a new kind of mined net was being laid in the Dover Straits in addition to the indicator nets. Nevertheless the barriers did not sink any U-boats in this period because few U-boats attempted to traverse them: they could achieve all they wished without passing through them on their way to the south-western approaches.

Anti-submarine measures were also powerless to prevent the UC boats from laying their mines, but a vast minesweeping organization was able to keep a war channel swept along the east coast and so to keep the casualties within bounds. However half a dozen very small submarines were able to sink ten ships or so every month and keep well over a hundred minesweepers busy.

In August 1915, in an attempt to improve their effectiveness, all the auxiliary patrols to the west of the British Isles had been placed under a single command at Queenstown. These patrols often sighted U-boats and forced them to dive and they were able to rescue a dozen ships or so. Nevertheless their operations, which were on a vast scale, sank no U-boats and scarcely hindered them. Some new anti-submarine measures were introduced, including flying boat and seaplane patrols. The Flanders bases were bombed and deep minefields were laid but none of these measures had any success in this period. One U-boat was, however, sunk by a British submarine on an offensive patrol and another was run down by a merchant vessel. No armed merchant ship was sunk at this time, which was significant; but very few ships had guns, as there was an acute shortage of them.

Although the general merchant ship losses in this period, from June to September 1915, showed a marked increase, they were still small when compared with the total volume of trade. Even in the heaviest month of casualties in August they amounted to only 1 per cent, which was half what the French privateers achieved in the Napoleonic wars. However the rate of sinking had now overtaken that achieved by the cruisers and, what was more significant, had also overtaken the rate at which ships were being built. Although imports into the United Kingdom were maintained during this period, the prospect of a progressive decline in the size of the merchant fleet was particularly worrying when more ships than ever were required by the Allies for military purposes. It was therefore a great relief to them when the campaign was called off by the Germans.

The chief credit for the calling off of the first German submarine campaign must go to American diplomatic pressure, although the decoys could claim that they had made the waging of a U-boat campaign in accordance with international law impossible. Whether it was really impossible was hotly debated in Germany and there is no doubt that the decision was prompted by the fact that the North Sea U-boats were over-extended : at the end of the campaign they had only four ready for sea. The Germans also believed that if they were to be so restricted they could use the U-boats to greater effect in the Mediterranean, where Italy had entered the war on the side of the Allies and there was a great need to succour Turkey and prevent her collapse. It had therefore already been decided to send more U-boats to the Mediterranean where it was also hoped that they would be able to continue the war against shipping with less fear of complications with America.

The U-boat campaign against commerce now entered what the Germans called a twilight phase which was to last for a year, until September 1916. Whilst operations were continuous in the Mediterranean and from the Flanders bases, the North Sea U-boats, which were under the command of the High Seas Fleet, were withdrawn from the attack on trade except for a period of two months in March and April 1916. The operations against commerce that did take place were carried out under restrictions, the severity of which varied with the political situation from month to month.

The centre of gravity of U-boat operations now shifted from

54

Torpedoed without warning

Convoy

UNRESTRICTED SUBMARINE WARFARE   *Imperial War Museum photographs*

the south-western approaches to the Mediterranean. Here, as well as *U21* which had made the passage from Germany in May 1915, there were nine small submarines of the UB and UC types which had been sent overland in sections and assembled at Pola. During August and September 1915 this flotilla was reinforced by five new medium U-boats sent out from Germany. The North Sea flotilla which provided this reinforcement was reduced to a dozen U-boats most of which were in urgent need of repair, and the winter of 1915-16 had to be spent in refitting them.

The Mediterranean, as well as being a main artery of trade from the east, was of course of great importance to French and Italian shipping. The Salonika landing took place in October and Gallipoli was not evacuated until the end of 1915, so important military communications still passed through the Mediterranean. Most of the damage was done by the six 'Mittel U' submarines which had made the voyage from Germany. They ranged from Cretan and Egyptian waters to the Algerian coast and the Gulf of Lyons, sinking eighteen ships in September, seventeen in October, and no less than forty-one in November. But they could not keep this up and the total fell to twenty-four in December and, because of their need to refit, to only six in January. The great majority of the sinkings were with the gun but some torpedo attacks without warning were made, mostly on troopships and naval auxiliaries, which were of course perfectly legitimate targets. During this time not a single U-boat was lost in spite of the fact that the Allies had sixty-six destroyers, seventy-nine sloops and two hundred trawlers available for anti-submarine work in the Mediterranean. Although nominally all under the French Commander-in-Chief, these forces were divided among eighteen separate areas; they patrolled in a disconnected way and proved quite ineffective. In September, drifters and nets were sent out to form a barrier across the Straits of Otranto and so block the U-boats in their Adriatic bases. This was a formidable task, as the straits were much wider and deeper than either the Straits of Dover or the North Channel. The only cheering fact for the Allies was that a number of defensively-armed merchant ships had escaped by using their guns.

The Flanders U-boats were used mainly for minelaying in the southern North Sea and this campaign exacted a toll of twelve to fourteen ships a month. In December 1915 *U24* of the North Sea flotilla made a raid into the south-western approaches with the object of pinning down anti-submarine forces and preventing them from being transferred to the Mediterranean. In the whole of the period from October 1915 to February 1916 in all areas the Germans lost only three U-boats, not one of these losses being due to any of the Allies' anti-submarine measures.

Throughout the winter of 1915-16 the debate on the resumption of the U-boat campaign continued in Germany. In September Admiral von Holtzendorf, a great protagonist of U-boat warfare, had become Chief of Naval Staff and he was already making calculations which showed that Great Britain could be totally defeated by U-boats alone in a period of six months, provided that they were allowed to be quite unrestricted in their operations. The politicians were still firmly opposed and believed that an unrestricted campaign would be certain to bring America into the war against Germany. Support for a U-boat campaign also came from General von Falkenhayn, the Army Chief of Staff. Although he was confident that the Verdun offensive could defeat France, he saw no way in which the conventional German armed forces could bring the war against Great Britain to a successful conclusion. Invasion was out of the question without command of the sea and the only solution seemed to be a U-boat campaign against her sea communications. He held the view that politically the risk of unfavourable neutral reaction could now be accepted; Bulgaria had just joined the central powers and this would be bound to have a beneficial effect on other neutrals.

In November 1915 the United States had occasion to complain about certain aspects of the British blockade and Germany at once took the opportunity to step up the operations of the Flanders flotilla in the Channel. In January the United States sent a note to the Allies, affirming that a U-boat campaign against commerce could be perfectly legal provided the crews of merchant ships were allowed to leave before the ship was sunk, but also asserting that merchant ships must not be armed or they could be treated as naval auxiliaries. Such an interpretation of international law was of course greatly to Germany's advantage and was quite unacceptable to Great Britain. As a result, in February 1916, the Germans felt that the situation was sufficiently favourable for them to reopen the submarine campaign in home waters.

The orders to revive the campaign with the full strength of the U-boat fleet were given on 29 February 1916 and the Germans were so heartened by the American views that they allowed armed merchant vessels to be attacked without warning, provided that the armament could definitely be seen. However they soon lost their nerve and stipulated that this concession did not apply to passenger ships even if they were armed. Admiral Scheer, who had just taken command of the High Seas Fleet, did not think that these orders were really practicable. It would be very difficult for a U-boat to see whether a ship was armed before torpedoes had to be fired, and to examine all ships to see if they carried passengers would play into the hands of the decoys.

The Germans, as well as renewing activity in the western approaches, continued operations in the Mediterranean, the Channel and the southern North Sea. In March there were eight U-boats at sea in all these areas, two being normally to the west of the British Isles. In home waters they sank thirty-nine ships in March, half by gun and half without warning by torpedo, but only four ships were sunk in the Mediterranean. In April the number of U-boats at sea rose to no less than eighteen and these sank fifty ships in home waters and another sixteen in the Mediterranean. Mines continued to take a steady toll of a dozen ships a month, mainly in the southern North Sea and Channel.

In March and April the Germans lost six U-boats, one to a Q ship, one in a barrier and two to the patrols, the others by accident and nothing to do with British anti-submarine measures. These poor results were not for want of trying and the Allies persevered with their anti-submarine measures, but these were still quite insufficient to defeat or even check the U-boats. The Auxiliary Patrol had done rather better by sinking two U-boats and the arming of merchant ships was proving an undoubted success, only one such vessel having been sunk by gunfire by a submarine. A defensive armament was of course no protection whatever against being torpedoed and six armed ships were sunk without warning. In the Mediterranean the Otranto barrage was proving almost useless, since the U-boats were able to see the drifters with their indicator nets and pass through the gaps between them at periscope depth.

The German Navy were very disappointed that they were not allowed to wage a completely unrestricted campaign. Only in this way did they believe they could prevent neutrals from trading with the Allies, and compete with the decoys and armed merchantmen, which were the only counter measures which caused them any concern. They continued to press their case, and on 4

March 1916 the Kaiser actually consented to an unrestricted campaign to begin on 1 April. After two days he withdrew his permission, at which Admiral von Tirpitz, the Minister of Marine, who had not been consulted, resigned. On 13 March, in an attempt to compromise, the orders to the U-boats were altered to allow them to sink all British ships in the war zone, except passenger ships whether they were armed or not. These orders were much more than the Americans could accept and matters came to a head on 24 March when the French cross-Channel packet *Sussex* was torpedoed without warning by *UB29*. The campaign continued until 20 April when a very strong protest was received from America about the *Sussex*, threatening to break off diplomatic relations. Orders were at once given for the U-boats to operate in accordance with international law. Admiral Scheer, believing this to be completely impracticable, recalled all the U-boats under his command, thus for the second time withdrawing half of the U-boat fleet from the attack on commerce.

After this second withdrawal of the North Sea U-boats, the Mediterranean and Flanders submarines struggled on throughout the summer of 1915 with the attack on commerce under the restrictive policy that they were not allowed to attack without warning. For nearly five months, from May to September 1916, half of the U-boat fleet was occupied in the North Sea, co-operating with the High Seas Fleet as described in Chapters III and V.

In the Mediterranean there were now between three and five U-boats at sea at a time. The vast majority of their victims were sunk in accordance with international law by the gun, but one or two ships were sunk without warning by torpedoes and the Germans, finding that there were no protests from America, attacked in this way more often. In July and August 1916, *U35* made the record cruise of the war, sinking no less than fifty-four ships in the western Mediterranean, nearly all by gunfire. The majority of the casualties in the Mediterranean were French and Italian, but those British ships which were sunk were large and so constituted a considerable proportion of the total tonnage.

The anti-submarine policy in the Mediterranean consisted of sailing merchant ships on fixed routes which were patrolled by anti-submarine vessels. The hope was that the patrols would keep the U-boats away from the routes. The U-boats, however, dived as the patrols appeared and, after they had passed, surfaced and continued their depredations. There was no shortage of targets, as some 350 ships were at sea in the Mediterranean at a time and the fixed routes made them comparatively easy to find.

The Flanders flotilla was composed of an increasing proportion of the later UB and UC types which were larger and could pass the Straits of Dover without much difficulty. They were able to extend their operations over a much wider area, appearing as far west as the Bristol Channel.

Allied anti-submarine measures were prosecuted with great energy but were still quite unable even to check this campaign, although it was waged by only half the German U-boats working in accordance with international law. On 6 July 1916, however, *UC7* was detected by hydrophones and sunk by depth charges. This sinking inaugurated a completely new method of dealing with the submarine.

The hydrophone, which had been under development since 1915, was an underwater microphone which could hear the noise of a submarine's machinery or propellers and was the first device capable of detecting a completely submerged submarine. It was still of very limited value, as all ships in the vicinity had to stop so as not to mask the sound of the U-boat. In calm weather the noise of a U-boat could then be detected and its direction ascertained. By using several hydrophone-fitted ships, the U-boat's position could be plotted by cross bearings. The depth charge was a great advance, as it provided the first effective way to attack a submerged submarine. It was simply a large bomb with a hydrostatic fuse. It was dropped over the stern of a moving ship and sank to its set depth when it exploded. It had the great advantage over the former towed explosive sweep that it exploded whether contact was made with the U-boat or not. It therefore had a chance to cause some damage or at least unsettle the crew even when it missed. Depth charges were however still carried only in small numbers by a few ships.

The most effective anti-submarine measure of all at this time, however, was the defensive arming of merchantmen. By September 1916 nearly two thousand ships had a gun, which meant that five out of every seven passing through the Mediterranean were armed. The vast majority of armed ships escaped when attacked by gunfire.

After the Battle of Jutland at the end of May 1916, Admiral Scheer was convinced that the Germans could never gain command of the sea by defeating the Grand Fleet. Its immense

59

superiority and strategic position were more than Germany could compete with. He was sure that, if the war was to be won, the command of the sea must be disputed by an unrestricted U-boat campaign. He believed that the success attained at Jutland had sufficiently impressed neutrals to allow an unrestricted campaign to take place without serious repercussions. This policy was as usual strongly opposed by the civilian members of the government headed by the Imperial Chancellor.

Attempts were made by the German High Command during the summer to get Admiral Scheer to agree to resume the campaign with the North Sea U-boats, pointing out that, in spite of the restrictions, the Mediterranean U-boats were achieving considerable success. However he remained adamant in his belief that an unrestricted campaign was the only way to operate submarines. He also suggested that the High Seas Fleet's policy of waiting for a favourable opportunity to engage the Grand Fleet should be changed, and that the High Seas Fleet should now be entirely auxiliary to an unrestricted U-boat campaign against commerce. Its function should be to defend the U-boat bases, protect the minesweepers which kept the channels swept for the U-boats, escort the U-boats to sea and raid the Dover barrage.

In August 1916 a conference took place with the German High Command at Pless to try to resolve these issues. In the debate between the Navy and the Imperial Chancellor about an unrestricted submarine campaign, the Army High Command, in which von Falkenhayn had been replaced by Hindenburg and Ludendorf, came to be a sort of referee. They saw that there was great force in the arguments for an unrestricted submarine campaign and indeed in their heart of hearts could see no other way to win the war. They looked at the problem of how much they could try neutral patience entirely from a military, as opposed to an economic or political, standpoint. Rumania had just come into the war against the central powers and this had absorbed all available German troops so that the frontiers with Holland and Denmark were unguarded. The resumption of the U-boat campaign was consequently delayed. Early in October 1916, when the Rumanian campaign had been successfully concluded, Hindenburg ordered the resumption of restricted U-boat warfare by the North Sea U-boats. The twilight period of the U-boat attack on commerce was at an end.

The effect of this year, the 'twilight period', of U-boat operations against trade had been an irritation rather than an anxiety to the Allies (see p. 103; fig. 11, i). Throughout the winter of 1915, the Allied shipping losses had been a steady drain when yet more tonnage was needed to sustain military operations. France and Italy suffered heavy losses in the Mediterranean; shipbuilding in both countries was at a standstill and the additional burden of supplying them fell upon Great Britain. The decline in British shipbuilding, due to the mobilization of shipyard workers and a shortage of steel, meant that the replacement tonnage was still less than the losses. Nevertheless, during the twilight period, the Allies were stimulated into great improvements in the efficiency with which they operated merchant ships, which resulted in there being no loss of carrying power. As a result of diplomatic pressure, neutral losses were diminished and their carrying power was also put to good use by the Allies.

In March and April 1916 when all the U-boats had returned temporarily to the attack on commerce, the result was to raise the monthly rate of sinking nearly to the level of August 1915 which was still the worst month of the war to date. This rate of sinking was over twice that at which ships were being built and, although such losses could be absorbed by the immense size of the British mercantile marine for some years, it was bound progressively to hinder the Allies' capacity to make war.

The losses had decreased again during the last five months of the twilight period but gave the Allies an irritating time. The casualties to merchant ships from both the Mediterranean and Flanders U-boats were some fifty ships a month from May to July 1916, rising in August and September, with more U-boats at sea, to 115 ships a month. These losses were still heavier than the building programme in Britain, whilst the French and Italian losses were not being replaced at all. There was consequently a decline in arrivals of ships in the United Kingdom but, due to a still more efficient use of shipping and ports, the actual weight of cargo landed was little less than before. Nevertheless the shortage of shipping was acute because of the insatiable demands for military purposes and for the unquestionable needs of the Allies. All had to be met by British or neutral shipping which was now nearly 10 per cent smaller than it had been in 1914.

Of much more significance than the shipping losses during the twilight period, however, was the great expansion of the U-boat arm (see p. 103; fig. 11, ii).

61

When Admiral von Tirpitz resigned in March 1916, he had left no less than 120 U-boats under construction. Admiral von Capelle, who succeeded him, ordered another fifty-six U-boats in May. Eighty new boats had been delivered in the twilight period for the loss of only seventeen so the number available was doubled. Strength in all theatres had risen steadily, but the greatest increase was in the North Sea flotillas which trebled in size from twelve to thirty-five boats in this period of a year. During the last five months of the twilight period in the summer of 1916, although only half the U-boats were operating against trade, the numbers so employed were in fact greater than the whole U-boat fleet during the first campaign in 1915.

Improvement was not only in numbers; the new boats of the standard 'Mittel U' type, on which the brunt of the war to date had fallen, had higher speed, greater endurance and more torpedoes. The new UBII type was twice the size of the original UB boat and was comparable to the British coastal submarine of the C class. Two new types of minelayer came into service, the *U71* class of 'Mittel U' size which greatly extended the area in which mines could be laid and the new UCII type which was over three times the size of its predecessor and carried torpedo tubes and a gun as well as mines.

Admiral von Capelle's policy was to obtain longer range and greater offensive power in order to spread operations over a wider area. Twenty-two of the U-boats he ordered were therefore of a new and larger type than the Germans had built before and the smallest ordered were of a new UBIII type which were nearly as large as the original 'Mittel U'.

During the summer of 1916 the Germans found a new use for the submarine. In June the commercial submarine *Deutschland*, the first of six building, made a voyage to the U.S.A. and brought back a cargo of nickel, tin and rubber. For the *Deutschland's* second trip *U53* was sent with her to give protection should the British be waiting for her off the U.S. coast. *U53's* protection was not however needed, but before returning she sank five ships off the American coast. *U53* was a new 'Mittel U' submarine and had to embark extra fuel in her main ballast tanks for this voyage. But this cruise showed the astonishing range of the new U-boats and how with still larger submarines the campaign could be extended.

*   *   *

The instructions for the resumption of the restricted campaign against trade by all U-boats came from the German High Command on 6 October 1916 as a direct order. Admiral Scheer strongly disagreed with this policy but felt that he could not protest against such a definite command. Although the resumed campaign was officially restricted, the Germans reserved the right to sink armed merchantmen without warning. The number of U-boats available for the campaign was greater than ever before and in October 1916 numbered eighty-seven operational out of a total of 119. In this third and final period of the German restricted submarine campaign, which lasted from October 1916 until January 1917, U-boat strength rose to 103 operational boats out of 148 altogether. The North Sea, Flanders and Mediterranean flotillas were all reinforced and only the number of submarines in the Baltic declined. The campaign was widespread: in October, ships were sunk off North Russia and west of Gibraltar as well as in the south-western approaches, the Mediterranean and the Channel. The operations of the larger UB and UC boats from Flanders spread right down the Channel into areas hitherto only reached by the northabout route. The Mediterranean was reinforced by seven of the new UC boats which had just sufficient endurance to reach the area if they went by the Straits of Dover.

In the four months of this campaign (see p. 103; fig. 11, i) the shipping casualties rose to very nearly twice the level they had reached in August 1915, which had been the heaviest month of the war up to this time. Three-quarters of the ships were sunk by the gun but some 20 per cent were destroyed without warning by torpedo. Mines added their quota which was slightly larger than usual during this period. One hundred and forty steamers and large sailing vessels were sunk in October 1916, 113 in November, 128 in December and 135 in January 1917, as well as many more small sailing ships. The 'exchange rate' rose to sixty-five ships destroyed for every U-boat sunk.

In December 1916, through traffic to Australia, New Zealand, India and the Far East was diverted from the Mediterranean right round the Cape with the resulting loss of carrying power. The casualties were now far greater than the shipbuilding programme and the total imports into the United Kingdom began to decline. It was no longer possible to obtain space for supplies which had heretofore been regarded as essential. The destruction of shipping had become a serious anxiety rather than an inconvenience. Casualties at this rate, if continued unchecked for a year or so, would decrease the tonnage to an extent which would make the support of the Allies and the overseas expeditions impossible. The British Admiralty now realized that the U-boat had become of paramount importance in the war at sea and Admiral Jellicoe was moved from the command of the Grand Fleet to be First Sea Lord in this crisis. Conditions, however, in the Allied countries, although admittedly there were shortages, were still good compared with the privations that the Germans themselves were suffering from the British blockade.

The principal reasons for the U-boats' success were the increase in their numbers and the continued ineffectiveness of any of the Allied counter measures. In the whole of the four months the Germans lost only eleven U-boats, five of which were sunk by the Russians in the Black Sea and off their northern Arctic coasts by mines and patrols. Two were not really to the Allies' credit, one being stranded and the other sunk by the explosion of its target. British counter measures could claim only four, two of which were sunk by Q ships and two by destroyer patrols. In the same period seven 'Mittel U' and thirty-six UC boats were delivered.

The poor anti-submarine results were not for want of trying and the British exerted an immense effort. The barrages in the Otranto and Dover Straits were strengthened, but the Germans continued to use both without losing a single U-boat. In October 1916, to make matters worse, the Dover barrage was raided by German destroyers and the patrols suffered some losses. The mined nets of the Dover barrage were supplemented by deep minefields but the winter weather caused havoc with this system and by the spring it had become as dangerous for the patrols as the U-boats. A start was made with a huge semi-circular anti-U-boat mine barrier in the Heligoland Bight, but these fields were very quickly discovered by the German minesweepers and passages swept through them. The expanded decoy service had sixteen Q-ship battles in the period but the U-boats were much more wary, with the result that there were only the two sinkings already noted. British submarines were used more extensively to patrol against U-boats, and hunting flotillas of destroyers and P-boats were stationed in the Channel. The aim of these hunting flotillas was to proceed in force to areas where U-boats were reported and to try to keep them down until their batteries were exhausted. It was hoped that when forced to the surface, they could be sunk by gunfire. The hunting groups, however, usually arrived so long after the reports of submarine activity that the U-boats had already moved on. Even if they were still there, they had only to dive until nightfall when they could surface and seek targets elsewhere. In some areas, where the patrols were very persistent, the U-boats had to move further to seaward but were still able to find plenty of targets.

The British, seriously worried, pressed on most vigorously with all the counter measures they could think of. These included the mass production of depth charges and the further development of hydrophones, as well as the arming of more merchantmen and an expansion of the decoy service. They were also developing much better mines, which had hitherto proved very inefficient against submarines. Few of these measures could reach fruition before the middle of 1917 and the British could discern no radically new way to deal with the problem.

This final so-called 'restricted' submarine campaign in which the majority of ships were sunk by the gun has been subsequently condemned by the Germans, as they consider it stimulated counter measures prematurely and, by being restricted, lost them many sinkings. Admiral Scheer was right in thinking that it could not be decisive, but it was nevertheless a considerable success for the Germans, and his fear that it would lead to heavy casualties at the hands of the decoys was not substantiated.

In the whole period of two years, in which the German U-boats had waged their campaign against commerce, the restrictions imposed upon them varied greatly from phase to phase of the struggle. In the most restricted form it meant that the U-boats had to operate entirely in accordance with international law and had to apply the rules of visit and search, sinking ships only if they were carrying contraband. At the other end of the scale the U-boats were allowed to sink without warning all enemy merchant ships found in the war zone, whether armed or not, and only neutrals were spared. In general the Germans went as far towards a totally unrestricted campaign as their relations with neutral states allowed. The term 'restricted campaign' has not therefore a very precise connotation.

It has been seen that the general effect of restrictions was that the submarine could not always be used in the way in which it had been designed : that is, to submerge and make surprise torpedo attacks on ships. It could use its quality of being able to make itself invisible only to evade patrols and penetrate barriers to reach the trade routes. When operating against merchant ships it had to act as a surface gunboat in the same way as the old privateers. Although there were distinct advantages in this form of attack, as more ships could be sunk for each sortie, it had the disadvantage that it could be countered by the universal arming of merchant ships and it rendered the U-boat vulnerable to decoys.

Throughout the campaign the number of ships sunk was almost entirely a question of how many U-boats were operating and the Allied anti-submarine measures had very little effect. This is confirmed by the steady increase in the 'exchange rate' of ships sunk to U-boats destroyed. The main Allied counter measures of a vast patrol system and of barriers, on which they expended most of their effort, were in general ineffective. The most efficient anti-submarine measure of this period was not naval in character and was probably American diplomatic pressure, which kept the campaign restricted and worked for the general application of international law among belligerents.

For two considerable periods during these two years, the High Seas Fleet U-boats were withdrawn and the campaign was left to those in the Mediterranean and working from Flanders. Nevertheless the U-boats sank over $3\frac{1}{2}$ million tons of world shipping, 2 million tons of which were British. In spite of this huge rate of destruction, the British merchant marine, by the end of the two years, was still 94 per cent of the size it had been at the beginning of the war. In the last four months of the campaign, the rate of destruction had risen to $3\frac{1}{2}$ million tons a year, but, even had there been double the number of U-boats and had the British taken no new counter measures, it would still have taken another two years to defeat them by this means alone. In other words, the submarine when restricted, although far more efficient than a surface ship as a commerce raider, could still not be a war-winning weapon on its own and this was in line with the analysis of the history of the *guerre de course* in the past.

66

V

The Submarine as a Warship in the First World War
(June 1916–November 1918)

It had been obvious for some time that the British offensive submarines were not being used to the best advantage. Their deployment to coincide with surface operations, such as a minelaying
expedition to the Bight or a sweep by the Grand Fleet, never
seemed to lead to results. But keeping them in harbour and sending them into the Bight only when there were signs of enemy
activity was even less successful: they never arrived until after
the enemy had returned to harbour. There was little doubt that
the solution was to occupy the patrol areas continuously. By June
1916 there were ample submarines available to do this but the
heavy mining in the Bight by both sides seemed bound to lead to
increased losses. It was this that so far had made the Admiralty
hesitate. The German swept-channels out of the Bight were, however, by now fairly well known and it was where they debouched
into the North Sea that the British submarines normally patrolled:
they penetrated right into the Bight only on special occasions and
to lay mines. Continuous patrols in these areas, even if they led
to greater casualties, would also give a better chance to sink
U-boats which used the same swept-channels. There was also the
hope that, in spite of the limitations of the new wireless sets, the
submarine would be of value for reconnaissance.

After Jutland, in May 1916, therefore, British submarines
settled down to occupy a number of patrol positions with a succession of boats relieving each other on station (see p. 67; fig. 8).
The Harwich submarines kept four or five at sea north of Terschelling to watch the western exits from the Bight and the Blyth
and Tyne submarines patrolled in the Horns Reef–Jutland Bank
area to watch the northern exits. Their principal aim was still to
act as offensive outposts although they would clearly be useful as
a reconnaissance screen for the Grand Fleet.

In August, Admiral Scheer renewed his plan for the bombard-

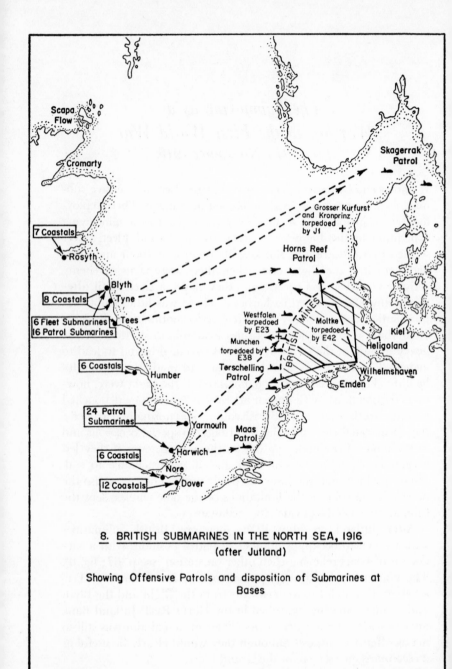

8. BRITISH SUBMARINES IN THE NORTH SEA, 1916
(after Jutland)

Showing Offensive Patrols and disposition of Submarines at Bases

ment of Sunderland. But this time he decided to place the U-boats more for reconnaissance than attack, in the hope that he could prevent himself from being surprised by the Grand Fleet. In order to control their operations the Commander of the U-boat flotillas sailed with the fleet. This operation, in August 1916, is not well known; the Main fleets did not make contact, but it is of very great interest from the submarine point of view as they were used extensively by both sides (see p. 70; fig. 9). Admiral Scheer deployed twenty-four U-boats in all and, as the quadrants in which he had disposed them before Jutland were out of favour, he placed them in five patrol lines. The lines were designed to cover the flanks of the High Seas Fleet whilst it was bombarding Sunderland and to use them, in Scheer's words, as mobile mine-fields. One line of U-boats was stationed on each side of Sunderland; two other patrol lines guarded the approach from the Flanders Bight whilst the fifth line was in the Heligoland Bight to secure his retreat. These lines were co-ordinated with the positions of existing minefields and with the Zeppelin patrols.

The Admiralty, as usual, got wind that some sort of an operation was imminent and the British counter measures included the deployment of twenty-six submarines. Three were already on patrol off the western approaches to the Ems and two more were at once ordered into the Heligoland Bight. Six patrol submarines were stationed at gun range off Lowestoft, Yarmouth and Harwich and this time were where the Admiralty wanted them. The rest of the submarines were in three groups, each with a destroyer. One group from Blyth set out to take up a defensive position to protect the Tyne and Whitby areas, and the other two from Harwich and Yarmouth were sent into the Flanders Bight.

When leaving the Heligoland Bight, the German High Seas Fleet was ambushed by *E23* which made in all three attacks on various formations. She finally hit the dreadnought *Westfalen* which was badly damaged and had to return to base. The British Battle-Cruiser Fleet in its early movements passed near the end of the line of U-boats off Sunderland and was reported by *U53* and *U52*, the latter torpedoing and sinking the light cruiser *Nottingham*. In spite of several reports from the U-boats, the High Seas Fleet was unaware that it was about to run into the whole Grand Fleet and turned to engage a non-existent force reported by a Zeppelin to be to the south-east. No fleet action therefore took place but, as the Grand Fleet was returning to harbour, the light

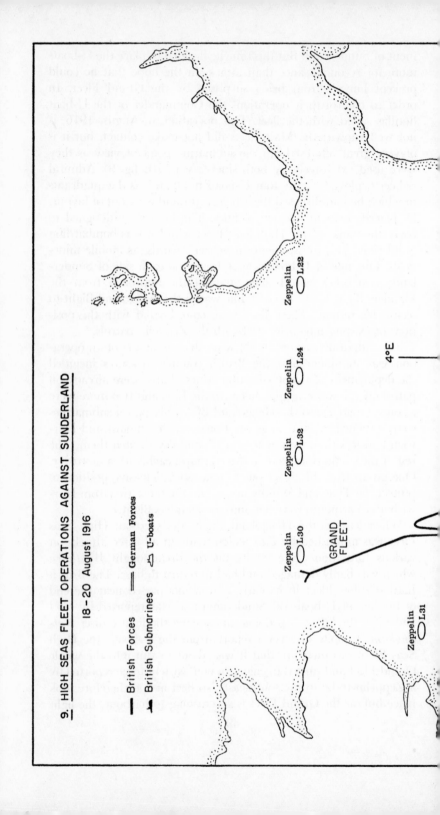

9. HIGH SEAS FLEET OPERATIONS AGAINST SUNDERLAND

18–20 August 1916

British Forces —— German Forces ══

British Submarines

Zeppelin L22

Zeppelin L24

Zeppelin L32

Zeppelin L30

GRAND FLEET

Zeppelin L31

4°E

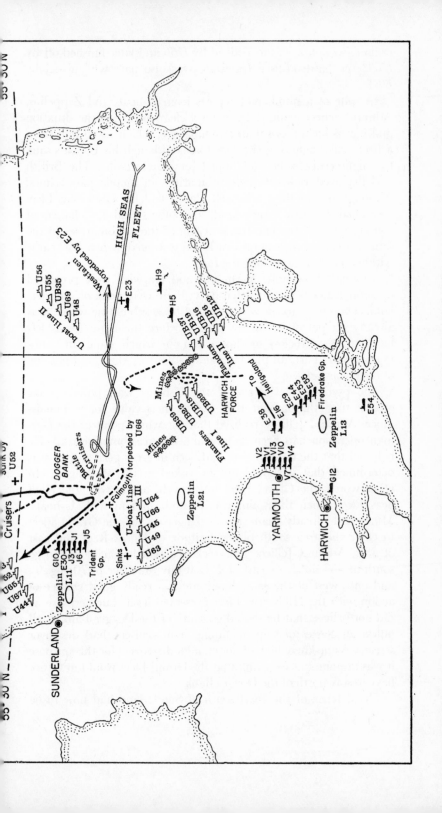

cruiser *Falmouth* was torpedoed by *U66* and later finished off by *U63*; the battle-cruiser *Inflexible* was also narrowly missed by *U65*.

In spite of a number of reports from U-boats and Zeppelins, Admiral Scheer again did not get a clear picture of the situation and it was luck, more than anything else, which saved him from a fleet action against a superior force. Although his U-boats sank two light cruisers, he had hoped for better results. The British had deployed most of their submarines in mobile patrol lines. Although one of these was well placed had the High Seas Fleet continued towards Sunderland, the others had no chance of coming into action. The manœuvring of these submarines in the same areas as surface ships nearly led to tragedy when *E30* came within an ace of torpedoing the *Lion*.

Although Lowestoft, Yarmouth and Harwich were protected by submarines deployed defensively, there were none off Sunderland. The only success was obtained by a submarine which was already on patrol in enemy waters before the main forces left harbour. Nevertheless in this action, in which some fifty submarines took part, all the damage was done by them and not one of them was lost.

The psychological effect of the U-boats was, however, far greater than the damage they did or their value for reconnaissance. Admiral Jellicoe realized that the whole point of the German operation had been to lure him into a submarine trap. He believed that the Grand Fleet had been in great peril and he was determined that it should not be risked in this way again. In other words, the Grand Fleet must avoid action with the High Seas Fleet when their aim was to ambush him with U-boats. Mines had already made it too dangerous for the Grand Fleet to enter the area south of the latitude of Horns Reef and east of 5°E. Admiral Jellicoe now reckoned that he ought not to go south of 55° 30′ N or east of 4°E at any time (see p. 70; fig. 9), and only west of the same longitude if a really good chance of action with the High Seas Fleet presented itself. Furthermore he did not believe that he should go south of the Dogger Bank at all unless all classes of ship, including light cruisers, had destroyer screens. As he knew he had not enough destroyers for this purpose it was tantamount to saying that the Grand Fleet would in future have to stay north of the Dogger Bank.

The defence of the coast south of Sunderland had now to be

left to local defence forces and they could no longer depend on support from the Grand Fleet. It was thereby admitted that the Grand Fleet had virtually lost command of over half the North Sea, including much of the British coast line. It was the tactical use of U-boats and not the High Seas Fleet or minefields which had brought about this situation. Furthermore they had the effect of denying this area to the Grand Fleet whether they were there or not. In fact the U-boats were withdrawn from fleet work almost at once to return to the attack on trade, but the restrictions they imposed on the Grand Fleet remained.

The German U-boats did not operate in close co-operation with their fleet again during the war, and their absence had a cramping effect on the High Seas Fleet. Admiral Scheer tried one more sortie without U-boat support but felt that he could not move freely in the North Sea without them. He did not come out again with his whole fleet until his final sortie in April 1918.

After the High Seas Fleet's operation against Sunderland, all the British submarine flotillas on the east coast were strengthened and an additional flotilla was put under the command of the Grand Fleet. The idea that a submarine was primarily a defensive weapon being still uppermost in the British High Command's mind, this increase in strength was to be used defensively by holding back a number of patrol submarines in harbour in readiness to be used in this way. It was thus hoped to compensate for the new restrictions on the movements of the Grand Fleet.

Nevertheless it was the continuous patrols in enemy waters which secured results. The Germans were never able to come out again without being detected by the submarine patrols. In the sortie of the High Seas Fleet in October *E38* damaged the light cruiser *München*. When in November a German battle squadron came out to try to help two U-boats aground on the Danish coast, both the *Grosser Kurfürst* and the *Kronprinz* were torpedoed and damaged by *J1*. These results were not achieved without a price, eight submarines being lost in the North Sea during the year.

The British were not at all satisfied with the co-operation of submarines in fleet operations. Their hopes for improvement did not lie, however, in the development of patrol lines. They had been trying since before the war to develop the submarine to be

73

part of the fleet. In 1914 two submarines (see Note 8) of a higher speed for fleet work were under construction but, being of an experimental nature, were discontinued in order to hasten the production of patrol submarines. Early in 1915 information, false as it turned out, reached the British Admiralty that the new German U-boats were very fast on the surface. The figure of 22 knots was mentioned which could only be to allow them to work with the High Seas Fleet. As a counter measure the British considered it of great importance to produce high speed submarines themselves so that the Grand Fleet would not be caught at a disadvantage in action. Admiral Fisher, the First Sea Lord, therefore decided to build a fleet submarine with known and tried machinery as soon as possible. By using existing designs of diesel engines and packing in as much power as possible, the new J class were expected to make from 18 to 19 knots on the surface which would just allow them to keep up with the fleet.

Before the completion of the J class it was considered that submarines must try to work with the fleet in spite of their low speed. In the autumn of 1915 a new flotilla of submarines was formed and stationed at Blyth to co-operate directly with the Grand Fleet. It was comprised of G and E class submarines which could not sustain a sea speed of more than 14 knots. The plan was that they should leave harbour at the same time as the Grand Fleet in groups of three accompanied by a destroyer. They would make their way at full speed along a set route to the eastwards to join the fleet. It was recognized that the sea speed of the Grand Fleet was too fast for them, but it was hoped that they would join near the point where a battle would be fought and so be able to take part in it. Once they had joined they were to try to keep as close astern of the screening cruisers ahead of the fleet as possible and maintain full speed to avoid losing ground. If the Grand Fleet overtook them they were to follow up in case they could be of use. If all else failed they were to make at full speed for the Heligoland Bight and try to cut off the enemy's retreat. Although submarines set out in this way several times, notably before the Battle of Jutland, they were never able to catch up with the fleet. As a result they were generally used for ordinary offensive patrols in the Horns Reef area or the Skagerrak and on occasions were used defensively north of Flamborough Head.

It was obvious that patrol submarines were far too slow but it was now realized that the higher speed of the J class was not going to be enough. The Admiralty had anticipated this and were determined to produce fleet submarines with a substantial margin of speed over the fleet and to get sufficient horse power they had to use steam turbines. The result was the K class which were three times the size and seven or eight times the horse power of any former British submarine. Fourteen of them were ordered in 1915 and *K3*, the first one, was completed in the remarkably short time of eighteen months. With a sea speed of 24 knots these submarines could actually accompany the fleet and form part of it.

Two flotillas of fleet submarines were formed in 1917 as the K class were completed and they became an integral part of the Grand Fleet for the rest of the war. At sea they were stationed close astern of the advanced light cruiser screen, accompanied by a light cruiser or flotilla leader. On the approach of the enemy they were to be spread in pairs five miles apart and would endeavour to get on the far side of the enemy and interpose themselves between him and his base. They would then be well placed if the enemy attempted to avoid action by turning away. They would of course miss no opportunity to attack and they had twice the torpedo armament of the average patrol submarine. No opportunity occurred for these submarines to be tested in action. They were unfortunately not very handy when submerged and, like all steam submarines, took a good five minutes to dive. They therefore earned for themselves a bad name but in fact the whole venture was a remarkable achievement. The Grand Fleet, which was unique in having submarines to form part of it, was thereby increased in strength probably equivalent to a division of battleships.

By the end of 1916 the need for the British to do everything to counter the German U-boat campaign against trade was paramount. The Admiralty were anxious to use British submarines in an anti-submarine capacity and a Grand Fleet committee sat towards the end of 1916 to study the subject. Admiral Beatty, who had just assumed command of the Grand Fleet, was very critical of the present use of submarines and their disposition. He pointed out that only ten submarines were normally on patrol out of eighty-six in the North Sea; the remainder, apart from those resting or under repair, were kept back ready to act defensively. The submarines on offensive patrols achieved very little considering their high losses. He wished to organize no less than forty submarines under Grand Fleet command to ambush U-boats on their way to the Atlantic. Coast defence was to be left to the small C class submarines as at the beginning of the war. Up to date British submarines had made nearly sixty contacts with German U-boats, which had resulted in only half a dozen attacks and the destruction of four U-boats. Two of these had been by C boats working with decoy trawlers and the other two in the course of ordinary offensive patrols. There was therefore little at this time to indicate that the submarine had much potential as an anti-submarine vessel.

Opinion varied widely on how best to use submarines against the U-boats. Two U-boats sunk in over two years did not seem to suggest that offensive patrols off the enemy bases were the answer. The Grand Fleet wanted to use them to attack the U-boats on passage and had plans to co-ordinate submarine patrols with destroyers and trawlers working mined-nets in large anti-U-boat operations. There were other suggestions to use them on the trade routes where the U-boats operated against shipping and even that they might escort merchantmen. At the beginning of 1917 no firm conclusion had been reached, and in the end nearly all of these methods were tried with some degree of success.

All the usual offensive patrols concentrated on sinking U-boats as their first priority, and eight C boats at Harwich were diverted from their defensive tasks to be used offensively off Zeebrugge to waylay the UC boats. The Commander-in-Chief of the Grand Fleet started to use his submarines to form a continuous patrol line across the North Sea from the Long Forties to the Skagerrak. At the end of March 1917, the Admiralty moved some patrol submarines from the North Sea to the western approaches and based them at Queenstown and Lough Swilly to work against U-boats in the Atlantic. The flotilla of submarines from the Tees was then moved to Scapa Flow to patrol on the U-boat passage routes round the north of Scotland and later in the year submarines were also used against U-boats in the Channel.

The aim in all types of anti-U-boat patrol by submarines was to catch the U-boat on the surface and torpedo her. This was far from easy, as a U-boat was not a large target and submarines of those days had only two, or at most four, torpedoes which could be fired in one attack. Nevertheless U-boats spent a very great deal of their time on the surface on passage to their operating areas, when searching for targets and in attacking by gunfire.

Anti-submarine patrols could be conducted by day either on the surface or submerged. A submerged patrol had the advantage that the patrolling submarine was unlikely to be seen first by the enemy but the disadvantage that the range of vision using a periscope was small. The surface patrol was generally preferred, as an enemy U-boat could be seen at a much greater distance and the hunter could dive at once and head her off submerged. At night a surface patrol was the only way to sight a U-boat, the torpedoes being fired from the surface as well. The principal detecting device was therefore the lookout, both by day and night, using binoculars when on the surface and the periscope submerged. Although primitive hydrophones were fitted in submarines before the end of the war, they were never more than auxiliary to the lookout. Attacks on completely submerged submarines were not possible and the two cases in which submerged U-boats were rammed were more by chance than anything else. Anti-submarine patrols had to be conducted with a high decree of alertness or the hunter could easily become the hunted. Two British submarines were sunk by the U-boats they were supposed to be hunting and there were a number of near misses.

During 1917, therefore, anti-submarine patrols became the primary task of British submarines and this shift of emphasis soon began to show results (see p. 78; fig. 10). Seven U-boats were sunk during 1917 and a further six in 1918, making a total of eighteen for the war. This was a substantial contribution to the defeat of the U-boat. Of these results, six U-boats were sunk off their bases, four were caught on passage and eight whilst operating on the trade routes. In the large operations in which submarines worked with other forces they did not secure any results and seemed to do better on their own. The intense anti-submarine activities of other air and surface forces and the difficulty of identification made operations against U-boats on the trade routes a hazardous business. Many attacks were made in error on British submarines and three succumbed to their own side during the war.

Whilst the majority of British submarines were deployed widely against the U-boats in 1917 and 1918, they never relaxed their grip on the exits from the Heligoland Bight. Such patrols were monotonous and dangerous and little happened until March 1918,

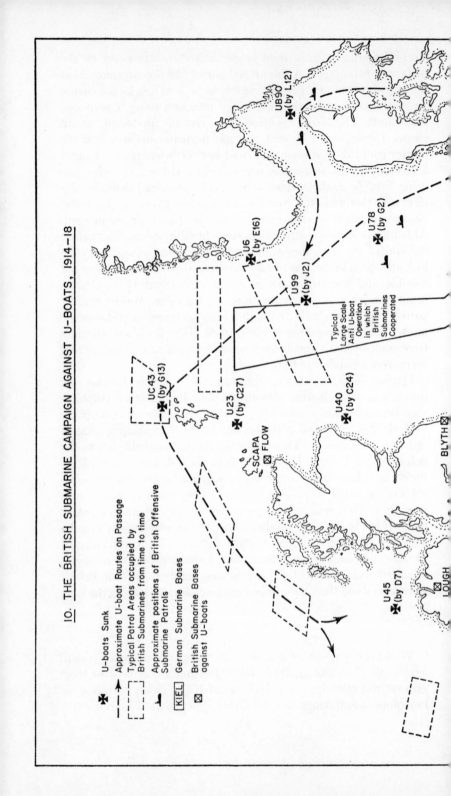

10. THE BRITISH SUBMARINE CAMPAIGN AGAINST U-BOATS, 1914–18

✠ U-boats Sunk

➝ Approximate U-boat Routes on Passage

☐ Typical Patrol Areas occupied by British Submarines from time to time

⌐ Approximate positions of British Offensive Submarine Patrols

☐ KIEL German Submarine Bases

⊠ British Submarine Bases against U-boats

UB90 (by L12)

U6 (by E16)

U78 (by G2)

U99 (by J2)

Typical Large Scale Anti U-boat Operation in which British Submarines Cooperated

UC43 (by G13)

U23 (by C27)

U40 (by C24)

SCAPA FLOW

BLYTH

LOUGH

U45 (by D7)

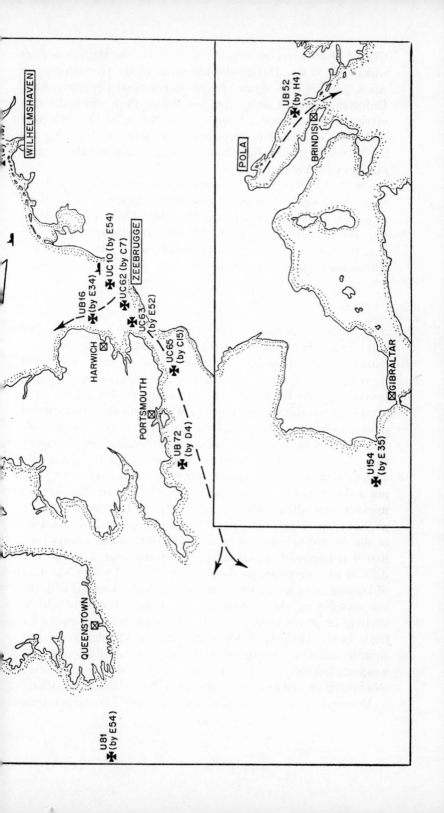

when *E44* attacked but missed some units of the High Seas Fleet which put to sea. During the last sortie of the German fleet in April, its ships were sighted by *J6* on patrol off the Horns Reef. Unfortunately they were taken for British ships which the submarine had been warned might enter the area. On their way back *E42* succeeded in torpedoing and severely damaging the battle-cruiser *Moltke*. For these few excitements ten British submarines were lost.

On 21 October 1918 Admiral Scheer withdrew all U-boats from attacking trade into the North Sea, intending to use them to assist with a final sortie by the High Seas Fleet. These U-boats were concentrated off the Firth of Forth and in the southern North Sea, but the High Seas Fleet mutinied and its plan to raid the Thames estuary did not come off.

As a military weapon the submarine proved itself a far more versatile warship than had been foreseen before the war. The submarine had been adopted by most of the navies of the world for defence and it was in this role that manœuvres seemed to have proved its value before the war. Both sides used it defensively a great deal and this use was uppermost in the minds of many naval officers right up to the end of the war. Although a considerable proportion of British submarine strength was allocated to defence throughout the war they proved a complete failure in this role. In all the raids by the German fleet on the east coast of England not a single ship was intercepted. It can be argued that the submarines were often badly placed or kept in harbour when they ought to have been at sea, but the reason is deeper than this. One of the great disadvantages of defensive warfare has always been that it is impossible to be strong everywhere and that it is very difficult to concentrate at the decisive time and place. The lack of knowledge of where the enemy would strike, coupled with the low mobility of the submarine, meant that they were seldom likely to be in the right place. The German defensive use of U-boats in the Heligoland Bight and off the Flanders coast was equally ineffective. So much for the peacetime evaluation of new weapons, but this was the submarine's only real failure; in every other role it proved its worth and in many it exceeded expectations.

Although towards the end of the war anti-U-boat operations

took priority, the principal role of British submarines was to help the Grand Fleet to deal with the German High Seas Fleet. The main strength of the British submarine force was kept in the North Sea throughout the war for this purpose. Co-operation with the fleet took three forms. The first was the diving patrol watching the exits from the Bight with the aim of sinking enemy ships which emerged and to report them by wireless. Submarines employed in this way succeeded in damaging four capital ships and a light cruiser of the High Seas Fleet and sinking a light cruiser and two destroyers. For these successes in enemy waters the British suffered the loss of eighteen submarines. In the reconnaissance role they did not detect the High Seas Fleet emerging from the Bight until after the Battle of Jutland, when their patrols became continuous, but all subsequent sorties were intercepted. Bad communications coupled with bad staff work, however, prevented any of these sightings from being of value to the Grand Fleet. The reconnaissance role did not have the importance that it merited, mainly because other sources of intelligence were so much better : the Grand Fleet generally knew that the High Seas Fleet was at sea long before it reached the submarine patrols. If this had not been so, submarine reconnaissance would have assumed a much greater importance. Although the going was tough, the diving patrol in the Bight was unquestionably a proper role for British submarines in which they did better than when employed in other ways in the North Sea.

The second type of co-operation with the fleet was in mobile patrol lines which, it was expected, could be moved as necessary during enemy sorties to intercept them. It was hoped in this way to cause damage which would reduce the enemy's speed and so bring on a fleet action. They did not succeed in doing this during the war, mainly because the low mobility of the submarine could not compete with fast ships, and because the British seldom had the initiative. It was very difficult to predict the course of an action and get the patrol line in the right place. However this malady was not confined to submarines and formations of all types of warships had the same difficulty. The submarines could, however, have been put to better use in enemy waters.

The third method of co-operation was the fleet submarine, two flotillas of which formed part of the Grand Fleet for the last eighteen months of the war. No action took place in this period and so they never had a chance to show what they could do. There were no fleet submarines in the High Seas Fleet and the Grand Fleet had a decided advantage by their presence, especially as they offered a solution if the High Seas Fleet tried to avoid action.

The Germans also used their U-boats to assist the High Seas Fleet for two short periods. In the first of these early in the war, they were used independently as weapons of attrition but the U-boats were diverted to a war against commerce before they had time to achieve very much. This campaign continued, however, as a side line throughout the war and the total casualties suffered by the British Navy from the U-boats were six battleships, ten cruisers, forty-two smaller warships and sixty-six auxiliaries including eleven armed merchant cruisers. In addition 225 auxiliary vessels were sunk by mines mostly laid by submarines. This list is impressive but was not enough to achieve the aim of reducing the British Fleet to a size that the High Seas Fleet could engage. All the battleships were old and so were most of the cruisers and, when the vast size of the British Navy is remembered, they did not alter the balance very much in Germany's favour. It is of interest that they did not succeed in hitting a single Dreadnought, which was the type that really mattered. This leads us to believe that, even had they used all their U-boats throughout the war to attack warships instead of commerce, the U-boat was not powerful enough in those days to have been decisive.

In the second period in 1916, Admiral Scheer used patrol lines but these were really more a stiffening of offensive patrols than mobile patrol lines of the British type. On more than one occasion major formations of the Grand Fleet went through them but the total casualties were only two light cruisers sunk. Although a patrol line looks very formidable on a map, a fast-moving force, such as Admiral Beatty's battle-cruisers, would at the most expose itself to attack by one U-boat as it passed and so to the danger of two, or at the most four, torpedoes: the damage from these, even if they all hit, could not be disastrous. Although these patrol lines reported many contacts, the picture of the situation given by them was always incomplete. This is not altogether surprising considering their restricted field of view, the prevailing poor visibility and the vast size and dispersion of fleets of those days. But the effect of the submarine on fleet operations could not be gauged solely by the casualties it caused or its efficiency in reconnaissance. Its effects on the endurance and maintenance of a fleet have already been discussed and the limits it imposed on where a fleet

82

would venture were profound. It is of great interest that much of this effect was psychological and often the submarines achieved it without being there at all. This effect alone more than justified the use of the U-boats against warships and it did more to dispute command of the sea than the High Seas Fleet itself.

The British use of the submarine as an anti-submarine vessel was not in any way a decisive factor in the campaign against the U-boats but was a very acceptable bonus. The eighteen U-boats sunk represented 10 per cent of the total U-boat casualties : it was twice as many as the famous Q ships achieved and three times the number sunk by aircraft. When these results are compared with the forces engaged they appear in a still more favourable light. There were only thirty-five submarines employed fully on anti-submarine patrols and another fifty which were used from time to time. The eighteen U-boats sunk by them compare favourably with the forty-one sunk by 300 destroyers, sloops and P-boats or the thirty-two sunk by 4,000 Auxiliary Patrol vessels. The Admiralty's diversion of the main strength of the British submarine force to this role, which was not based on any solid evidence that it would be effective, was well justified by these results.

It was as an independent weapon of attrition in enemy waters, however, that the submarine achieved its best results. It proved most effective when it operated where its own surface fleet could not go and where the enemy really needed to use the sea. For the Germans this meant everywhere outside the Baltic and the Heligoland Bight and for the British inside the Baltic and in the Sea of Marmora. In these areas the full potential of the submarine could be realized : its ability to operate in enemy waters, unsupported by other forces; its endurance, which allowed it to wait patiently in the right place until targets appeared; and its apparent ubiquitousness which made counter measures so difficult. Almost all the damage done by submarines was in enemy waters : three-quarters of the British results were achieved in the Baltic and the Sea of Marmora alone. In these areas their value was out of all proportion to the effort put into them; for example, the Allied submarines at the Dardanelles represented a smaller effort than that needed to sustain a single pre-Dreadnought battleship of which the British had ten in that area alone. Many of the submarine's apparent failures were because its true character had not been discerned by those who operated it. It could not bar the way like a battleship, but it could take a toll as the enemy passed. It was the attempts to manœuvre submarines like ships, or to keep them back in readiness in harbour, which led to disappointments. A routine which kept submarines on patrol in enemy waters whenever available, only allowing for proper rest and maintenance, was what led to success.

Unlike the battleship, the submarine's influence was not obtained by being invulnerable but by being replaceable, and throughout the war both the British and German submarine fleets were built and manned substantially faster than they were depleted. The British submarines were employed almost entirely on military operations and in all they lost fifty-four boats. These losses were mostly caused by mines; eight are definitely known to have been sunk in this way and the fate of eleven more is unknown but more probably due to them than anything else. Five were torpedoed by enemy U-boats, four were sunk by surface ships and three while penetrating into the Baltic and the Dardanelles. Finally one was bombed by an aircraft in harbour. The enemy can take the credit for destroying these thirty-two submarines. Of the rest, no less than nine were lost by collision or accident of some sort, three were sunk in error by Allied forces and three more ran aground and were wrecked or interned. The remaining seven were trapped in the Baltic and had to be scuttled to avoid them falling into the hands of the enemy. In all 150 new submarines joined the fleet between 1914 and 1918. There was, therefore, a steady increase in size in the British submarine force. Some older boats were disposed of and seven were sold to Italy when she entered the war, but at the Armistice there were 137 submarines in commission which was double the number in 1914.

If the total damage caused to warships by either the British or German submarines had been gained in a fleet action, it would undoubtedly have been hailed as a great victory. But purely as a warship, as opposed to a commerce raider, the submarine in the First World War was not powerful enough to rival the Dreadnought battleship as the arbiter of sea power. On the other hand it became a serious factor which influenced all operations and this influence on occasions was capable of denying whole areas of sea to the enemy. Although its protagonists' hopes that it would replace the battleship were not realized, its influence was certainly as important as, and probably greater than, most other types of warship.

VI

The German Unrestricted Submarine Campaign 1917-18

The unrestricted U-boat campaign, which was to last for the remaining twenty-one months of the war, was not begun by the Germans without misgivings. The debate on whether to proceed with it had continued throughout the winter. The Navy school, led by Admirals Scheer and von Holtzendorf, were fully conscious that Germany's unenviable position was largely due to the British blockade and the failure of the German Navy to break it. They saw no hope of the High Seas Fleet regaining command of the sea but were anxious to show that the Navy had a way to restore the position. They were convinced that this was by allowing U-boats to operate against trade in the way in which they could achieve the best results. In their view this meant, whatever international law said, a totally unrestricted campaign.

Von Holtzendorf rightly saw that the British merchant service was the backbone of the Allies. The industry of Great Britain, upon which the war effort depended, relied upon it and it kept the Allied armies overseas supplied. Great Britain's allies themselves would not be able to continue the war without its support and indeed Great Britain could not even feed herself without it, as three-quarters of her food had to come by sea. If an attack on British sea communications could reduce her tonnage sufficiently, the war could be won without regaining complete command of the sea but merely by depriving her of the use of it. Von Holtzendorf's information on the amount of British shipping used for military purposes, to support her allies and for her own imports was substantially correct, as was his estimate of the tonnage being built and under repair. He believed that, if he could prevent any neutral tonnage from working for the Allies and could reduce the volume of shipping available by some 39 per cent, Great Britain would only have enough left to supply the homeland: she would be unable to support her military operations overseas or her allies or indeed import sufficient raw materials to keep her war production going. As there could be no possibility of such a heavy loss of shipping being replaced during hostilities, the whole Allied war effort would collapse and the Allies would have to sue for peace.

During the summer of 1916, half the U-boats, working in accordance with international law, had sunk an average of 130,000 tons of shipping a month. The full U-boat strength, under the restrictions in force at the end of 1916, were sinking over 300,000 tons a month. The greater number of U-boats that would be available in 1917 would be able to do better than this, but to reduce British shipping by 39 per cent in the six months available before having to face another winter, it would have to be sunk at the rate of 600,000 tons a month. This was clearly more than was possible in a restricted campaign.

The main weapon of restricted submarine warfare had been the gun, which had made it possible to sink more ships in a patrol than by torpedo attack delivered when submerged. This advantage no longer held good. The arming of more and more British merchant vessels meant that not only did many escape from attacks by gunfire, but that a much heavier expenditure of ammunition was required to sink a ship which resisted, as this meant fighting a battle, generally at long range. All the newer types of U-boat which were coming forward carried more torpedoes: the new 'Mittel U's', for example, had ten instead of six or seven and so could sink more ships in this way. Although U-boat losses had not been serious in 1916, the Q ships had proved to be the most dangerous opponents. Surface attack by gun and every restriction which involved the examination of ships played into their hands, but they could be completely countered by a torpedo attack without warning when submerged. Torpedo attack therefore promised to give better results than the gun in the future and everything pointed towards a completely unrestricted campaign. The Navy school were sure that it was in this way that the required 600,000 tons a month could be brought within the capacity of the number of U-boats that would be available in 1917.

The civilian politicians, headed by the Imperial Chancellor, were rigidly opposed to unrestricted submarine warfare. They doubted the validity of the naval figures and did not believe that the U-boats were capable of achieving the results postulated for them. They were certain that neutrals, especially the United

States, would be antagonized to an extent which would probably bring them into the war against Germany and this would make her defeat inevitable.

On the other hand the Army High Command felt above all that whether or not an unrestricted U-boat campaign should be started was a matter for the military and not the civilians: Hindenburg and Ludendorf were determined that they would have the last say in this matter. They now believed that the war had reached a stalemate which the German army could not break and that it could no longer be won by a land campaign. The effect of the British blockade was such that they feared that they could not stand another winter. It was imperative that something should be done during the summer of 1917 to finish the war. They realized that the neutral countries would be antagonized by an unrestricted U-boat campaign, but the German army was in a position to deal with the minor European neutrals if they entered the war. America, having no army on a continental scale, would have to raise and train one before she could really have any effect. This would take time and, if von Holtzendorf's calculations were right, the war would be won before they could do this. Hindenburg and Ludendorf were therefore now prepared to accept a break with America and, indeed, believed that they had no other course if the war was to come to a favourable conclusion. At a conference at Pless in January 1917, the decision was finally taken, against the advice of the Chancellor, to start an unrestricted submarine campaign on 1 February.

By 1 February, the Germans had 111 operational U-boats (see p. 103; fig. 11, ii) out of a total of 152. Another 105 were in various stages of construction and this total was increased by an order for another fifty-one U-boats, mostly of the smaller UB type so that they could be built quickly. A larger programme was not embarked upon, as the Germans believed that the unrestricted campaign should win the war before it could be completed. In February nearly fifty submarines were at sea, twenty-four of which were actually cruising round the British Isles and in the Mediterranean, destroying the record number of 250 steamers (see Note 9). In March they did better still and sank over 330 ships. In April, when there were no less than thirty-nine U-boats cruising in the operational areas, they achieved the highest score of the war and sank some 430 steamers. Most of these ships were sunk by torpedo without warning. A few British armed steamers were attacked with the gun and half of them defended themselves and escaped. The gun was used mainly against unarmed steamers, generally Allied or neutral, and against small sailing ships, coasters and fishing vessels which were not worth a torpedo. On an average, in all areas, over ten merchant ships were being sunk by every U-boat on station each month, which meant that they were doing twice as well as in the restricted campaign at the end of 1916. The High Seas Fleet U-boats based on German ports were beginning to use the Straits of Dover again, thus saving many days on passage, and the Flanders U-boats were operating as far as the south coast of Ireland and the Bay of Biscay. The UC boats continued their minelaying offensive on a larger scale than ever, but the counter measures to their mines were reasonably effective and only twenty-five ships a month were sunk. The average sinkings for the whole campaign were therefore up to von Holtzendorf's calculations and from the German point of view everything seemed to be going according to plan.

In April a quarter of the ships setting out from the United Kingdom were being sunk before they could complete a round voyage. To make matters worse, neutrals were being terrorized and their traffic with the Allies fell to a quarter of the normal. The losses the British were now suffering were so large that they realized that, at this rate, they would have to arrange a peace by November (see front end paper diagram, also Note 10).

The Allied counter measures were proving totally inadequate. The barrages in the Dover and Otranto Straits were not stopping the U-boats. They passed through them unchecked and the numerous patrols in the barrier areas seldom even saw them. They succeeded in sinking only one U-boat in the first three months of the unrestricted campaign. The mines laid in the Heligoland Bight were inefficient and were, in any case, swept up by the German minesweepers almost as soon as they were put down. The vast number of auxiliary vessels which patrolled round the waters of the British Isles and in the Mediterranean succeeded in sinking only one U-boat in this period. They hurried from sinking to sinking, arriving only in time to pick up survivors; the U-boat was then either miles away or submerged and invisible. Their activities forced the German U-boats more to seaward, but this did not worry them as there were still plenty of targets to be found. Q ships and British submarines were rather more successful and sank two U-boats each. Three others were lost by accident of some sort not attributable to Allied anti-submarine measures. These casualties were totally insufficient to check the campaign and German submarine strength was still increasing. The effectiveness of the campaign can be gauged by the 'exchange rate' of the steamers sunk for every U-boat destroyed, which was fifty-three in February, seventy-four in March and no less than 167 in April.

In April the unrestricted submarine campaign brought America into the war on the side of the Allies and it was at once apparent to them, as well as to the British, that if they did not do something about the U-boat campaign very quickly the Allies would lose the war. It was clear that such rates of sinking upset the whole strategic theory of naval warfare. The Grand Fleet still commanded the surface of the sea and prevented the Germans from using it, but it could do little or nothing, except to cover the operations of the anti-submarine vessels, to protect commerce from the German submarines. Notwithstanding the supremacy of their battlefleet, the British were gradually losing the power to use the sea and the theories of the past, which held that a *guerre de course* could never be more than a nuisance, were rapidly being disproved. The threat of the High Seas Fleet was moreover still there and, by remaining 'in being', it materially helped the U-boats by forcing the Grand Fleet to retain its 100 destroyers which were urgently required to help in the anti-submarine campaign. The Americans readily agreed with the British that it was destroyers above all that were required in the eastern Atlantic and not their battlefleet. Without hesitation they unbalanced their fleet by sending all the destroyers they could to join the Queenstown command and reduced most of their battleships to a training status.

In May the number of U-boats at sea fell slightly and their losses increased. In June an immense effort was made to regain the high sinkings of April and even more U-boats were got to sea. However it was not found possible to sink more than seven merchant ships for each U-boat on station (see Note 11). In July, after this supreme effort, the number of U-boats at sea fell sharply and consequently the shipping casualties too. U-boat losses increased in these three months to sixteen. Five of these went to patrols of some kind and three were sunk by seaplanes with bombs. Q ships and British submarines again secured two each and a merchant ship managed to sink one in self-defence. Four others were lost by accidents of one kind or another. Although twenty-two new U-boats were delivered in this period, the losses showed a sharp rise from the previous three months, nevertheless the average 'exchange rate' was as high as seventy-three merchant ships sunk for every U-boat destroyed. These improved results for the Allies were due to the anti-submarine measures set in train the year before and also to an increase in the anti-submarine forces employed, especially destroyers, thirty-five of which were American. During the last three months, moreover, the British had at last begun the strategy which was to get the measure of the U-boats. They had experimented with a system of convoys, two of which sailed in May, four in June and fifteen in July.

The six months postulated by von Holtzendorf as necessary to win the war had now passed. The Germans had in fact sunk well over the required 600,000 tons a month : $3\frac{3}{4}$ million tons of world shipping had been lost and the repair yards were choked with another half a million tons which had been damaged. Admiral von Holtzendorf's calculations and predictions of sinkings were therefore substantially correct, but the Germans had not won the war. Carrying-power had indeed been considerably decreased not only by the sinkings but by delays, deviations and evasive routing, all directly attributable to the U-boats. Tonnage was already insufficient for all needs at the start of the campaign, but nevertheless the vast army in France and the expeditions overseas at Salonika, in Mesopotamia and East Africa were maintained, and there was only an 8 per cent decrease of imports into the United Kingdom. The import of materials required for war purposes and for making munitions actually rose. The only serious anxiety was oil fuel, stocks of which fell to under three months' and were expected to be exhausted before the end of the year. The Germans had, therefore, failed to bring about the collapse of the Allies in six months by an unrestricted U-boat campaign.

Credit for the failure of the first six months of the German unrestricted campaign is often given to the convoy system. The convoy system was, however, only experimental in May and June and had hardly got into its stride by July. In these three months only about 350 ocean-going ships had been convoyed, out of over 3,000 voyages. The convoyed ships suffered two casualties and it is improbable that they would have lost more than thirty-five if the ships had sailed independently. Convoy in the first six months of the unrestricted campaign, therefore, saved only about thirty-three ships out of nearly 2,000 casualties (see Note 12). The German failure was certainly not due to Allied anti-submarine measures, the average 'exchange rate' during the period being over seventy ships sunk for every U-boat destroyed: the Germans possessing eight more U-boats at the end of the campaign than they had had at the beginning. Nor could the success be attributed to shipbuilding, for Britain was still replacing only a fifth of her losses.

Although von Holtzendorf's figures and calculations proved accurate, his deductions from them were seriously in error, as the civil members of the German government had suspected. The whole of his plan depended on terrorizing the neutrals and depriving the Allies of the carrying power of their ships and of their building capacity. The Germans did succeed at the beginning of the campaign in scaring away a very great proportion of neutral shipping from British trade. Diplomatic skill, hard bargaining and pressure exerted in various other ways managed, however, to get a great deal of this back before the end of the period and by July the entrances of foreign ships were only 20 per cent less than the normal. A consequence of this was that the U-boats had to expend a great deal of their effort in sinking neutral ships and only 400,000 tons a month, out of the average sinkings of 600,000 tons, was British. As a result the British merchant fleet lost a total of $2\frac{1}{4}$ million tons instead of von Holtzendorf's estimate of over $3\frac{1}{2}$ million tons. In this period Great Britain had built only half a million tons, as the Germans had estimated, but another half a million tons had been built by the rest of the world and a further half a million tons of German shipping in American and neutral ports had been seized. These additions amounted to only half the losses but were nevertheless much greater than the Germans had thought possible, as they had not counted on world replacements being available to the Allies and had hoped to sabotage their interned ships before they could fall into the Allies' hands.

In spite of the fact that the U-boats sank what they said they would, therefore, the tonnage available to the Allies was not reduced by anything like what they had hoped. Moreover von Holtzendorf had underestimated the flexibility of the world's merchant shipping and the immense skill with which it was being organized. A great gain in carrying power was achieved by concentrating shipping, with a total disregard for financial and economic factors, on the shorter routes to North America instead of the longer routes to South America and the East. There was also a very great improvement in turn round and in easing the congestion of the ports. At the same time the ships requisitioned for military purposes were cut down by over half a million tons without reducing the commitments. The tonnage available was, therefore, put to much better use than before and carrying power was not reduced to the same extent as the tonnage sunk. Imports were restricted to those things absolutely necessary for the prosecution of the war and, although this caused great inconvenience and discomfort, it was still nothing to the privations brought about in Germany by the British blockade. Production of food in the United Kingdom was greatly increased and rationing ensured no waste and its even distribution. The carrying power available was thus used to better effect and the dependence on imports lessened.

The laurels for the defeat of the first six months of the unrestricted U-boat campaign must therefore go to the British and Allied civil administrations, whose diplomacy kept the neutrals working for the Allies and whose organization of shipping, import control, food production and rationing was superb and prevented the prodigious destruction of the U-boats from being decisive.

It was obvious to the Germans that the enemy's collapse was not imminent. Doubts were openly being expressed in Germany about the efficacy of the U-boat campaign, but the Navy were not particularly dismayed as they believed they had sunk over five million tons of shipping in the first six months and that victory was only a matter of time. They were only annoyed that they had raised hopes by setting a date by which the U-boats would win the war. The result of the U-boat failure to succeed in six months was, in any case, no longer fatal. The collapse of Russia, the supplies obtained by the overrunning of Rumania and the successful bridging in other ways of the gap to the 1917 harvest, made it possible for the Germans to last another winter. The U-boats, in spite of greater numbers at sea, were, it is true, sinking fewer ships but there was still room for considerable hope : the rate at which U-boats were being destroyed was not crippling and sinkings of merchant ships were well above the world's capacity for replacing them. Furthermore there was no sign of the U.S. Army in Europe. The obvious policy to adopt, which was fully supported by the Army High Command, was for the U-boats to redouble their efforts in an all-out attempt to win before the U.S. Armies could deploy in France.

There did not seem to be any way in which each U-boat, already totally unrestricted, could sink more ships in each patrol. Indeed they had already passed their peak, and so the solution must lie in getting greater numbers of them to sea. A special bureau under a vice-admiral was set up to hasten the construction of the 120 U-boats already on the stocks and to take charge of U-boat production generally, including the new 'Hindenburg' programme in which another 113 U-boats were to be built as rapidly as possible.

The story of operations over the next six months, from August 1917 to January 1918, is of the gradual thwarting of the U-boats by the institution and extension of the convoy system. Most inward-bound ocean-going shipping of under 12 knots was already in convoy by August, in which month twenty-nine convoys arrived in the United Kingdom and a start had been made with outward convoys. In September all outward-bound shipping was in convoy and thirty-three convoys arrived whilst thirty-seven left the United Kingdom. In October through convoys were started in the Mediterranean and the traffic no longer had to go round the Cape. Thereafter an average of thirty-five convoys sailed inwards and outwards each month. Although thirty to thirty-five U-boats were kept at sea in the operational areas, the shipping losses fell steadily from 211 ships sunk in August to 150 in January. The ships sunk for every submarine at sea each month also fell from seven in August to only five in January.

The convoy system had succeeded in the past because the escorts were able to protect the merchant ships from the enemy's attack. In anti-submarine warfare the escorts were certainly able to do this if the U-boats attacked on the surface with their gun, and this form of attack became completely out of the question by day. But, having no method of detecting submarines when submerged, they were not often able to frustrate a torpedo attack before it took place, unless the U-boat was very careless with its periscope. With its small silhouette, a U-boat was generally able to make a surface torpedo attack at night without being seen. But, whenever a ship was torpedoed, the escort could at once counter attack by steaming along the tracks of the torpedoes and dropping depth charges. Depth charges became available in quantity towards the end of 1917 and the firing of a torpedo by a U-boat was invariably followed by a liberal plastering of the vicinity by the escorts. U-boats did, however, manage to torpedo eighty-three ships in convoy in this period for the loss of six U-boats, only one of which was sunk before firing. Ten times as many ships were, however, sunk when independent. In September these casualties were mostly among outward-bound ships not yet in convoy, but in October the U-boats moved into the coast where they were able to find unescorted coastal shipping or ships from convoys which had been dispersed to their destinations.

The concentration of the U-boats on independent shipping was not because of the danger or difficulty in attacking convoys, but because the U-boats could not find them and so had no alternative. The first effect of the convoy system was that the ocean suddenly seemed to the U-boats to be devoid of shipping. This was because, strange as it may seem, a convoy of ships was not much more likely to be sighted than a single vessel. A single ship will probably be seen by a U-boat lurking within ten miles of its track. A convoy of twenty ships is only two miles wide and so would be seen by a U-boat lying within eleven miles of the centre of the track of the convoy. Five convoys of twenty ships each were not, therefore, very much more likely to be seen than five single ships and were obviously much harder to find than a hundred independents. The result was that the vast majority of ships when in convoy were never seen, and the greatest advantage of the system was the difficulty the U-boats had in finding the convoys at all.

It is also true that the British intelligence of U-boat movements at this period was surprisingly good. The U-boats used their radio a great deal and their positions could be fixed by direction-finding stations on shore. The distress calls of merchant ships also gave information which enabled the U-boats to be tracked with considerable accuracy. With ships in convoy and the better control it gave over them, this information could be used to divert them into safer waters.

When all shipping sailed independently, U-boats were presented with a long succession of targets at which to fire, and they had time to take deliberate aim and then reload before the next victim

94

appeared. With convoy there would be only one chance to fire as the enemy swept by *en masse*. Whilst the selected ship was being attacked, the rest of the convoy would slip by unscathed and a second shot was seldom possible even if the escorts permitted it. With only two, or sometimes four, torpedo tubes, only one ship, or at most two, would generally be hit. Moreover the attack was complicated by the presence of the escorts and the anticipation of the heavy counter attack which was likely to descend on the U-boat after firing. Convoy brought the escorts into the vicinity of the U-boats at a time when they had to reveal their position by firing. When the anti-submarine vessels patrolled at random they could never find the U-boats, but with a convoy system, the U-boats, when they did find the convoys, could not help bringing themselves into contact with the anti-submarine vessels.

Convoy also had the great advantage that it could give the same protection to neutrals as to British ships, which had not been the case when they had been independent and unarmed. Convoys therefore achieved their great success not so much because the escorts protected them, but because they were much harder to find, gave only a fleeting chance of attack as they swept by and then offered the escorts a better chance to destroy the U-boats than they had ever had before.

In this period the Germans extended their attack by using the large converted merchant submarines of the *U151* class to patrol round the Azores and Canaries and off the west coast of Africa. These submarines were armed with two 5.9-inch guns and twenty-two torpedoes and were able to remain at sea for three months. They sank a considerable number of independent ships, although not at the same rate as the U-boats close in round the British Isles.

Allied anti-submarine measures showed a very marked improvement during these six months. The 'exchange rate' had now fallen to only sixteen ships sunk for every U-boat destroyed. In all forty-six U-boats were sunk, whereas only forty-two new submarines were delivered, so that the Germans were unable to increase their strength which remained steady at about 135 operational U-boats out of a total of 170. In the autumn the British manufactured a reliable mine in large quantities and began laying a huge quadrant of them in the Heligoland Bight and elsewhere off the U-boat bases. Six U-boats were sunk in these fields, indeed the German minesweepers had such difficulty in clearing the channels in the Bight in October that the U-boats had to leave by the Kattegat for several weeks. These mines were also used in the Dover barrage, where they began to replace the ineffective mines and mined nets with row upon row of deep and shallow mines which made a veritable wall of high explosive. Patrols forced the U-boats to remain submerged and prevented their passing over the fields on the surface at high water. Four U-boats were sunk by the barrage and by December the passage had become very difficult.

The return of the U-boats to operations in coastal waters also proved costly; the patrols sank five U-boats and another six were lost in trap minefields and mined nets in British waters. British submarines continued to take a toll and sank four more U-boats in this period, but the Q ships had their last success in August. The institution of convoys had made the Q ships an anachronism and the U-boats, being unrestricted, were able to torpedo them without warning. In August no less than four Q ships lost their duels with U-boats and it was clear that the decoy had had its day. The Flanders U-boats were now having a hazardous time, not only when at sea and off their bases but in harbour also. The air raids on Bruges, Zeebrugge and Ostend, although they sank no U-boats, were continuous and air patrols in the southern North Sea were becoming dangerous.

During this second six months of the unrestricted campaign the world losses were another $2\frac{1}{4}$ million tons of shipping, against which over $1\frac{1}{2}$ million tons had been replaced by building and another half a million tons of enemy ships brought into the service of the Allies. The total shipping available was therefore still declining. Strenuous efforts were being made to increase the output of the shipyards and indeed in 1917 Great Britain had already built twice the tonnage and the U.S.A. three times that constructed in 1916. Great Britain hoped to produce no less than 3 million tons per annum by the end of 1918, but the requirement for shipping was greater than ever. True, Russia was no longer a shipping liability, but there had been poor harvests in France and Italy and much tonnage would be required to transport the U.S. Army to Europe and to keep it supplied. In spite of further increases in efficiency by pooling inter-allied tonnage, an even greater concentration on the shorter routes across the Atlantic and rigorous measures to get more neutral ships back into Allied service, imports by the end of 1917 were 20 per cent down on 1916. By rigid control and the exclusion of all but essentials and strict rationing the situation was, however, just kept in hand and even the oil fuel crisis was surmounted.

In November the shipping losses had been the lowest since the unrestricted war began and the Allies were much more hopeful about the future. In Germany, on the other hand, the General Staff had now lost faith in the U-boat as a method of winning the war. With the release of the armies from the eastern front, Hindenburg and Ludendorf now pinned their faith on a great offensive in the west by the army. Obviously a continuation of the U-boat campaign would help, but in their view this was now a secondary operation. The German Navy were still optimistic and another hundred U-boats were ordered during the winter. They hoped that, if they could increase the output of submarines sufficiently, they could still force up the losses to a point where they could win the war.

The final phase of the unrestricted campaign lasted for the first nine months of 1918 and continued until a week or two before the Armistice. During this period the Germans made great efforts to get more U-boats to sea, not only by hastening new construction but by shortening their time in harbour. They were, however, unable to average more than thirty-six at a time in the operational areas, with a peak of forty-two in July 1918. Operational strength varied from 120 to 130 out of a total which reached 179 in October 1918. The rate of sinking fluctuated between three and four ships sunk by each U-boat in the operational area every month, but had declined to less than two by October. Total sinkings each month varied from 188 ships in March to 99 in September, with a grand total of 1,133 ships for the whole nine months. Of these only 134 were sunk in convoy, the rest were sailing independently. The main reason for their inability to sink more ships was the steady expansion of the convoy system, which now took ships right into their ports and gave still fewer occasions for attack.

Sixty-one U-boats were lost in the final nine months but this rate of destruction, although very high, was less than in the second half of 1917. Eighty-three new U-boats were delivered in the same period so that German U-boat strength continued to rise slowly. Their losses were not therefore crippling, but they were sufficient to prevent any large expansion of the U-boat fleet.

By February the Dover barrage was proving extremely troublesome and the North Sea U-boats again ceased to use the Dover Straits and had to make the voyage round the north of Scotland. This added six days to the passage and decreased their time in the operational area accordingly.

In May the Germans made a supreme effort and got the same number of U-boats to sea as they had had in April 1917, which was the most during the war so far. They also started operations by a few of the large long-range U-boats right across the Atlantic off the American coast. This measure was conceived as a way to attack the American transports and it was hoped to catch them weakly escorted. In fact they sank no transports and the casualties caused by these U-boats were much smaller than could have been produced by a similar number of submarines operating round the British Isles. Psychologically it was an astute move and but for the strategic sense of Admiral Sims, who commanded the U.S. Naval Forces in Europe, it might well have caused the withdrawal of a number of American warships from the vital eastern Atlantic to deal with it.

The Germans realized that, if the U-boats were to regain their effectiveness, they would have to find a way not merely of sinking independent ships in remote areas or ships which had left their convoys, but of mastering the convoy system itself. In the middle of May eight U-boats were on patrol in the south-western approaches to the British Isles, deployed to intercept convoys. In operations which lasted for about a fortnight, thirty-six convoys passed through the area, but the U-boats made contact with only five of them. All five were attacked and three merchant ships were sunk : two independent ships were also sunk in this area. In a similar period a year before against unescorted shipping, this number of U-boats would probably have sunk a hundred ships or more. On the other hand, the convoy escorts did not prevent any of the U-boats from completing their attacks nor did they sink any of them.

The U-boats simply could not find the majority of the convoys and it is clear from their movements that they had very little idea of where the other convoys were, or which way to go to intercept them. Admiral Scheer believed that the convoys were being diverted clear of the U-boats but, in fact, few diversions were made during these two weeks. These operations are a good illustration of the working of the convoy system and the way in which it achieved its success.

The German Navy still believed that if they had enough U-boats they could win the day and in June ordered yet another 132. They planned that the output by April 1919 would be twenty-two per month and by early 1920 no less than thirty-three per month. In July the sinkings of Allied merchant vessels fell to the lowest since the start of the unrestricted campaign, in spite of another concentration of U-boats off the North Channel and the sinking of the large liner *Justicia*. These concentrations against the convoy system, however, failed and the U-boats achieved the results they did against independent shipping far out at sea or right inshore off the coasts.

Allied anti-submarine measures made matters very uncomfortable for the U-boats, but failed to sink them faster than they were being built or to impose a heavy enough casualty rate to drive them from the seas. The 'exchange rate' varied from thirty-seven in March to ten in May when the Germans suffered the heaviest loss of U-boats in the whole war, this being the only month in 1918 in which the losses exceeded the replacements. However, this rate of destruction was exceptional and in the following month only three U-boats were destroyed.

Strategically the counter measures can be divided into three groups: first, offensive measures against the U-boats before they reached their operating areas; secondly, the counter measures against them on the trade routes where they were operating; and finally, the defence of the convoys themselves. Twenty-six U-boats were sunk under the first group by blockade measures and the barriers, sixteen under the second group by sea, air and sub-marine patrols and thirteen under the third group by the counter attacks of escorts. The depth charge proved the most effective weapon, sinking twenty-three U-boats; the mine came next with thirteen, British submarines sank six and other methods including the ram, gunfire, seaplanes and mined nets accounted for the remaining thirteen.

In April 1918 the famous attacks on the submarine bases at Zeebrugge and Ostend took place. It is true that after them few U-boats operated in the Channel and sinkings there almost ceased, but the entries and exits from these bases show that they were blocked for only a few hours and that the relief in the Channel was entirely due to the increased effectiveness of the Dover barrage. From this time on, the Flanders U-boats seldom tried to penetrate into the Channel and confined their operations to the North Sea. This increase in the efficiency of the Dover barrage was due to the combination of patrols and the vast complex of new minefields. The patrols at night, aided by searchlights on shore, forced the U-boats to dive into the minefields and, in all, thirteen of them were destroyed during 1918. The effectiveness of the Dover barrage is in sharp contrast to the failure of the Otranto barrage. Here it was too deep to use mines and, although the U-boats were often detected by a screen of hydrophone-fitted trawlers, only two were sunk during 1918. The U-boats had little difficulty in passing the Straits of Otranto right up to the evacuation of the Adriatic bases, in spite of the large concentration of 280 ships in the barrage force. The success of a barrier strategy depended entirely on whether it was practicable to impose a sufficiently high casualty rate to force the U-boats to abandon the attempt to pass as too dangerous. If it could, then the passage was as good as sealed; if not, then the very great effort was largely wasted.

The large quadrant of mines laid in the Heligoland Bight sank only one U-boat although it did force them to use the Kattegat route on occasions and add another two days to their passage. But here the Germans were now able to sweep the mines and clear a passage for the U-boats. A very big effort was made during 1918 by the British and American Navies to repeat the success of the Dover barrage right across the top of the North Sea, where the Germans would be unable to sweep the mines. A vast number of mines were manufactured and laid during the summer and it began to achieve results in September and October, when six U-boats were sunk in it. Nevertheless it is very unlikely that it could have been developed sufficiently to prevent the U-boats from coming out at all.

By September the Flanders U-boats were practically neutralized by the incessant air attacks and the difficulty of entering and leaving their bases. The continual decline in sinkings per U-boat now made it clear to the German Navy that, even taking into account the vast number of U-boats building, the total tonnage of shipping sunk in the future would be unlikely to increase. Allied counter measures were in fact developing faster than the U-boat expansion and there was little chance that Allied shipbuilding could be overtaken again. By this time trained men were lacking for the U-boats and the counter offensive was steadily expanding and improving. The perils of mines, depth charges, air patrols and hydrophone-fitted ships were making the task of the U-boats extremely difficult. No U-boats passed the Straits of Dover after September and in October the Flanders and Adriatic bases had to be evacuated because of the situation on land. On 21 October all U-boats were recalled in order not to prejudice the Armistice negotiations and so ended the German submarine campaign against commerce.

In the last nine months the Germans sank another $2\frac{1}{4}$ million tons of world shipping, but in the same time 4 million tons were built, half in the United States and the remainder in Great Britain and the rest of the world. There was, therefore, $1\frac{3}{4}$ million tons more shipping at the end of the nine months than at the beginning. Although the Germans did not know it, the campaign had in fact been defeated in March 1918, when the replacements for the first time exceeded the shipping losses. The greater number of ships available was used even more efficiently than before and the U-boat campaign reverted to being merely a nuisance. Throughout the summer the U.S. Army crossed to Europe in large numbers and the Germans simply had not enough U-boats to attack the transports as well as trade. They decided to continue against trade in the south-western approaches and the vast majority of the transports carrying the American Army passed well to the south of them, direct to France, with negligible loss. During the summer very large troop movements were also carried out in face of the U-boat threat in the Mediterranean.

So ended what the British official historian has called 'the greatest sea fight in history'. In this titanic struggle the Germans had thrown 373 U-boats into the fray and had lost 178 of them with casualties amounting to nearly 5,000 officers and men. In the unrestricted campaign and the restricted operations against trade which preceded it, they sank 5,708 ships of over 11 million tons, which was a quarter of the world's total tonnage. Over half of the ships sunk were British and this was roughly one-third of their tonnage in existence at the beginning of the war. The overall exchange rate was, therefore, thirty-two ships sunk for every

U-boat destroyed. Nearly half of this tonnage was sunk round the British Isles by U-boats based in Germany. One-third was sunk in the Mediterranean and a fifth by the Flanders U-boats in the narrow seas. The remainder, under 2 per cent, was destroyed by the U-cruisers in remote areas. The main weapon had been the torpedo fired without warning, which was responsible for 60 per cent of the tonnage sunk. The gun, combined with other methods of finally despatching the target, had accounted for 32 per cent as well as a large number of small craft such as fishing vessels. Over 11,000 mines laid by U-boats sank the remaining 8 per cent.

At the end of the war the Germans had 179 U-boats in commission, 121 of which were operational and 58 engaged in trials or training. These were manned by about 13,000 men, and the total personnel required for training, overhaul, repair and building amounted to 113,000. On the Allied side, over 300 destroyers, sloops and P-boats were used exclusively on anti-submarine work, as well as 35 submarines, 550 aircraft, 75 airships and nearly 4,000 auxiliary vessels. This was in addition to the immense effort needed to produce and lay a vast number of mines and nets. The number of men required to man this gigantic force was approximately 140,000 with probably another half a million to build, refit and support them generally.

In spite of the prodigious destruction wrought by the U-boats, the campaign failed to prevent the Allies from exerting their military strength through sea power wherever they wished : notably by maintaining the British Expeditionary Force in France, by transporting the U.S. Army to Europe and by supplying other Allied armies in the Middle East and elsewhere overseas. They failed to cut down the imports into the United Kingdom to an extent which seriously impaired the war effort or reduced food supplies below that necessary to maintain health. Furthermore, Great Britain and the United States were able to support France, Italy and Russia with supplies of all kinds without which they would not have been able to continue the war.

On the other hand, the U-boats themselves were thwarted more than defeated and they were not driven from the seas. It was only for a few months in 1917 and early in 1918 that their losses exceeded the building rate. Their strength steadily increased throughout the war and was still increasing at the time of the Armistice. Although very difficult to find and so to destroy, the

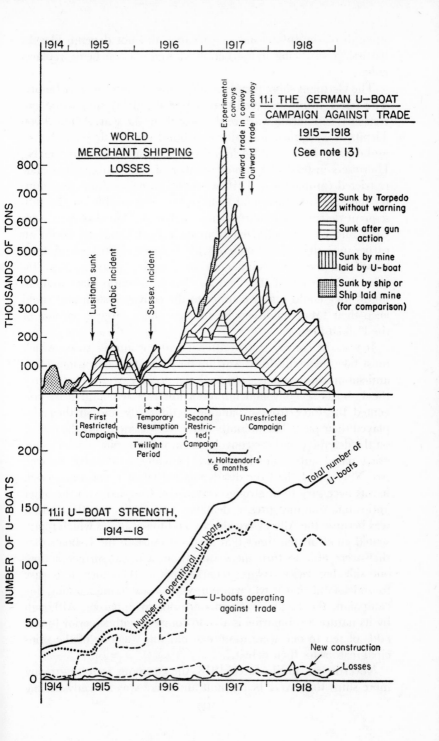

strength of the submarine as a weapon did not depend, like the battleship, on being indestructible so much as on being replaceable.

The Germans subsequently made many excuses for their failure. The Navy firmly believed that it was the delay in starting unrestricted submarine warfare that lost them the war. Admiral von Tirpitz was blamed for failing to build enough U-boats before and during the war and Admiral von Capelle for building the big U-cruisers instead of a larger number of small submarines. The restricted campaigns of 1916 were said to have stimulated counter measures too early and to have been responsible for the subsequent defeat of the unrestricted campaign. These reasons were valid and clearly detracted from their efforts, but no doubt an earlier unrestricted campaign with fewer U-boats would have stimulated the same counter measures earlier with the same results. It is clear that they had no chance to restore the situation, unless they could find a counter to the convoy system and could keep their losses small enough to carry out a large expansion of the U-boat fleet.

It was the convoy system after it had got into its stride which must take the credit for thwarting the U-boats. The various other anti-submarine measures, although not decisive, were able to harry the U-boats severely and impose a loss rate which at least prevented the force from expanding significantly and so they also played their part. The ubiquity of the submarine threw the enemy on the defensive and the convoy system was, in spite of what some great naval authorities have said, basically a defensive strategy (see Note 14). It had the disadvantage that, it if was to succeed, it was necessary to be strong everywhere. Coupled with the other anti-submarine measures, it demanded an enormous effort and it was because the Allies were able to send to sea forces which represented an effort ten times that needed to sustain the U-boats that they were able to turn the scales. If, in a naval surface action, one side has twice as many battleships as the other, it is easy to understand that it will win but, when considering a submarine campaign, the relative strengths are not so apparent. Although by its nature a submarine is able to compete with superior forces, odds of ten to one were too great and this was one of the principal reasons for their defeat.

Nevertheless, until March 1918, the Germans were destroying more ships than were being built and there was a steady decline in the total tonnage available. That this did not have a more serious effect was due to the civilian organization for getting more out of the ships than was normal in peacetime. Improved agriculture in Great Britain and rationing alone saved over 6 million tons of shipping. These, combined with a cutting down of the need for imports by excluding all but essentials, bridged the gap until an increase in shipbuilding was able to overtake the losses. The decline in shipbuilding during the early part of the war was responsible for much of the trouble. Its expansion later, especially in the U.S.A., was of extreme importance and succeeded in the end in building ships twice as fast as the U-boats could sink them. The immense flexibility of the economic system was a surprise to the Germans and these civil counter measures were at least as important as the naval anti-submarine measures in the defeat of the U-boat campaign. The gigantic international effort, both naval and civil, necessary to defeat the U-boats certainly detracted from the Allies' ability to wage war in other ways. All this was achieved by fewer men in the U-boats than in a single army division, and for economy of force the submarine was quite unrivalled.

Both Great Britain and Germany had their respective interpretations of international law in the war at sea and did not pay much attention to the rights of neutrals. But whereas Great Britain used her control of the world's coaling stations and marine insurance as well as her geographical position to 'persuade' neutral tonnage to work for her, Germany used terrorism and force to try to prevent them from doing so. Great Britain threatened their pockets but Germany their lives and Great Britain's actions were morally and legally more acceptable. Great Britain exploited illegal German actions with great skill and her campaign of indignation at the inhumanity of the U-boats was a potent anti-submarine measure in itself. The German policy led to their defeat in the end. They failed to prevent neutrals from trading with the Allies and so pitted themselves not only against Allied shipping but against that of the world. The result was that the immense size of the world's shipping was able to absorb the losses and with its flexibility to minimize the effects. The German U-boat fleet was simply not large enough to be decisive against such a huge target.

Above all, the Germans under-estimated the effect of America's entry into the war which was directly due to the unrestricted submarine campaign. They thought of this as solely a question of how big an army they could raise and how soon they could bring it to bear in Europe. In fact, the timely help of the U.S. destroyers strengthened the anti-submarine forces sufficiently to make the convoy system possible. An extra half a million tons of ex-German shipping was released from internment in American ports when losses were most serious, and the concentration of shipping on the shorter routes across the Atlantic became possible on a scale which Great Britain could never have afforded without U.S. assistance. Finally, the great output of the American shipyards produced ships faster than the U-boats could sink them.

It is, of course, easy to jump to the conclusion that the defeat of the German submarine campaign supports the analysis of history which, up to 1914, showed the *guerre de course* to be an indecisive method of warfare which could never succeed on its own. Indeed, the failure of the U-boats to interfere with the Allies' overseas expeditions or imports to an extent which impaired the war effort seems to support this contention. The German U-boat campaign was, however, never capable of stopping the movement of troops or of supplies directly, and the cargoes lost when ships were sunk were never likely to be enough to win the war. The campaign was directed against ships which, when sunk, virtually took with them all the cargoes they could have carried for the rest of the war. It is only after enough ships have been sunk that imports will fall catastrophically, and this stage was never reached, although it came within sight in April 1917. It was not, therefore, the loss of imports that was significant but the sinkings of merchant ships relative to the shipbuilding effort.

Nevertheless, the fact that the U-boats failed does not mean to say that, if the Allies had not taken the measures they did, the U-boats would not have won. There is no doubt that, if the loss rate of April 1917 had been continued for a year, the British expeditions overseas would have collapsed for lack of support, the Allies would have been unable to maintain their war efforts, the U.S. Army would never have reached Europe and the British would have come near to starvation. The defeat of the U-boats was not because the *guerre de course* could not by its nature be decisive: it was because the Allies were able to be strong everywhere and make a gigantic effort.

Contrary to all the teaching of the past, the *guerre de course* must now, therefore, be considered potentially a decisive method of waging war. There is little doubt that, unlike all wars of attrition in the past, it could now not only dispute but also prevent another power from exercising command of the sea. An important reason for this change was Great Britain's greatly increased reliance upon the sea and her vulnerability to the loss of the command of it. This was due to other factors, such as the growth of population, the decline of agriculture and her development as a manufacturing country using raw materials from abroad. Nevertheless, it was the submarine which made the throttling of this lifeline possible in face of Great Britain's command of the surface of the sea by a superior fleet. The lessons of the *guerre de course* in the past applied with even greater force to cruisers and surface raiders in the steam era, but the characteristics of the submarine as a warship were the principal reason for this great change. The fact that the German submarine campaign was actually defeated does not alter this conclusion.

Whatever the reasons for the defeat of the U-boats, therefore, it was now clear that the submarine had become a potentially war-winning weapon. In future a power wishing to command the sea must not only have a superior battle fleet and cruisers to counter surface raiders, but be prepared also to provide a huge armada of anti-submarine vessels, aircraft and obstructions ten times the size of any likely enemy submarine force : in future the sea could be commanded only by such a diarchy.

When used as a commerce raider, therefore, the submarine, before it had been established for twenty years as a unit of the fleets of the world, had shown itself capable of being one of the decisive weapons of seapower. It had altered the theories of the past even more than the change from sail to steam.

VII

The Inter-War Years

Although the Allies had defeated the German submarine campaign, they had been severely shaken by it. The very first article of the Naval Armistice terms imposed by them on the Germans was that they should surrender all their U-boats with their armament and equipment complete. One hundred and seventy-six U-boats were accordingly handed over and, except for a few which were retained by special permission in the French Navy, all were broken up or used as targets during the next three years. Some U-boats were unfit to make the passage to an Allied port and, together with the 224 in various stages of construction, were broken up in Germany under the supervision of the Allies. Thus the largest and most powerful underwater fleet that the world had yet seen came to an ignominious end only twelve years after its inception. The Treaty of Versailles confirmed this policy and allowed no submarines in the very small fleet the Germans were permitted to keep, and the construction or acquisition of any submarine, even for commercial purposes, was forbidden.

The demise of the German U-boats left the British submarine fleet, with 137 boats, the largest in the world. At the end of the war, they scrapped ninety of their older submarines, including all of the small defensive type, and cancelled thirty-one new submarines building. At the same time they completed twenty-four vessels under construction and made experiments with surrendered German U-boats. They pushed forward with the development of the submarine by carrying out trials with some of the new types they had developed during the war and which had been completed too late to take part in it.

During the war it had been found difficult to hit with torpedoes except at close range and, even when a hit was obtained, it was not enough to sink a Dreadnought battleship. Ranges of over 1,000 yards were long for torpedoes but were still point-blank for a heavy gun. In the first of these experimental submarines the British therefore decided to try a heavy gun as an alternative to the torpedo. Three submarines of the M class, often known as

'Monitor' submarines, were built and armed with a single 12-inch gun, which could be kept loaded submerged. This made it possible for the submarine to attack by surfacing and opening fire instantly. Hits would undoubtedly be secured at a far greater range than with a torpedo, but it was obvious that it rendered the submarine very vulnerable to return gunfire especially from a warship. The M class were not completed in time to be tried in action, and peacetime trials were difficult to make conclusive, but the alternative plan of mounting a much heavier torpedo armament was clearly a far better principle for a submarine.

The E class, which had been the principal patrol submarines during the war, were armed with a pair of 18-inch torpedo tubes in the bow, a single tube on each beam and a single tube in the stern. Although this disposition made a close attack easy, as one of the tubes could always be brought to bear, it meant they could never fire more than a pair of torpedoes at a target. Many long-range attacks therefore missed and modern heavy warships, although hit, were seldom sunk. During the war, therefore, the number of bow torpedo tubes was increased in successive designs at the expense of beam and stern tubes. Torpedo diameter was increased from eighteen to twenty-one inches, doubling the weight of the weapon and giving it a greater range and heavier explosive head. These improvements culminated in the design of the L50 class which had a salvo of six 21-inch bow tubes. The increase in power of these submarines, which were able to launch six large torpedoes in one attack instead of two small ones, is obvious. Not only would they have a better chance of hitting the target at long range by spreading a salvo, but they would also make it possible to sink a Dreadnought battleship by getting a number of hits at close range with these more powerful torpedoes. This armament was a great advance, equivalent to the advent of the Dreadnought battleship itself as a capital ship, and it became standard in new British submarines.

The anti-U-boat operations by British submarines during the war had been carried out mainly by patrol and small defensive types. Although moderately successful, they could clearly be improved upon for this specialized task and twelve submarines of the R class were specifically designed to sink other submarines. To ensure that they would always sight the U-boat first either by day or night, they had a very small silhouette on the surface. By day they would be able to dive unseen and complete the attack submerged. They were given a high underwater speed with which to close to an effective range and six 18-inch torpedo tubes which would give them an excellent chance to secure at least one hit, which was all that was required to sink a U-boat.

Finally, the British pressed on with the development of the fleet submarine and built *K26*, which was greatly improved and armed with the new six-torpedo salvo. Great Britain, therefore, not only had the largest submarine fleet at the end of the first world war but undoubtedly led in its development as well.

The U-boats had brought Great Britain nearer to defeat at sea than at any time since the Battle of Beachy Head in 1690. Although they now had the largest submarine fleet in the world and were in the lead in its development, the British believed that the submarine, in the hands of an enemy, was potentially so dangerous that it outweighed any advantage they themselves could gain from using it. In other words, they had come to the conclusion that the total abolition of the submarine was to their advantage, so returning to the policy of Earl St. Vincent of 1803.

When, in 1921, the five largest naval powers assembled in conference in Washington to avoid an armaments race and negotiate a treaty of limitation, the British strongly advocated abolition. They maintained that the submarine was effective only as a commerce raider and then only if it disregarded international law. They spoilt their case, however, by asserting that it was of no use as a military weapon, which was obviously untrue. Abolition was opposed by all the other countries at the conference, particularly France. The United States, with the second largest submarine fleet (see Note 15), was opposed to total abolition but was prepared to accept some limitation. She pointed out that the submarine was a very effective and perfectly legitimate weapon against warships and valuable as a scout and that there was no need to use it contrary to international law any more than any other type of warship. She therefore proposed that the submarine should be limited in the same way as the conference had agreed to limit capital ships and in the same ratio. The French, although they had not been able to use their submarine fleet in the war as effectively as either the Germans or the British, were still the submarines' greatest protagonists. They stoutly maintained their pre-war policy that, in order to redress the balance, submarines were an essential part of any navy which had an inferior battlefleet. As they had accepted a smaller battlefleet than any other country at the conference, except Italy, they were not prepared to accept a small submarine fleet as well. Logically, they argued, a nation with a weak battlefleet needed a larger submarine force than the nations with powerful battlefleets, and they demanded a tonnage of submarines at least three times the size that the capital ship ratio would have given them. In this general view they were supported by Japan and Italy, who also had inferior battlefleets. Japan had at this time very few submarines, but the acquisition of eight ex-German U-boats of various types had stimulated her interest and she had already twelve more under construction.

The Washington Conference of 1921-2 halted the armaments race and achieved much in limiting capital ships and aircraft carriers, but it failed to agree to limit submarines in any way. In the end Great Britain could do no more than persuade the members to sign a declaration that, in war, they would not use their submarines for the wholesale destruction of commerce after the German fashion. There was, subsequently, considerable doubt whether this agreement outlawed the use of submarines for commerce raiding altogether, or whether it merely confined them to international law, that is, to the rules of visit and search as for surface ships. In the end this part of the treaty was not ratified by France.

In the decade that followed the conference, the British, having failed to secure the abolition of the submarine, pushed forward experiments with counter measures. Existing battleships, at the sacrifice of some speed, were fitted with 'bulges' to protect them against torpedo hits. All new capital ships had 'internal bulges' as an integral part of their design, and the anti-torpedo protection for cruisers was also improved. By far the most important experimental work of this period was, however, on a new method to detect submerged submarines. Any way to find submarines when they were totally submerged would obviously revolutionize anti-submarine warfare by producing a counter to its greatest asset of invisibility. This device was developed in great secrecy and was called the Asdic after the initial letters of the Allied Submarine Detection Investigation Committee of 1917.

The Asdic was an acoustic system which, unlike the hydrophone which was passive and merely listened for any sound the submarine might make, was active and so could detect a completely silent submarine. This was done by emitting a loud supersonic 'ping' underwater which was reflected by the metal hull of a submarine and gave an echo at ranges of a mile or so. This system had the added advantages over the hydrophone that it could be used with the searching ship steaming at moderate speed and could give the range as well as the bearing of a submarine. Accurate location of a submarine in this way would greatly improve the accuracy with which depth charges could be dropped and was bound to lead to a much better kill rate against submarines. It would enormously enhance the protection of fleets and convoys whose escorts, instead of having to wait for the submarine to reveal its presence by firing a torpedo, would be able to detect it first and counter attack before it could do any harm.

The signing of the Washington Treaty meant that all the parties to it except France could develop the submarine only as a military weapon and not as a commerce raider. In spite of their desire to abolish submarines, the British kept their lead and began a series of new experiments. In the same year as the treaty was signed they authorized the construction of the biggest submarine that had ever yet been built. This was the *XI* and she was designed as a cruiser submarine with the heavy gun armament of four 5.2-inch guns in addition to the new salvo of six torpedoes. A design for a cruiser submarine had been suggested as early as 1915 but although thought to be practicable was not proceeded with, as no strategic need was seen for it then. It seems that the protagonists of this vessel saw it as a small cruiser which would be able to submerge. Its gun power made it superior to destroyers which it could fight on the surface. It was a step towards the dream of a fleet composed of all types of warship which could submerge. *XI* was not, however, fast enough to work with the fleet and was obviously of much more use as a long-range commerce raider, a purpose for which the British had no intention whatever of using her.

The British then converted one of their Monitor submarines to a submarine seaplane carrier and another to a large submarine minelayer. A seaplane launched from a submarine would clearly be useful for reconnaissance, especially of distant enemy bases. The use of seaplanes with submarines was not an entirely new idea. During the war the submarine *E22* had put to sea with a seaplane on its fore-casing to carry it closer to the enemy coast, so

112

that it could bomb the Zeppelin sheds. This was obviously only possible in very calm weather and, if the submarine was forced to dive, the seaplane would probably be lost. By removing the gun from *M2*, a watertight hangar was installed which enabled the submarine to dive with the seaplane on board. Although the seaplane was extremely small, the design was technically a success and *M2* could surface, catapult the seaplane and dive again in five minutes. The conversion of *M3*, the other Monitor submarine, to a minelayer increased the capacity from the eighteen mines of the L class to no less than a hundred.

The Washington Treaty, whilst limiting the size and number of capital ships and aircraft carriers, had other clauses which quite unintentionally stimulated the building of submarines. It had been agreed to preserve the *status quo* in the Far East and not to build new naval bases or extend existing ones outside Japan. The acceptance of the one power standard by Great Britain and the United States, and the fact that they could not now base their fleets closer to Japan than Singapore or Pearl Harbor, meant that they relinquished command of the sea in the early stages of a war in the Far East to the Japanese. As they were now, therefore, the weaker powers in that area, the importance of submarines for them greatly increased. These clauses of the treaty thus had a profound effect on the submarine-building policy of the three major naval powers.

The British soon found that the L class, which were their largest patrol submarines and had been developed during the war for the North Sea, were too small for the Pacific: they had too short an endurance and lacked habitability in a hot climate. They therefore embarked on a programme of much larger and improved patrol submarines, the first of which, ordered in 1923, was the *Oberon*. These were not only of greater endurance and improved habitability but had a higher speed, were able to dive deeper and carried the new salvo of six torpedoes. Eighteen of these submarines of the O, P and R classes, as well as a mine-laying version developed from *M3*, were built during the next ten years.

Although some of the American submarines had crossed the Atlantic and had operated from British bases during the war, their submarines still constituted strategically a defensive force. Their S class were large enough to operate offensively at moderate range but, because of the vast distances involved, they had to be stationed on both coasts and in the canal zone in a purely defensive posture. The appearance of the German U-boats off the American coast and their ability to operate from Germany without refuelling showed that a great extension of the range of operations was possible. One of the U-boats surrendered to the U.S.A. at the end of the war was *U140*, one of the very large cruiser submarines. Prompted in this way, the U.S. Navy began to build submarines of over twice the size of their S class to operate offensively across the oceans from American bases. Three of the six V class, as these new submarines were called, were of nearly three thousand tons and armed with two 6-inch guns : they were considerably larger than *U140* and not much smaller than the monster British *XI*.

In their study of a war against Japan in the Pacific, the U.S. Navy believed it important to use all arms, air, surface and subsurface, in close co-operation in the fleet. In the 1924 manœuvres the S class submarines were found to be quite inadequate in speed, endurance, habitability and reliability for this purpose and were the subject of adverse comment by the Commander-in-Chief. For working with the fleet, it was doubtful whether the very large submarine cruisers with a heavy gun armament, then building, were the answer either. Development, therefore, now centred on obtaining speed, endurance and habitability with a good torpedo armament in a slightly smaller submarine. Development was slow, however, and only nine V class submarines were completed in the ten years following the Washington Treaty.

The Japanese had accepted the ratio of three to five in capital ships relative to the Americans, and so would be inferior if the whole weight of the U.S. Navy was brought to bear upon them. The success of submarines in the Great War and the French example suggested to them that it was in this arm that they could look to redress the balance. They therefore started to build up their submarine fleet from a comparatively minor defensive one into a formidable long-range force able to operate with the fleet : they intended to rely upon it to reduce the strength of the American fleet if it attempted to attack Japan across the Pacific. By the end of ten years they had actually taken the lead in large ocean-going submarines in the Pacific.

After the Washington Treaty the French began a steady submarine construction programme which, in spite of their declared policy that they were to redress the balance of their small battlefleet, were of a type very suitable for commerce raiding. Their latest submarines of the Redoubtable class were well over a thousand tons and clearly much larger than was required for defence. In 1926 they laid down the large cruiser submarine *Surcouf*, armed with two 8-inch guns and carrying a seaplane, which could only be intended to attack trade. The French Navy had for many years been known to favour the strategy of the *guerre de course* and, indeed, some of their writers claimed that a submarine campaign against trade had been a French invention from the start. This line of development and increase in the French submarine fleet, coupled with their failure to ratify the part of the Washington Treaty restricting submarines as commerce raiders, was regarded by Great Britain with very great suspicion.

A more sinister move than the French submarine building programme was, however, afoot in the late nineteen-twenties. Secret preparations were being made by Germany to reconstitute her submarine fleet. A design office was set up in Holland disguised as an engineering firm and two submarines were laid down to their designs in Spain and Finland, purporting to be speculations by the private companies who built them. The German naval mission to Finland was also able to use its position to secure training facilities for German personnel in Finnish submarines. These moves were not in fact contrary to the letter of the Versailles Treaty, although they were undoubtedly a breach of its spirit. Although financed by the German government, the money was not voted directly for these purposes, but there is little doubt that this diversion of funds was intentionally overlooked in high places.

The Washington Treaty was due to expire in 1936 and, in 1930, the main naval powers met in London to try to reach agreement on what was to follow it. Since the Washington Conference the British had never ceased to advocate the total abolition of the submarine and this was still their view when the delegates assembled in London. Their submarine fleet, from being the largest in the world at the Washington Conference, had now been halved, making it the second smallest of the five great naval powers. It had fifty-three units and the remaining wartime vessels, including all the steam-driven fleet submarines of the K class except one, had been scrapped. British submarines were, however,

115

now armed exclusively with the 21-inch torpedo and over half had the powerful six-torpedo salvo, so that in armament they had a lead over all other countries. Development continued, but at a less ambitious pace than during the period immediately following the war. The giant *XI* was now seen to have been a mistake: she had continual engine trouble and the British wished they had never built her. Experiments with *M2*, the seaplane carrier, ceased when she was lost by accident shortly after the London Conference. Although all the fleet submarines of the K class except *K26* had gone, this was not because fleet submarines were out of favour but because, by a technical advance, they were being replaced by the diesel-engined Thames class. These submarines could make 23 knots on the surface and had the immense advantage over the K class that they had good handling and diving qualities and could patrol in enemy waters.

Although coast defence submarines had ceased to be part of the British Navy, the custom of having some small submarines in the fleet persisted. The British began to replace the small and ageing H class with the S class which were small patrol submarines of almost exactly the same size as the E class of the Great War. They had a very similar performance except that they mounted the six-torpedo salvo. In this period of development there were fewer specialized types and all submarines, whether of the fleet, minelaying, large or small patrol types, were capable of operating offensively off an enemy coast.

Of the other four nations at the London Conference the Americans, with eighty-one, now had the largest number of submarines, but they were almost entirely of the small S or earlier classes and they still only had six of the new long-range V type completed. France now had sixty-six submarines, two-thirds of which were of the sea-going patrol type. Nearly all of these were modern vessels built since the Washington Treaty and, with another forty-one building, they were rapidly coming into first place. Japan, with seventy-two, had more than doubled her submarine fleet since the Washington Conference and, although this number included many obsolete vessels, she now had the lead in modern ocean-going submarines for the Pacific. Italy, with forty-six, came last and the majority of her submarines were of the smaller patrol and coastal types and only half were modern: nevertheless twenty-one new ones were building or projected.

Great Britain again failed to secure the abolition of the submarine at the London Naval Conference. Italy alone was prepared to support abolition, but only if all the other powers would scrap their battlefleets as well, a suggestion which was not taken seriously. The conference did, however, manage to agree not to build submarines of over two thousand tons or with a gun larger than 5.1-inch. Special provision was made to keep the British *XI*, the French *Surcouf*, and the U.S.S. *Argonaut* and others which already exceeded these limits. Great Britain, the U.S.A. and Japan agreed to limit themselves to the size of the British submarine fleet, that is to 52,700 tons each. France and Italy would only agree not to increase the size of their present and projected submarine forces and not to replace individual vessels under thirteen years of age.

Although the London Naval Treaty of 1931 achieved more than the Washington Treaty of 1922, in that it secured some limitation of the world's submarine fleets, its practical effect was negligible. Some obsolete submarines in the U.S.A. and Japan had to be scrapped but it did not reduce the French submarine force, which was the most dangerous one and which, with 82,000 tons of submarines, now became the largest as well as the most modern in the world. The limitation in size was an empty concession, all countries having already ceased of their own accord to build very large submarines and those with guns of over 5.1-inch being already considered freaks. Size and gun power were formidable characteristics only if submarines were to be used against trade strictly in accordance with international law; the real threat lay in numbers of boats of moderate size armed with torpedoes.

During the nineteen-thirties, two new and large submarine fleets were built to join the five belonging to the principal naval powers. The first of these was that of Soviet Russia, who had inherited the remains of the Czarist fleet which had included a few submarines but was now largely obsolete. Their concept of the purpose of a navy was for coast defence as a sort of projection of the army frontier guard into the sea. The poor showing of the submarine for defence in the Great War seems to have escaped their notice, for they decided to base their defence in the future mainly upon it. This radical naval policy led to the construction in the ten years from 1928 onwards of some 150 submarines and by 1939 they had numerically the largest submarine fleet in the world. The power of this underwater armada was, however, much reduced, as it was split between the four fleets in the Arctic, Baltic, Black Sea and Far East and had a high proportion of small patrol and very small coast defence submarines.

The second of the new submarine fleets was added by the rebuilding of the German U-boats. When Hitler came to power in 1933, the German Navy lost no time in manufacturing U-boat parts in secret. In 1934, twenty-four small U-boats of the type already tested in Finland and two of the type tried in Spain were laid down. It seems true that the German aim at this time was limited to a desire to improve their defence against France and Poland : this is supported by the small size of the U-boats which were suitable only for use in the Baltic and North Sea and were too small for the Atlantic. Nevertheless the building up of a force on which they could expand later was clearly in their minds.

In 1935 Hitler repudiated the Treaty of Versailles and the Anglo-German Naval Agreement was concluded. In this, Great Britain agreed to Germany's building up to 35 per cent of the tonnage of all types of warship allowed to Great Britain by the London Naval Treaty and up to 45 per cent of her submarine tonnage. A special provision was made for Germany to build up to 100 per cent of British submarine tonnage at some future date should the situation warrant it. Germany also undertook to sign an agreement, which Great Britain was negotiating with all the other naval powers, that submarines in war would sink merchant ships only in accordance with international law and that the crews must be rescued and not left in open boats. This treaty, called the London Submarine Agreement, was finally signed in 1936.

With the foreknowledge of how much damage the German U-boats were to cause in the Second World War, the Anglo-German Naval Agreement seems now to have been a most imprudent move. At the time, however, the British knew that the Germans were building U-boats and that the only way they could stop them was by force. As they were not prepared to go as far as this, the agreement was simply a recognition of what was happening and was in line with the general appeasement policy of the day. It seems that the British genuinely believed that, if they released Germany from the Versailles Treaty, she would keep to the new agreement. Hitler probably intended to do so at the time and hoped that, if he accepted a permanent position of inferiority to the Royal Navy and allowed the British to control the sea, they would give him a free hand in Europe.

In signing the agreement, the British were undoubtedly influenced by the development of their Asdics, which had given encouraging results on trials and during exercises. Over half the destroyers of the fleet were now fitted with it : all new destroyers and sloops were to have it on completion, and a programme was approved to equip the rest of the existing destroyers and sloops with it as well. These Asdic-fitted destroyers and sloops carried thirty depth charges and, when they detected a submarine, were able to run over the position and explode a diamond shaped pattern of five charges. Such a weapon system was expected to be lethal and it was widely believed that the Asdic was the 'answer' to the submarine. This view was shared by many officers of the British submarine branch, who spent much time giving the Asdic-fitted destroyers practice in its use. The concession allowing Germany to build submarines, was, therefore, not thought to be at this time a very great risk. If the Germans could be kept quiet by allowing them to play with U-boats, this was all to the good, Asdics being thought to have made them into a comparatively harmless toy.

It was inevitable that a belief in Asdics should decrease British faith in their own submarines, but, as they did not think any other country had Asdics, they still visualized a war role for them. Nevertheless, there was a marked decrease in experiments with submarines and most of the advanced ideas of the nineteen-twenties were dropped. The new fleet submarines of the Thames class, only three of which were built, never really had a chance to show what they could do, as they were shortly to be completely outpaced by the fleet. The speed of the new capital ships rose to 28 knots, leaving any fleet submarines far behind : they were subsequently used only as fast patrol submarines. The new patrol submarines for the Pacific, which had been produced since the war, were great improvements but their design requirements had been set too high. The O, P and R classes had defects in their hulls and engines and began to fall off in performance and give a great deal of trouble. They had difficulty in making their fuel tanks really oil-tight and leaks were common. It was obvious that reliability in a submarine was more important than high performance and that oil leaks which gave away their position when

E   119

submerged were quite unacceptable. In the next designs of patrol submarine, therefore, the requirements were reduced and oil fuel was put back inside the pressure hull with a consequent sacrifice in endurance. The new designs were confined to large and small patrol submarines of the T and U classes and a new minelayer, the performance of which, if not spectacular, was at least reliable. They had only one new feature. It was clear that, if an enemy had got Asdics, it was going to make a short-range torpedo attack very difficult. The armament of the larger patrol submarines of the T class was therefore increased to one big salvo of no less than ten torpedo tubes, so that they could fire from outside Asdic range and still have a chance of success.

The new American submarines suffered from many of the same difficulties as the British and this was one of the reasons for their slow development. But they did not lower their standards and persevered with the high design requirements, concentrating their efforts on one type of large fleet submarine of trans-Pacific endurance. This eventually became, in the Sargo and Tambor classes, a magnificent warship of high performance. They were approximately of the size of the German U-cruisers of the First World War but were faster, being able to make 20 knots on the surface. They were, like the British T class, armed with ten torpedo tubes but they were split between the bow and the stern. As the older American submarines built during the Great War reached the age limit, they began to replace them with this type which they built in quantity, and soon overtook the Japanese.

Between the wars, developments in radio greatly improved the communications of submarines with the shore. High-frequency transmitters, coupled with a world-wide network of receiving stations, made it possible for their messages to be received from almost anywhere on the globe. At that time such signals were unlikely to be intercepted or give away the submarine's position. Although experiments had been made with periscope aerials for use when submerged, they still had to surface to transmit. It had been found that the very powerful low-frequency radio station at Rugby, which had originally been built for long-range imperial communications, could be received in a submarine which was totally submerged. Messages could therefore be sent to submarines anywhere in the Eastern Atlantic or the Mediterranean without their having to surface to receive them. This development of these long-range two-way communications opened the way for a far more satisfactory control of submarine operations and greatly improved the value of the submarine for reconnaissance.

When Captain Doenitz was appointed to command the new German U-boat service in 1935, he had no doubt whatever that its function was to expand and be ready to fight a new campaign against British commerce. He rightly believed that the key to the whole problem lay in producing a counter to the convoy system. For this purpose he invented the 'wolf pack', by which he intended to oppose the concentration of escorts round a convoy with a counter concentration of U-boats. He hoped to help the U-boats to find the convoys by using air reconnaissance or, failing this, to spread the wolf packs in a scouting formation. It appears that Doenitz knew that Asdics existed but did not believe that it was the 'answer' and set about convincing the U-boat crews that they could compete with it. By the end of 1935 the theory of pack tactics had been formulated and they were tried out with success in the Baltic in 1937. During this period the 500-ton Atlantic U-boat was developed from the successful UB 111 type of the Great War and a number were laid down to bring the strength up to 45 per cent of the British tonnage. There was considerable argument between Doenitz and the German naval staff, who wished to build large ocean-going U-boats with a heavy gun armament which would be capable of operating in distant areas in accordance with international law. Doenitz rightly pointed out that attack on convoys was the only way to obtain decisive results and that distant operations could always be defeated by an extension of the convoy system. In the end his policy of building 500-tonners suitable for pack tactics prevailed.

By 1938 Hitler had found that he was not to be allowed to do as he wished in Europe and invoked the clause of the Anglo-German Naval Agreement which permitted him to build up to parity in submarines with the British. British protests that there was no reason to justify this expansion programme, which was of course directed at them, were brushed aside. At a secret conference Hitler reminded the German military leaders that Great Britain's weakness lay in her sea communications and Doenitz' policies received official blessing. In the winter of 1938-9 a war game showed that 300 U-boats would be required to defeat the convoy system in a war with Great Britain. A hundred of these would be kept on station in the Atlantic with another hundred on passage and the remaining hundred in harbour, resting or under repair. After Munich, Hitler embarked on a naval expansion programme in order to be ready to fight Great Britain at sea by 1945. This Z plan, as it was called, included a large surface navy and also the 233 more U-boats required to build up to the three hundred which were to be completed by 1943.

The technical development of the submarine in the twenty years between the wars was, in fact, less spectacular than in the twenty years before 1918. After a number of far-sighted experiments, the submarines of the world's fleets settled down to a type designed for offensive patrol and all were propelled by the now universally accepted diesel and electric combination. The greatest advances were in armament and communications. Salvoes of larger torpedoes, capable of sinking any ship afloat, greatly increased their power and their operations could now be effectively controlled from the shore. Submarines were much more reliable, were able to dive faster from the surface and were easier to control submerged. They could also dive deeper, but surface endurance, speed and submerged mobility were hardly improved at all. The average size had increased somewhat, but varied from the 2,000-ton trans-Pacific types of the U.S.A. and Japan to the 200-ton coastal defence boats of the Russians. Taking all factors into consideration, the submarine was a much more potent weapon than in the Great War. On the other hand the Asdic had been developed by the British and this, combined with the depth charge pattern, was obviously going to be a formidable opponent.

The strategic purpose for which the various submarine forces had been built varied widely. Great Britain had, since 1921, never ceased to advocate the total abolition of the submarine, but now, with her secret Asdic detecting device, she felt fairly confident that the submarine menace was a thing of the past. Her own submarine force, fifty-seven strong, was kept principally to train her anti-submarine forces. It was to be used in war for reconnaissance and to operate against enemy warships and U-boats and so assist the battlefleet and anti-submarine forces to command the sea.

Of the countries that had refused to agree to abolish the submarine, the United States was one of the strongest sea powers. Nevertheless they had an important role for their large force of over a hundred boats, which was not only to help other forces to defend their coasts, the Panama canal and the Philippines, but to contest Japan's initial control of the sea in the Far East. Japan, Italy and France all hoped to use submarines to make up for their weaker battlefleets. Japan, with fifty-nine units, hoped to cut down the strength of the American Navy if it attacked across the Pacific and to reduce it to a size with which her own battlefleet could compete. Italy, with a hundred submarines, hoped, in co-operation with the rest of her fleet and air force, to deny the Mediterranean to the superior British Navy. France, with another hundred submarines, clung to her policy of the turn of the century and this large force was to compensate for her small battlefleet, but in her case it was not clear whether this was to be achieved by attacks on warships or by a *guerre de course* against trade.

In the two latest navies to build major underwater fleets, the submarine constituted the principal and most important arm. But, whereas Soviet Russia's hundred and fifty submarines were to defend her coasts, the new German U-boat fleet, fifty-seven strong but with over two hundred more building, was preparing for a direct attack on commerce.

Of the seven major submarine fleets in existence at the end of the inter-war period, all except those of Great Britain and Germany were larger than at the end of the Great War. Whereas, in this era of disarmament, strength in every other type of warship had declined, there were more submarines in the navies of the world and they had a more important place than before.

VIII

The Submarine as a Warship in the Atlantic in the Second World War

In 1939, at the outbreak of the Second World War, both the British submarines and the German U-boats were used in much the same way as at the end of the First World War. The Germans were deployed against commerce, as will be described in a later chapter, and the British against warships. There was, however, a new and important British requirement which was to train Asdic-fitted anti-submarine vessels : eight of the older boats were initially allocated for this purpose and a substantial proportion of their strength was used in this way during the rest of the war.

The British operational submarines in home waters, eighteen strong, were moved at first to bases at Blyth and Dundee to act as outposts of the Home Fleet in the North Sea. Some were sent to patrol in the Heligoland Bight itself and others to form a reconnaissance line south-west of Norway. Maritime aircraft could not, at this stage, reach the Norwegian coast, and these submarines were disposed to fill the gap. The submarines were too late to intercept the raiders *Deutschland* and *Graf Spee*, which had left before the outbreak of war, and in November did not sight the *Scharnhorst* and *Gneisenau* when they came out and sank the armed merchant cruiser *Rawalpindi*. In these early stages the weather was the main adversary and difficulties were experienced in keeping 'friendly' forces apart. The new submarine *Triton* torpedoed and sank her elder sister, the *Oxley*, shortly after the outbreak of war and the *Sturgeon* narrowly missed the *Swordfish*. Several British submarines were bombed by Coastal Command aircraft and, in spite of every precaution, these difficulties continued in home waters for the rest of the war : in all, five British and Allied submarines were sunk by their own forces. Nevertheless the submarine patrols in the North Sea made a number of sightings of German warships engaged in minelaying, and attacked but missed several U-boats.

In December the submarine *Salmon* not only sank *U36* but

torpedoed and severely damaged the German cruisers *Leipzig* and *Nürnberg* which were on a minelaying mission. As she returned to base the damaged *Leipzig* was again attacked by the *Ursula* in the Heligoland Bight, but the torpedoes missed and hit an escort vessel. Shortly afterwards the submarines *Undine*, *Seahorse* and *Starfish* were sunk in quick succession by German anti-submarine vessels in the Heligoland Bight. The German ships had not got Asdics but achieved these results by sweeps and hydrophones in very shallow water. Two other submarines were severely damaged, one by a mine, and the British patrols were then moved further out.

By the end of 1939 there were twenty-three British submarines operating in the North Sea and they had been joined by the two Polish boats which had escaped from the Baltic. They were organized in three flotillas at Rosyth, Blyth and Harwich. Early in 1940, attempts were made to interfere with the German iron ore traffic from Norway but, as this could only be done in accordance with international law, only two merchant ships were sunk. In general, in these operations of the 'phoney' war period, the British submarines cannot claim to have influenced the war at sea very much, but nevertheless gained useful experience and established that they could compete with the German anti-submarine measures.

In this early period, although the German U-boats were employed mainly against trade, *U47* entered Scapa Flow and sank the battleship *Royal Oak*. It was fortunate for the British that the rest of the Home Fleet was at sea at the time, but this exploit was possible only because the harbour defences were incomplete, and it could not be repeated. Nevertheless, as in the First World War, the Home Fleet base had to be moved further west. In December the battleship *Nelson* exploded a mine laid by a U-boat and the battleship *Barham* was torpedoed and damaged by *U30*. By the end of the year the small U-boat force had, therefore, put a third of the Home Fleet battleships out of action which was quite an achievement, especially as these operations against warships were a sideline.

It was in the Norwegian campaign in April 1940 that the British submarine first came into prominence and the U-boats were concentrated for military purposes. The German invasion of Norway appeared to violate the long-accepted maritime principle that an overseas expedition should not be attempted without command of the sea. The German surface forces were in a relatively weaker position than they had been in the days of the Grand Fleet in 1914-18. The plan to rush the first waves of troops to Norway in warships, which were to return at once to Germany before the British could react, was ambitious and would have been foolhardy had it not been planned in conjunction with the large-scale use of U-boats and shore-based aircraft. The full strength of the U-boat arm, including all the training boats, was deployed in support of the operation (see p. 129; fig. 12). Thirteen were sent to establish defensive patrols off Narvik, Trondheim, Bergen and Stavanger with the aim of protecting the German landings: thirteen more were deployed offensively in three groups to attack the British Home Fleet if it attempted to interfere: finally four patrolled to protect the lines of communication from Germany to Norway across the Skagerrak.

It had been expected that the British minelaying operation which had been planned to take place early in April off the Norwegian coast might stimulate German counter moves. British submarines on patrol were therefore reinforced to a strength of twelve boats. Eight more put to sea the day before the invasion at the first sign of German activity. Before the landings two of the German supply ships masquerading as innocent merchant ships were intercepted and sunk in the Skagerrak by the *Trident* and the Polish submarine *Orzel*. Of the five groups of German warships which constituted the invading force, the four which sailed from bases in the North Sea were not detected by the submarines: four submarines were, in fact, well placed to intercept but did not sight them in the darkness. The fifth group was sighted but unsuccessfully attacked by both the *Triton* and the *Sunfish* in the Kattegat. Next day the submarines achieved more substantial results: the *Truant* sank the cruiser *Karlsruhe* and the *Spearfish* heavily damaged the pocket battleship *Lützow* on their way back to Germany.

As soon as it was realized that Norway was being invaded, the British Government gave permission for submarines to sink merchant ships on sight in the Skagerrak, so allowing them to wage unrestricted warfare which was indeed the only way in which they could achieve results. The submarines were then concen-

126

trated to attack the German communications off the Danish coast and across the Skagerrak to southern Norway. In the three months up to the end of June they sank nineteen ships totalling 89,000 tons. The British submarines were opposed by aircraft and anti-submarine vessels and had a very difficult time because of the short summer nights in these high latitudes. With some twenty-one hours of daylight and only three hours of darkness they had little time to recharge their batteries. The German patrols, which had not got Asdics, in fact needed no detecting devices : they simply had to patrol the area and the submarines would eventually have to withdraw to charge their batteries. The Germans were greatly assisted by their very efficient radio interception service which gave them the positions of many British submarines. The British submarines were therefore progressively driven from out of the Skagerrak and away from the Norwegian coast. Nevertheless in June the *Clyde* succeeded in torpedoing the battlecruiser *Gneisenau* in constant daylight off Trondheim, so preventing her from making a raid on shipping. In the first three months of the Norwegian campaign the British had lost four submarines, but in July and August another five were sunk. Three of these were destroyed by German anti-submarine craft, three by mines, two by German U-boats and only one by aircraft.

Early in the campaign, the German U-boats stationed off the Orkneys and Shetlands sighted some British formations but achieved no success against them and they were soon moved north to counter the British landings in Northern and Central Norway. U-boat operations for the rest of the Norwegian campaign were completely abortive due to the inefficiency of their torpedoes : the magnetic exploders were adversely affected by the high latitude and the degaussing of the British ships, and because of their poor depth-keeping were no better when set to fire on contact. Some twenty attacks on British major warships, four of them on the battleship *Warspite* alone, failed and, of ten attacks on transports, only one succeeded. Allowing for possible misses from other causes, the U-boats were robbed of almost certain success against the *Warspite*, seven cruisers, seven destroyers and five transports and, to make matters worse, they lost five of their number.

Although nearly the full operational strength of both the British and German submarine fleets was deployed in Norway, their intervention did not have a decisive effect on the campaign. Nevertheless their operations are of considerable strategic interest. Many of the German U-boats were deployed defensively and had little success. Their failure, however, was not a strategic one, as in the past, but was due to technical faults in their torpedoes. If their torpedoes had worked, although they still would not have exercised a decisive influence, the British would have suffered severe casualties and, without the *Warspite*, the second Battle of Narvik would probably have had a different result.

Early in April 1940 after the first contacts between the Home Fleet and the Luftwaffe, the British Commander-in-Chief decided that he could not operate off the southern part of Norway and that operations in this area would have to be left to submarines. By this decision he in fact admitted that his superior battlefleet had lost command of the sea to aircraft in this area and was powerless to prevent the invasion of Norway. The submarines could still dispute command of the sea, but the toll they were able to take was insufficient to have a serious effect on the campaign. Out of the six army divisions which the Germans sent to Norway, submarines were only able to prevent the arrival of two battalions and they destroyed under 2 per cent of the stores. Nevertheless this was more than any other arm was able to do. The significant point was that, whereas the battlefleet was shown to have another limitation on its operations and suffered a diminution of its power to command the sea, the submarine proved that it could operate in face of shore-based air power and so gained in stature.

The Norwegian campaign saw the biggest concentration of British submarines in home waters during the war. Towards the end of 1940 they began to move to the Mediterranean, which thereafter became the main theatre, and only a few were kept operational in home waters. For the rest of the war they were used for a variety of purposes but especially against the German heavy ships and U-boats. In summer, because of the constant daylight, they were unable to operate close in to the Norwegian coast and had to patrol well out in the open sea. They were sometimes used to escort convoys which were threatened with attack by the German heavy ships and from the fall of France they patrolled in the Bay of Biscay. There were so few of them that patrols

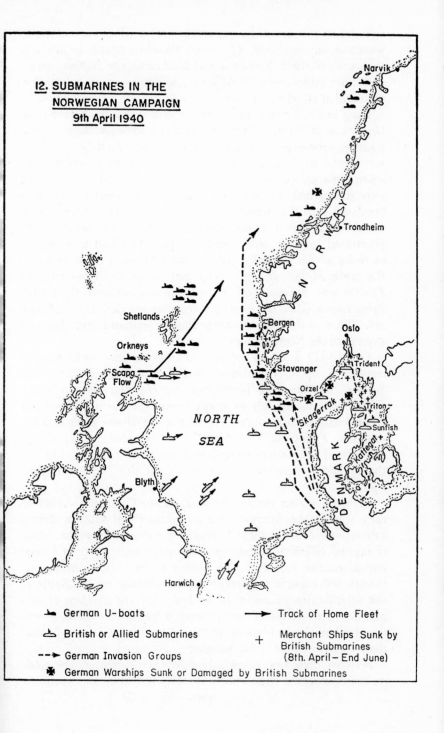

12. SUBMARINES IN THE NORWEGIAN CAMPAIGN
9th April 1940

Narvik

Trondheim

Shetlands

Orkneys

Bergen

Oslo

Scapa Flow

Stavanger

Trident

NORTH SEA

Orzel

Skagerrak

Triton

Sunfish

Blyth

Kattegat

DENMARK

NORWAY

Harwich

- ⊶ German U-boats
- ⊷ British or Allied Submarines
- --▸ German Invasion Groups
- ✠ German Warships Sunk or Damaged by British Submarines

- ⟶ Track of Home Fleet
- + Merchant Ships Sunk by British Submarines (8th. April – End June)

were by no means continuous and few submarines were in enemy waters at any one time. They were therefore unable to intercept the sorties of the *Scharnhorst* and *Gneisenau*, the *Hipper*, *Scheer* and other raiders into the Atlantic and there were no submarines on patrol at all when the *Bismarck* broke out.

Early in 1942, when intelligence indicated that the *Scharnhorst*, *Gneisenau* and *Prinz Eugen* were about to leave Brest, all the training submarines, mostly veterans of the First World War, were sent into the Bay of Biscay where they were joined by other submarines on passage to and from the Mediterranean. They were nicknamed the 'iron ring' and were disposed to prevent a break-out into the Atlantic. The *Sealion*, one of the few operational submarines at home, was sent to patrol close off Brest and penetrated into the outer roads. At night she had to withdraw to recharge her batteries and the three German ships passed to the north of her at high speed and turned up Channel. The *Trident* was, however, off Trondheim and damaged the cruiser *Prinz Eugen* when she arrived there after her dash up the Channel. This was the only success against a German heavy ship subsequent to the Norwegian campaign.

From 1942 onwards, operations to cover the North Russian convoys occupied the submarines a great deal. In March 1942, *Seawolf*, on patrol off Trondheim, reported the German battleship *Tirpitz* as she left to attack one of these convoys and this report enabled carrier-borne aircraft of the Home Fleet to intercept her. Finally in September 1943, the whole of the British operational submarine strength in home waters was used to tow the midget submarines to the attack on the *Tirpitz* in Alten Fjord.

In home waters during the war, eleven German U-boats on their way to the Atlantic were intercepted and sunk by British submarines. Most of these U-boats were destroyed in the course of normal offensive patrols but some were intercepted by special anti-submarine patrols on the passage routes. These sinkings, although not enough to exercise much influence on the Battle of the Atlantic, were a useful bonus and when the numbers of submarines used are taken into account, it transpires that an operational submarine in home waters was more likely to sink a U-boat than a convoy escort in the Atlantic.

Between these operations submarines were used against trade on the Norwegian coast and in the Bay of Biscay and up to the end of the war had succeeded in sinking forty-seven ships of 160,000 tons. Their total losses in home waters since the Norwegian campaign were eleven submarines, three of them by accident, and these casualties were lower than in the Norwegian campaign itself or in the Mediterranean.

The German U-boats returned to the attack on trade in the Atlantic in June 1940 and, except that plans were made for them to guard the flanks of the German invasion of Britain, they took no part in military operations again for a year. After the action between the *Hood* and *Prince of Wales* and the German battleship *Bismarck* a patrol line of seven U-boats was formed south of Greenland through which the *Bismarck* hoped to draw the pursuing British ships. The *Bismarck*, however, had to turn for France before she reached this line. Another patrol line was then formed south-west of Ireland with the same purpose in mind, but consisted of U-boats on their way back to base which were short of fuel and torpedoes. *U556* sighted the pursuing British battleship *King George V* which passed her at point blank range : she was unable to attack as she had no torpedoes left.

Except for minor operations, such as escorting surface raiders through dangerous areas on their way to the open sea, it was another sixteen months before the U-boats were again used in a military capacity, and then they attempted to oppose the Anglo-American landings in North Africa.

In October 1942, when the Allied expeditions sailed for this first large-scale amphibious operation of the war, the Battle of the Atlantic was at its height and the Germans had two hundred U-boats operational (see p. 133; fig. 13). The British were fully alive to the threat and estimated that some seventy-five U-boats could be deployed against the landings in the first few days. With the memory of what a single U-boat had achieved at the Dardanelles in 1915, they were apprehensive and took strong defensive measures. The British half of the expedition consisted of 240 ships in ten convoys for which no less than 94 escorts were provided. The American half consisting of 136 ships in four convoys with 75 anti-submarine vessels was relatively more strongly escorted still. The British assault forces alone included over 200 anti-submarine vessels, from destroyers to motor launches, and they had made arrangements to step up air patrols in the Bay of Biscay and in the Gibraltar area.

The Germans were completely unaware of what was afoot. They took the preparations which they had noted at Gibraltar to be for another convoy to Malta, so that, although U-boats were the only forces available to the Axis to counter attack this expedition outside the Mediterranean, no special deployment had been ordered. Just before the landings, six U-boats had been sent to reinforce the Mediterranean and had already passed through the Straits. There were twenty-two U-boats some 700 miles west of Ireland operating against Atlantic convoys and eight more southward bound for the Cape Verde Islands and the Azores. Three U-boats were outward bound in the Bay of Biscay and another seven off the Portuguese coast also on their way to reinforce the Mediterranean.

The American convoys passed south of the main U-boat concentration and most of the British supporting formations to the east of them. One formation of warships and two of the convoys were, in fact, sighted, but the U-boats were unable to attack and the Germans were not unduly suspicious. The southern group of U-boats, which was in the best position to intercept, made contact with SL125, an ordinary trade convoy coming up from Sierra Leone, and pursued it, sinking twelve ships. Whilst they were so occupied, the main invasion convoys slipped past them unobserved towards the African coast and the Straits of Gibraltar. Not a single attack was, therefore, made on the expedition in the Atlantic, but on the day before the landings an American transport was damaged by a U-boat inside the Mediterranean. This was the U-boat's only success and the total effect was that a single battalion missed the actual assault.

As soon as the U-boat headquarters learnt of the landings, the eighteen U-boats in the Bay and off the coasts of Spain and Portugal were ordered at full speed to the Moroccan coast. Ten Italian submarines at once left Cagliari in Sardinia for the landing areas in the Mediterranean. Shortly afterwards fifteen of the U-boats in mid-Atlantic, which had enough fuel, were ordered to close the Straits of Gibraltar. Two days after the landings *U173* arrived off Fedala on the Moroccan coast and sank the American transport *Hewes* and damaged a tanker and a destroyer. The next day *U130* sank the American transports *Routledge*, *Scott* and *Bliss* in the same area. At the same time the two large but

132

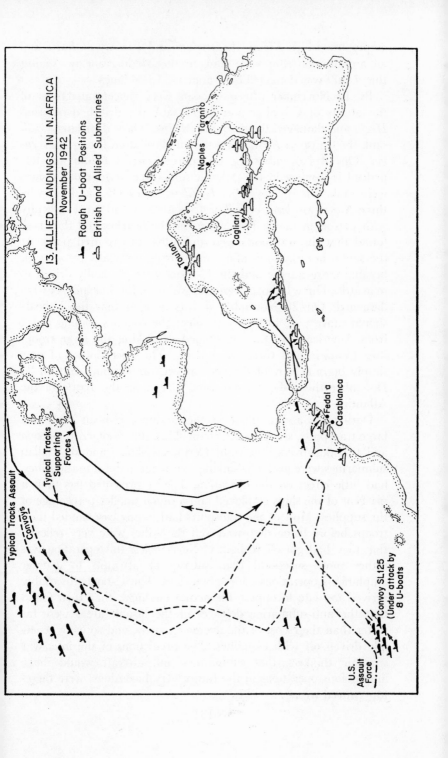

13. ALLIED LANDINGS IN N. AFRICA
November 1942

⊥ Rough U-boat Positions
⊂⊃ British and Allied Submarines

Taranto
Naples
Toulon
Cagliari
Fedal a
Casablanca

Typical Tracks Assault
Convoys
Typical Tracks Supporting Forces

U.S. Assault Force

Convoy SL125
(Under attack by 8 U-boats)

empty troopships *Nieuw Amsterdam* and *Viceroy of India* and an ammunition ship were sunk in the Mediterranean. Against this, *U509* was damaged by a mine off Casablanca.

By 12 November fifteen U-boats were concentrated west of the Straits of Gibraltar and *U515* sank the British depot ship *Hecla* and damaged the destroyer *Marne*. Three days later *U155* sank the transport *Ettrick* and the auxilary aircraft carrier *Avenger*. On 14 November the transport *Warwick Castle* was torpedoed in convoy in the Atlantic and three or four other ships were sunk. On 16 November *U173* was sunk off Casablanca by three American destroyers. The U-boats had had great difficulty with patrols in the shallow water off the beaches and they now found that the transports were unloading in captured ports. At the same time the anti-submarine patrols, especially by aircraft, became more intense and the U-boats were gradually driven to seawards. Three U-boats were lost west of Gibraltar and six were damaged. On 26 November it was decided that the U-boats should move west to try to intercept the convoys coming direct from America, and they succeeded in sinking the large troopship *Ceramic* and three other ships. The operations had now simply become part of the general war on shipping and on 23 December the U-boats were sent to resume the Battle of the Atlantic.

During the assault phase of the landings, U-boats sank nine large transports, six other merchant ships, the *Avenger*, the *Hecla* and two destroyers, but eight German U-boats and six Italian submarines were lost. The sinkings, although painful to the Allies, had little effect on the operation. They represented less than 5 per cent of the ships employed and a much smaller percentage of the supplies. Most of the transports had in any case landed their troops before being destroyed and the Allies were very relieved that they had got off so lightly. Nevertheless this operation was rather more successful than subsequent attempts to counter amphibious operations with submarines. The U-boats invariably arrived too late to oppose the actual landings; they then found that the anti-submarine defences of the assault areas were far stiffer than the escort of the average convoy, and so were generally driven off with casualties. The predictions of the inter-war strategic thinkers, that submarines and aircraft would make amphibious operations in the future very hazardous, were therefore proved wrong.

134

If the U-boat opposition to the North African landings was indecisive, their attempt to prevent the Normandy landings nearly two years later was a complete disaster. By this time the U-boats had been defeated in the Battle of the Atlantic and had failed, in spite of a number of technical advances, to regain the initiative. They were aware that an invasion was imminent and thirty-six U-boats were kept at six hours' notice in the Biscay bases and twenty-one in south-west Norway to oppose it. Only about a dozen of these were fitted with the schnorkel (see Note 16) which was by now practically essential for operations in confined waters The Allies had assembled 286 escorts of various types in the area south-west of the United Kingdom and had amassed several hundred anti-submarine aircraft to operate in the mouth of the Channel.

None of the U-boat group whose duty it was to oppose the invasion was at sea when it took place and, although thirty-five sailed at once from the Biscay ports, they were too late to oppose the initial landings. Nine U-boats fitted with schnorkel were ordered to make for mid-Channel and five other schnorkel-fitted U-boats from the Atlantic were called in. Seven others without schnorkels were ordered to operate in the mouth of the Channel and another nineteen formed a reconnaissance line in the Bay of Biscay in case the Allies attempted another landing there. The northern group of U-boats formed a patrol line south of Norway for the same purpose.

The Allied air patrols at the mouth of the Channel were able to keep up a half-hour coverage over the whole area and proved devastating. The U-boats without schnorkel suffered heavily, four were sunk and five were damaged in the first two days and even the schnorkel-fitted boats were reduced to a very low speed. It was nine days before the first U-boat arrived in its station in the middle of the Channel.

On 12 July all operations by the U-boats without schnorkel were suspended and those at sea were recalled. The schnorkel-fitted boats struggled on for another six weeks, but the Allied air and sea anti-submarine forces had the measure of them. They were in a superiority of something like ten to one and, operating in this confined space, were able to reduce the mobility of the U-boats to a crawl. Without mobility they became vulnerable to the swarm of Asdic-fitted ships in the confined area. Although the invasion target was a gigantic one, the Allied anti-submarine forces would have been strong even if spread over the whole Atlantic, and in this small area they proved decisive.

Over the whole period of the invasion the Germans lost twenty U-boats and managed to sink only twelve merchant ships, four landing craft and five escort vessels. These losses were scarcely noticeable amongst the immense volume of Allied shipping, and the defeat of the U-boat counter attack on the invasion was complete.

From its performance as a military weapon in the Atlantic the submarine could not claim to have exercised more than a minor effect, nevertheless it proved a useful warship, better able to compete against aircraft than ships and so more suitable in modern war. It forced its adversaries to expend much effort and suffer considerable inconvenience to compete with it. Its effect would have been far greater if the submarines of both sides had been more numerous, but the Germans used their U-boats to attack commerce and the main British submarine strength was in the Mediterranean.

IX

The Submarine Campaigns in the Mediterranean 1940-44

The British Navy as a whole was over twice the size of the Italian Navy and the British and French Fleets stationed in the Mediterranean also had a local superiority. Nevertheless before war broke out the British decided to divert their Mediterranean traffic round the Cape because they could not guarantee to command the sea in the central Mediterranean in the face of the enemy air forces. The Italians were content to control the routes to North Africa across the central Mediterranean and felt that there was nothing to be gained by seeking action : the British losses could be made good from outside the Mediterranean whereas their own would be permanent. This situation, in which the Allies controlled the ends and the Italians the middle of the Mediterranean, was one in which submarines, which were the only naval force able to operate continuously in face of shore-based air power, would clearly be of value to both sides.

At the outbreak of war the Italians had a large force of 120 submarines which was over twice the size of the British or German underwater fleets. Most of these were of a sea-going rather than an ocean-going type, but thirty were large enough to work outside the Mediterranean. It had been agreed with the Germans before the outbreak of war that the larger boats would co-operate in the Atlantic south of the latitude of Lisbon and on 13 June the submarine *Finzi* passed through the Straits of Gibraltar, to be followed by twenty-seven more. The rest, except for eight which were in the Red Sea, formed the Third Squadron of the Italian Fleet and came directly under the Italian Supreme Naval Command. They were divided among seven bases from Cagliari in the western basin to Leros and Tobruk in the eastern. They were to be used strategically for the defence of the central basin and were disposed mainly for reconnaissance to try and make up for their deficiency in maritime aircraft. The Italian submarines were in general reliable but inferior in performance to the U-

137

boats. They were trained to work by day and attack submerged and had not developed night surface tactics of the German variety.

Of the seventy submarines immediately available for operations in the Mediterranean, forty-nine, or well over half, were deployed on the outbreak of war. They were stationed in three groups, the first between Gibraltar and Sicily, the second in the Gulf of Genoa and the third between Greece and Alexandria. On 12 June the submarine *Bagnolini* sank the British light cruiser *Calypso* south of Crete and, on the 29th, the *Beilul* reported the British Mediterranean Fleet leaving Alexandra before the Battle of Calabria. These were, however, their only achievements and against this they lost six submarines in the first month to the British and French patrols. This large effort was, however, far too great to keep up, and patrols were soon reduced to about ten submarines at each end of the Mediterranean which achieved little for the rest of 1940.

Except for two elderly boats used for anti-submarine training, the British had withdrawn all their submarines from the Mediterranean in the early days of the war with Germany. When relations with Italy became strained in 1940 they moved ten submarines from the Far East and Indian Ocean to Alexandra. On the outbreak of war with Italy in June 1940, there were already forty-six French submarines in the western Mediterranean. Within ten days, however, the French had collapsed and all these submarines, except one, which joined the Free French, were withdrawn from the conflict.

On the outbreak of war on 10 June, Malta had to be abandoned as a submarine base for three months because of its weak air defences. Although attack on the Italian traffic to North Africa was an obvious use for submarines, there were no 'sink at sight' zones in the Mediterranean at the outset and any operations against merchant vessels had therefore to be in accordance with international law, which made them virtually impracticable. Thus the first patrols were made in the vicinity of the Italian fleet bases to act as outposts for the Mediterranean Fleet at Alexandria. A cruiser squadron and later two Italian battleships were missed by torpedoes at close range but the *Phoenix* sighted and reported the Italian battlefleet, which resulted in the two fleets making contact in the Battle of Calabria. Their only successes against warships were a torpedo boat sunk by the *Osiris* in the southern Adriatic and the Italian submarine *Diamante* sunk by the *Parthian* off Tobruk.

A 'sink at sight' policy within thirty miles of Italian territory was, however, approved in July. Up to the end of 1940, British submarines succeeded in sinking nine ships of 36,000 tons throughout the Mediterranean but this included less than 1 per cent of the traffic to Libya. Nine submarines were lost which was over half their strength. Although the Italians were aware of the principle of Asdics and had it under development, their anti-submarine vessels were not at this time even fitted with it; nevertheless they caused five of the British casualties. There is little doubt that these losses were due partly to the size and age of the submarines, which had been designed for the Pacific, and partly to a lack of realistic war-training in the Far East. The Italians laid over 12,000 mines in the first month of the war and these claimed another three of the casualties.

The British submarine operations in the first six months in the Mediterranean were, therefore, far from successful. Not only were the Italian communications with their armies in North Africa and Greece practically unimpeded, but they missed important opportunities to damage the Italian Fleet and, to make matters worse, they suffered heavy losses. Strength was, however, maintained by sending the four remaining boats from the Far East to the Mediterranean and four modern T class from home waters, and it is of interest that on arrival it was the latter which were responsible for half of the damage done so far. When the Italians invaded Greece in October, five Greek submarines became available and these were used to attack the sea communications with the Italian army in Greece and Albania.

At the end of 1940, therefore, in spite of what appeared to be splendid opportunities, the submarines on both sides had achieved little. Furthermore they had lost heavily and the Mediterranean seemed to be a dangerous place in which to operate them.

In the first six months of 1941, British submarine operations in the Mediterranean showed a very marked improvement. A flotilla of ten new submarines of the small U class was sent out from the United Kingdom and was based at Malta. The surviving large submarines were then concentrated at Alexandra and were reinforced by another three T class and a minelayer sent out from home waters. In March a third submarine flotilla was established at Gibraltar and, although this was originally intended to work in the Atlantic, in June it began to operate in the western Mediterranean. By the end of June there were, therefore, twenty-five British and Allied submarines available, so their strength since the outbreak of war had been doubled. It was not only in numbers that there was an improvement. The U class were modern and, although of moderate performance and armament, proved very suitable for the Mediterranean. All the reinforcements were manned by crews of high morale, trained and experienced in home waters.

In February the 'sink at sight' zone was greatly enlarged which made it possible to operate effectively against the Italian supply route to Libya (see p. 154; fig. 14). With the small U class it was now possible to patrol close to the Tunisian coast which was where most of the convoys passed. Patrols were maintained south of the Messina Straits and in the Ionian Sea and the submarines from Gibraltar worked in the Tyrrhenian Sea, which they could reach without having to cross the Italian mine barrier between Sicily and Cape Bon. On 24 May the *Upholder* sank the troopship *Conte Rosse* of nearly 18,000 tons south of Messina and over a thousand troops were drowned. In all, thirty-eight ships of 130,000 tons were sunk during these six months, mostly by day in submerged torpedo attacks, and in the same period only three submarines were lost. Two of the newly arrived U-class were mined and the Free French submarine *Narval* was sunk by an Italian torpedo boat. The exchange rate was therefore thirteen ships sunk for every submarine destroyed which was the best of the whole campaign. Nevertheless the rate of sinking was low and worked out at about one and a half ships sunk each month for every submarine on patrol.

In spite of these successes it was between February and May that the German Afrika Korps was transported to Libya. This was done in twenty-five convoys of an average of four ships each. In all, 82,000 men, who included considerable Italian reinforcements, and half a million tons of stores and equipment were got across. Of the ships sunk by submarines only about half a dozen were actually transporting German troops and stores and this represented only just over 5 per cent. These casualties were sufficient to cause General Rommel some anxiety, but the Italo-

140

German forces in Africa were built up to an extent which enabled them to retake Cyrenaica and advance to the Egyptian frontier. Although aircraft and some destroyers also attacked this supply line and the fleet bombarded Tripoli, German aircraft dominated the central Mediterranean and it was only the submarines which were able to make a sustained effort to oppose the movement.

The submarines, however, were not employed solely in attacking the Libyan supply lines. On 25 February the *Upright* sank the Italian cruiser *Armando Diaz* off the Tunisian coast in a night attack on the surface. Two Italian submarines also were sunk, the *Capponi* by the *Rorqual* north of Sicily in March and the *Salpa* by the *Triumph* off Mersa Matruh in June. Submarines were used also as beacons for landing operations at Bardia and Castellorizo and it was the *Truant* which led the fleet into the bombardment of Tripoli. Since the *Grampus* was sunk early in the war, the *Rorqual* was the only submarine minelayer left in the Mediterranean : she laid a number of fields which, in addition to sinking three ships, caused considerable delays while the minefields were swept.

In June 1941 the Germans attacked Russia and withdrew most of their aircraft from the central Mediterranean. This allowed a British air striking force to be built up at Malta and a force of cruisers and destroyers to return to the central Mediterranean. The attack on the communications of the Axis army in North Africa now began in earnest. With the success of General Rommel's offensive and his recapture of Cyrenaica, the Italians were able to route some of their supplies direct from Italy to Benghazi. Submarine patrols therefore paid more attention to this route but continued to operate off Tripoli, in the Tyrrhenian Sea and in the Aegean. British air reconnaissance from Malta was by now much more efficient and, although it was not often possible for submarines to take direct advantage of it, a great deal of intelligence was amassed on which submarine patrols could be planned.

From June to December 1941 submarines sank another thirty-eight ships of 175,000 tons, notably the troopship *Esperia* of 11,400 tons by the *Unique* off Tripoli in August and the troopships *Oceania* and *Neptunia*, both of over 19,000 tons and in the same convoy, by the *Upholder* in September. The Italians had been in the habit of running two fast troop convoys each month when there was no moon and their route had been fairly well established by various sightings by aircraft and submarines. The submarines *Upholder*, *Upright*, *Unbeaten* and *Ursula* were therefore sent out from Malta to lie to the north-east of Tripoli and intercept the second of these convoys in September. Three submarines were placed across the expected track of the convoy with the aim of attacking at night and a 'longstop' was placed fifty miles further on to attack after daylight. The convoy consisted of the *Neptunia*, *Oceania* and *Vulcania*, three large liners full of troops, and was escorted by six Fleet destroyers. *Unbeaten* sighted the convoy first but was out of torpedo range and so made a report by wireless and followed up astern. *Upholder* was the next to gain contact and fired a salvo of torpedoes hitting both the *Neptunia* and the *Oceania*. The *Neptunia* sank at once and the *Oceania* was damaged and she stopped. The third ship, the *Vulcania*, increased speed and was later missed by the *Ursula* at long range. *Oceania* was finished off after daylight by the *Upholder* who got there just before the *Unbeaten*. In October another convoy was sighted by aircraft, leaving Naples on a course to pass west of Sicily. *Ursula* was sent straight out from Malta and proceeded at full speed on the surface all night to intercept. She sighted the convoy next morning at very long range and damaged one ship. These examples of a pack attack and air co-operation were however, exceptions, and most of the sinkings were achieved by single submarines patrolling independently.

The Italian convoys consisted generally of about four ships with a similar number of destroyers or torpedo boats as escorts and they normally had an aircraft patrolling ahead of them. The convoy proceeded on a steady course, the escort zig-zagging about it. As the escorts had no Asdics it was their custom to drop deterrent depth charges every twenty minutes or so. The British submarines, however, found that the deterrent charges alerted them to the approach of a convoy and the sighting of the aircraft often gave them a good idea of its position. Nevertheless the aircraft were an anxiety, as the waters were very clear and the submarines could be seen by them submerged. After firing torpedoes the main danger was that an escort would steam along the torpedo tracks, dropping depth charges: the submarines would therefore turn off the torpedo tracks and proceed at full speed submerged for a

142

few minutes before slowing down to silent speed to avoid being heard by the Italian hydrophones.

In August the air striking force in Malta had been built up to a total of sixty-six aircraft including heavy, medium and torpedo bombers. They took an increasing toll of the traffic to North Africa until by the end of 1941 they were actually sinking more than the submarines. In November they did particularly well and a large convoy turned back to Italy when attacked by them. In this same month, Force K, consisting of two cruisers and two destroyers from Malta, put to sea and destroyed a whole convoy.

The effect of this combined assault on the communications of the Axis forces in North Africa steadily increased. In July the casualties had risen steeply and in August over a third of the traffic was sunk or damaged and failed to arrive. The 50,000 tons of supplies per month needed by the Axis armies were, therefore, for the first time, not met. In September matters grew worse and only a third of the army's requirements arrived. In October far fewer than the usual number of ships sailed from Italy and nearly two-thirds of the smaller total were sunk or damaged. In November three-quarters of the few ships that made the passage were sunk and less than a quarter of the Axis army's needs were supplied. There was only a very small improvement in December and it was clear that losses of this magnitude could not be borne for long. As it was, they had a decided influence on the land campaign. The Axis forces were kept so short of supplies that they were unable to take Tobruk or mount another attack on Egypt. During this period the British and Allied forces in Egypt were able to build up their strength, by the long route round the Cape, faster than the Axis across the central Mediterranean and in November they were able to advance and retake Cyrenaica.

Submarines proved to be the Axis' biggest enemy and caused 44 per cent of the casualties (see p. 159; fig. 15). Aircraft were responsible for 34 per cent and ships for 12 per cent whilst mines and miscellaneous causes made up the final 10 per cent. During the year the shipping available to the Axis in the Mediterranean declined by a third, and, although the Italians had been able to acquire some ships from France and Greece, they had very few building. It was clear that, if losses continued at this rate, they would not have the carrying power to supply an army in Africa for a long campaign.

Substantial results were also obtained by the submarines against warships, mostly in the course of normal anti-shipping patrols. The presence of a surface striking force at Malta stimulated the Italian heavy ships into putting to sea and there were other oppor‧tunities when the submarines were used to patrol off the enemy bases during the passage of a convoy to Malta in September. The *Upholder* damaged the Italian cruiser *Garibaldi* off Cape St. Vito in July and the *Triumph* hit and damaged the cruiser *Bolzano* north of Sicily in August. In November the cruiser *Abruzzi* was damaged by the *Utmost* in a night attack and in December the new battleship *Vittorio Veneto* was torpedoed and damaged by the *Urge*. Two more enemy submarines were sunk, the *Jantina* by the *Torbay* in the Aegean in July and the German *U95* by the Dutch submarine *O.21* east of Gibraltar in November.

Many other minor operations were carried out which seemed important at the time but which undoubtedly diverted energy from the main attack on the Axis communications to North Africa. With the fall of Crete in June and the British retreat to the Egyptian frontier, it became very difficult for ships to reach Malta. About a dozen storing trips had therefore to be made by submarines loaded with aviation spirit, ammunition, passengers and other stores. Some fifteen small landing operations were also carried out from submarines, some of which were to blow up the railway lines and bridges on the coast of Sicily and the Italian peninsula, others to evacuate soldiers from Crete or to land agents.

In the whole of this period the British lost another six submarines. The Italians had continued laying defensive minefields throughout 1941 and four of the lost boats were mined. The other two went to Italian anti-submarine vessels, one of them was sunk in a counter attack after firing at a convoy and the other after attacking a patrolling destroyer on the surface at night. Although the Italian air patrols were numerous and most of their convoys had air escort, they achieved no success. The exchange rate in the second half of 1941 fell to 6.3 Axis ships sunk for every Allied submarine destroyed.

In these six months thirteen new submarines arrived in the Mediterranean and by the end of 1941 total strength had risen to twenty-eight. It would have risen more, had not *Trusty* and *Truant* had to be detached to the Far East on the outbreak of war with Japan and some others to return to the United Kingdom to refit. During 1941 the British submarines proved not only that it was possible for them to operate with success in the Mediterranean, but that they were the best way to interfere with the Axis communications with North Africa. They showed themselves to be versatile warships and more than regained their reputation after the early failures. At the end of the year the British Commander-in-Chief in the Mediterranean asked for as many as possible to be sent out.

By the middle of 1941 the Germans were already worried about the communications of the Afrika Korps across the Mediterranean. Hitler was keen to render some naval assistance to the Italians but, except for small craft which could be sent overland, the only forces available were U-boats. Admiral Raeder was most reluctant to reduce the strength of the U-boats operating in the Atlantic and in July he managed to convince Hitler that U-boats could not help in the battle to get supplies across the Mediterranean. In August, however, Hitler's intuition won and he offered twenty U-boats to the Italians who accepted them. At the end of September six U-boats entered the Mediterranean and another four followed in early November. They had an immediate effect and, on 13 November, *U81* torpedoed the aircraft carrier *Ark Royal* east of Gibraltar and she sank next day. Twelve days later *U331* sank the battleship *Barham* off Sollum and on 14 December they had a further success when *U557* sank the cruiser *Galatea* off Alexandria. It was also in December that the Italian submarine *Scire* carried three human torpedoes (see Note 17) to Alexandria where they penetrated the harbour, seriously damaged the battleships *Valiant* and *Queen Elizabeth* and put them out of action for some time.

These successes not only destroyed the only aircraft carrier in the Mediterranean but put the complete battlefleet in the eastern basin out of action. Taken together they amounted to a serious defeat for the British. The German High Command now decided that the Mediterranean should be the main theatre for U-boat operations and that their strength must be built up to thirty-five and later to fifty boats. Although this policy was soon altered, the effect was to bring all U-boat operations in the Atlantic to a complete standstill for seven weeks. By the end of the year sixteen U-boats had passed through the Straits but they had lost four and had five damaged in doing so.

* * *

Whatever successes the new U-boat offensive was achieving, the Axis powers were acutely aware that they had to do something quickly about their sea communications if they were not to lose North Africa. It was obvious to the Italians that they had to improve their anti-submarine measures and, after consulting the Germans, they decided that the German version of the Asdic was the most advanced and in February they began to fit it in a number of ships. At the same time they laid down sixty anti-submarine corvettes. To compete with the air attacks on convoys and the surface striking force the Germans recalled the Second Air Fleet to the Mediterranean. Its first task was to bomb Malta and plans were made to capture the island during the summer.

At the end of December, as soon as the German aircraft had arrived, air attacks on Malta began. In January 1942 Italian shipping losses on the route to Africa were small and by the end of the month the Germans had sufficient supplies to take the offensive again. In February nearly 1,000 tons of bombs were dropped on Malta so that even the submarines began to have difficulty in using it as a base. At the same time German E-boats (see Note 18), which had been sent overland, began to lay minefields off Malta. The January improvement in supplies to Africa continued throughout February and March and this allowed the Axis forces to advance and retake Cyrenaica. Over 2,000 tons of bombs were dropped on Malta in March and three submarines were damaged in harbour. The cruisers and destroyers could no longer use the island as a base and the air striking force was reduced to impotence.

There were 233 air raids on Malta in April, 6,000 tons of bombs being dropped, and three British submarines and one Greek were sunk in harbour. The submarine base was not destroyed but it proved very difficult to maintain the boats which had to lie on the bottom all day, and their crews could get no rest. The E-boats had by now laid some 500 mines, all the minesweepers had been sunk, so the submarines had to abandon Malta and shift their base to Alexandria. As they left, two more submarines were lost in the minefields. Consequently in April the greatest weight of supplies was landed in North Africa of the whole war, losing only 1 per cent. More still would have crossed but for a general shortage of shipping. The Axis armies were now receiving sufficient to take the offensive again. At the end of May Rommel attacked, in June he captured Tobruk and by the end of the month was before El Alamein. The Germans, believing that they had permanently neutralized Malta, now transferred many of their aircraft back to the Russian front.

When Rommel arrived before El Alamein it was decided to shift the British submarine base at Alexandria further east to Haifa. The submarine depot ship *Medway*, on which all submarines in the eastern Mediterranean now depended, left Alexandria accordingly and was promptly sunk by *U372*. The submarines in the central and eastern Mediterranean were left without a supporting organization and this was not their only worry. In this period nine British submarines had been lost. In addition to the three sunk in harbour at Malta and the two mined just outside, another was mined in the Aegean and three more, including the famous *Upholder*, were sunk by Italian surface craft newly fitted with Asdics. Against this, eleven new submarines, mostly of the U-class, joined; but total strength fell steadily as three Dutch submarines working from Gibraltar were ordered to the Far East, a number of the older submarines had to be removed from operational duties and others had to return to the United Kingdom to refit. In April, although four new boats had just arrived at Gibraltar, there were only twelve submarines altogether in the Mediterranean.

Submarine patrols were, therefore, few and far between in the central Mediterranean. Some boats were off Crete and on the west coast of Greece but patrols had almost ceased in the Tyrrhenian Sea. Nevertheless they succeeded in destroying thirty-one ships of 117,000 tons, as well as the Italian cruiser *Bande Nere*. They also sank a destroyer and no less than six enemy submarines, all in the course of the normal anti-shipping patrols. Over the whole of the first half of 1942 only 6 per cent of the enemy supplies were destroyed on their way to North Africa but nearly all of this was due to the submarines (see p. 159; fig. 15) which were less worried by the neutralization of Malta than ships or aircraft.

In this period submarines were again used on many other tasks. Indeed the need for them to be so employed was greater than ever. At this time desperate efforts had to be made to relieve Malta by sea. The stores arriving in the surviving ships of the various Malta convoys were not enough and submarines had again to be used for transport. With the British battlefleet in the eastern Mediterranean completely out of action and with only cruisers to protect the convoys to Malta against the Italian battlefleet, submarine patrols off the enemy naval bases became more important than ever. In March it was the submarine *P36* which reported the Italian Fleet leaving Taranto and gave the first warning of their approach before the Battle of Sirte. In the convoy from the east to Malta in June, nine submarines, that is, almost their whole strength, were placed to the north of the route to try to protect it against the Italian battlefleet. Only one British submarine got in an attack on the Italian battlefleet and this missed but the cruiser *Trento*, which had been stopped by air attack, was finished off by *P35*. Nevertheless the British convoy had to turn back when faced with the Italian Fleet and this success for the Axis was the direct outcome of the elimination of the British battlefleet in December 1941.

At the beginning of 1942, there had been twenty-three German U-boats operating in the Mediterranean out of a total of ninety-one in all areas. These U-boats had been moved to the eastern end of the Mediterranean to attack the sea communications of the Eighth Army along the North coast of Africa. In March *U565* sank the cruiser *Naiad*, flagship of Admiral Vian, and on 16 June, during an attempt to get a convoy through to Malta, *U205* torpedoed and sank the cruiser *Hermione*. In the first six months of 1942, seven more U-boats were sunk in the Mediterranean but their successes included five destroyers and twelve merchant ships in the eastern basin. In July, as the Eighth Army was right back at El Alamein, it had no longer any sea communications, so the U-boats were moved to the western end of the Mediterranean to try to prevent convoys from getting through to Malta.

With the second departure of the German aircraft for Russia in May 1942 and the arrival of Allied air reinforcements, the Axis domination of the central Mediterranean began to weaken. In July, with fighter aircraft flown in from carriers, Malta made a remarkable recovery. A German attempt to renew the air offensive against the island was defeated by the newly arrived fighters and it was decided to reopen the submarine base. The submarine *P42* arrived at Malta on 20 July and by the end of the month the flotilla was re-established there. Submarine strength had very quickly returned to normal: not only were many new submarines of the 1940 war programme becoming available but some of the boats that had left the station to refit were returning. On 1 July the total number in the Mediterranean was twenty-three; there were also three Greek submarines available for limited operations but three of the British boats were old and of little use except for store carrying. In August the base of the flotilla in the eastern Mediterranean was moved into the former French submarine base at Beirut and the Gibraltar flotilla soon had its own quota of submarines as well as operating those on their way to the eastern basin. The British submarine force was, therefore, up to strength and with efficient bases again only a few months after it had been forced to abandon Malta and had lost the *Medway*.

Axis supplies reaching North Africa in June had been very low and there would have been a crisis if large quantities of British stores had not fallen into German hands at the capture of Tobruk. In July only 6 per cent of the supplies which left Italy were sunk but this still did not allow stocks to be built up for an offensive. As the Allied submarines were still reorganizing themselves, most of this damage had been done by aircraft. New British torpedo bombers with a greater range had arrived which could cover practically the whole Mediterranean. From now on, nearly every Italian convoy had to fight its way through to North Africa and most of them suffered several air attacks. In view of these heavy losses and the obvious need for the Axis to reduce the causes of them, their decision to cancel the amphibious operation against Malta seems to have been premature.

In August eight submarines took up positions to protect the important 'Pedestal' convoy from Gibraltar to Malta. One of these, the *P42*, torpedoed and damaged the Italian cruisers *Bolzano* and *Attendolo* north of Sicily. These two cruisers had already given up their attempt to attack the convoy because they had no air support and were, in fact, on their way home. Nevertheless they were both out of action for the rest of the war.

The Italian submarines on the other hand secured their greatest success of the war against the 'Pedestal' convoy. The Italian heavy ships were immobilized for lack of fuel and the convoy could be opposed only by submarines, aircraft and motor torpedo boats. Sixteen Italian submarines were deployed with five German U-boats in two groups south of the Balearic Islands and off Cape Ben. *U73* torpedoed and sank the aircraft carrier *Eagle* and so greatly weakened the convoy's air defence. The submarine *Uarsciek* reported the convoy north of Algiers and the *Cobalto*

149

made contact and attacked but was sunk by the escort. The submarine *Dagabur* then sighted the aircraft carrier *Furious* as she was returning to Gibraltar but she too was sunk by the escort. When the convoy arrived off Cape Ben in some disorder, the submarine *Axum* sank the light cruiser *Cairo* (see Note 19) and with the *Dessie* torpedoed the cruiser *Nigeria* and two merchant ships, one of which was the famous tanker *Ohio*. The *Nigeria* was the flagship of Admiral Burroughs; this and the *Cairo* were the only fighter direction ships, so this was a very considerable success for the Axis. The *Alagi* then sank another merchantman and the *Bronzo* finished off yet another which had been damaged by aircraft. Lastly the cruiser *Kenya* was damaged by an Italian submarine and these final operations were carried out without further loss to the Axis submarine force.

In August during the passage of the 'Pedestal' convoy to Malta, the Axis losses on the way to North Africa rose sharply and a quarter of the supplies which left Italy were lost. Rommel's failure at Alam Halfa was partly due to a shortage of fuel. This success for the Allies was a combined effort with aircraft but the submarines' share in it was the smaller as they were preoccupied with the 'Pedestal' convoy. In September only half the quantity of supplies required by the Axis armies arrived and the damage was almost entirely done by aircraft. In October the submarines got into their stride again and sank more than the aircraft. Over a third of the supplies to Africa were destroyed and two-thirds of the fuel. There is little doubt that Rommel's failure to take the offensive again and to push through to Cairo was largely due to these operations against his communications. At the end of October the British forces, again built up by the Cape route, passed to the offensive at El Alamein and the Axis armies, desperately short of fuel, retired and by 24 November Cyrenaica was in British hands again.

On 8 November 1942 the Allies had landed in North Africa and this was followed rapidly by the German occupation of Tunisia. In this month the British submarines were occupied in patrols connected with the North African landings and so aircraft again caused most of the damage. Axis losses to Tunisia were initially very light since most of the troops were sent by air and only the supplies by sea, but one-third of the cargoes to Tripolitania were destroyed. In December the Italians made a supreme effort and sailed over 200,000 tons of shipping for Tunisia;

150

twenty-eight ships were sunk, thirteen by air attack, eight by submarines, five by ships and two by mines. At the same time half the traffic to Tripolitania was sunk before the Eighth Army drove Rommel back into Tunisia.

The attack on sea communications was a major factor in assisting the Eighth Army in its victorious advance, but it seemed almost a failure that the enemy had been able to land in Tunisia and build up a large army there. The majority of the submarines were, it is true, occupied in October and November with the North Africa landings and, although they were released as soon as possible to resume the attack, it was some little time before they could be effectively redeployed. Nevertheless, over the whole period, submarines sank forty-three ships of 163,000 tons. This gave a greater rate of sinking than before and from August to October worked out at two ships sunk for each submarine on patrol each month. Although aircraft did by far the greatest damage to the Tunisian supply line, over all areas in the Mediterranean the tonnage sunk by submarines was 43 per cent, by aircraft 42 per cent, by ships 6 per cent and by mines and other causes 9 per cent.

These operations cost the British another six submarines, four to Italian anti-submarine craft and two to mines. This gave an exchange rate of 7.1 merchant ships sunk for every submarine destroyed, which was an improvement on the very low figure of 3.4 of the previous six months. The enemy losses now led to a general shortage of Italian shipping (see p. 161; fig. 16) but they were able to arrange for 120,000 tons lying idle in French ports to be transferred to them. Although many of these ships needed repair, they began to arrive before the end of the year.

During the Allied landings in North Africa, submarine strength was reinforced temporarily from home waters and by the end of October there were thirty-one British submarines in the Mediterranean and five more on the way out. Their first role was to patrol off the enemy bases to prevent interference by the Italian and French heavy ships (see p. 133; fig. 13). Four were stationed off Toulon to watch the French Fleet, seven between Sardinia and Sicily and five north and south of Messina to counter moves of the Italian Fleet at Taranto. The second role was to lie off the landing beaches to act as navigational beacons. Submarines were well suited to this task as they could approach submerged by day and, secretly and accurately, establish their positions. Lying on the bottom until the approach of the landing forces, they would then surface and lead them in. Six British submarines were stationed on the North African coast and four American submarines on the Atlantic coast for this purpose. A third but subsidiary task was to bring General Guiraud and his staff from France to North Africa and this was done by the submarines *P219* and *P217*.

The Italian Fleet was too short of fuel to intervene but two battleships left Taranto for Naples at economical speed and were missed at long range by the submarine *P35*. A minelaying sortie by the cruiser *Regolo* and six destroyers was, however, intercepted by *P46* and the cruiser was damaged. After the landings the beacon submarines were moved to the Tyrrhenian Sea and on 11 November all submarines were redisposed to attack the Axis communications with Tunisia.

The first six months of 1943 saw the culmination of the attack on the Axis sea communications across the Mediterranean. The seizure of Tunis as a counter measure to the Allied landings in North Africa was the last bid to maintain control of the central Mediterranean. The maintenance of the Italo-German sea communications with Tunisia for five months was a remarkable achievement. It was made under great difficulties: there were less than a dozen escorts available and fuel, even for them, was very scarce. Nevertheless the Italians ran over 100 convoys and over 500 trips were made by small vessels independently. At the same time eight fleet destroyers transferred 52,000 men to Tunis in over 150 passages.

The Allies used very large offensive air forces based near at hand in Malta and North Africa to attack the supply line. There were now thirty-two operational submarines in the Mediterranean and surface striking forces, including motor torpedo boats, were working from Malta and Bône. In the early stages submarines from Malta concentrated on the east coast of Tunisia where they had to work close inshore in shallow water under difficult conditions. Submarines from Algiers, to which port the Gibraltar flotilla had been moved, worked north of Sicily and submarine minelayers laid fields off Tunis itself. In January the Axis lost roughly a quarter of their supplies, mainly to submarines, but even so succeeded in getting 50,000 tons across. In February the result was much the same, but aircraft were now responsible for most of it. In March the Malta submarines were moved into the Tyrrhenian Sea to attack the routes from Naples and Leghorn and where conditions for them were more favourable. In March, April and May the Axis losses rose from under a half to over three-quarters of the traffic. After mid-April no large vessel reached Tunisia at all and the Axis forces surrendered in May.

In these months aircraft found it easier to dispose of the large number of small craft and sank four times as much as submarines on the Tunisian route. Of the convoys which sailed for Tunisia, half were attacked by submarines, which sank thirty-three ships, but nearly all were attacked by aircraft, many of them more than once, and seventy-one ships were sunk. After their success in December, the surface striking forces sank little. The submarine patrols were as usual not confined to the Tunisian traffic but were directed at Axis shipping wherever it could be found in the Mediterranean. Patrols were carried out off the south of France and in the Gulf of Genoa and round Sardinia and Corsica. Submarines from the base at Beirut patrolled in the Aegean. In the first five months of 1943, of the total losses of enemy merchant ships in the whole Mediterranean, 48 per cent were sunk by aircraft, 29 per cent by submarines, 21 per cent by mines or capture in ports or other causes and 2 per cent by surface ships. Well over half the ships sunk by aircraft were in harbour and submarines in fact destroyed more at sea.

The submarines did better in this period than ever before in the Mediterranean, sinking seventy-two ships of 221,000 tons. Furthermore their strength had not increased : on 1 April 1943 there were twenty-four submarines working from the three bases at Algiers, Malta and Beirut and three more on the way out. They had, however, been joined by eight French submarines from North Africa and a Netherlands boat and the three Greek submarines were still in the eastern Mediterranean. The rate of sinking was the highest yet attained and in February reached three ships sunk for every submarine on patrol. Seven submarines were lost in this period, four to surface anti-submarine vessels and three by mines. A particular disaster was the loss of the *Turbulent* which had been a most successful boat. Reinforcements from home

153

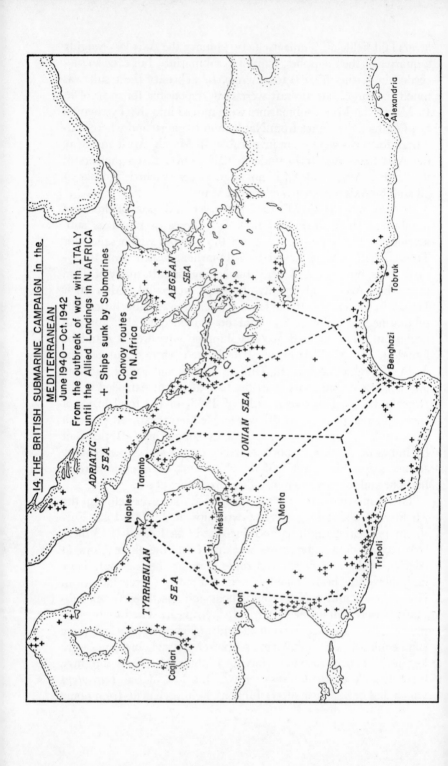

14. THE BRITISH SUBMARINE CAMPAIGN in the MEDITERRANEAN
June 1940 – Oct. 1942
From the outbreak of war with ITALY until the Allied Landings in N. AFRICA

+ Ships sunk by Submarines
--- Convoy routes to N. Africa

TYRRHENIAN SEA

ADRIATIC SEA

IONIAN SEA

AEGEAN SEA

Cagliari
C. Bon
Naples
Taranto
Messina
Malta
Tripoli
Benghazi
Tobruk
Alexandria

waters only just balanced these losses but the exchange rate rose again, to 10.2 merchant ships sunk for every submarine destroyed.

With the fall of Sicily the main work of the British submarines in the Mediterranean was done and the larger boats of the T class began to move to the Far East. With the collapse of Italy in September they were followed by the flotilla at Algiers, leaving two small flotillas, mostly composed of the U class, to operate on the south coast of France and in the Aegean. During the next eighteen months they succeeded in sinking five U-boats, three destroyers and fifty-five merchant ships of 190,000 tons for the loss of another six submarines. By the end of 1944 both these flotillas had been recalled to home waters and British submarine operations in the Mediterranean came to an end.

Of the forty-five submarines lost by the British in the Mediterranean, twenty-two are believed to have been lost on mines. The Mediterranean is in most places very deep, which meant that if a submarine was allowed to get out of control it could quite easily dive below its crushing depth. Although some of these boats may have been lost in this way, mines were probably responsible for nearly half the British submarine casualties in the Mediterranean. The total number of mines laid by the Axis in the Mediterranean throughout the war was 54,000 and this seems to have proved well worth while. Nineteen of the submarines were sunk by Italian surface vessels. Although in the early stages of the war some of the larger submarines were caught on the surface at night, in the later stages it was the combination of Asdics and depth charges which caused most of the losses. Although three submarines were lost in harbour in Malta through air attack, not a single British submarine was sunk throughout the war by an aircraft at sea.

The British submarines had a reliable torpedo and, in spite of primitive fire control, their marksmanship was good. Forty-three per cent of the attacks obtained at least one hit, the average number of torpedoes fired in an attack being three. British and Allied submarines sank twenty-one enemy U-boats in the Mediterranean, five of which were German. Fifteen of these were sunk whilst on the surface in daylight, and the rest at night. The British submarines were nearly always submerged by day and did not present themselves as targets to enemy submarines, and at night

155

they were careful when on the surface to zigzag. As a result only one British submarine was sunk by an Axis submarine in the Mediterranean.

The success of the British submarines in the Mediterranean was not just because the opposition was weak. They were nearly always pitted against convoys with air escort and, for the last eighteen months, with a force of Asdic-fitted escorts many times their number. Credit must go to their method of operation which seemed cautious by German standards, but was based on exploiting the fact that they were submarines rather than submersible torpedo boats. Two-thirds of their torpedo attacks were made submerged by day and only one-third on the surface at night. They tried to remain undetected at all times: passages were invariably made submerged in daylight which meant that they could not travel more than 120 miles a day. They made very few wireless signals and then only when absolutely essential. The water in the Mediterranean is very clear and submarines can be seen by aircraft on occasions down to sixty feet; they had therefore to patrol deep but with a porpoising motion, coming up to look through the periscope every ten minutes or so and keeping a sharp lookout for aircraft. British submarines were fitted with an air-warning radar from the end of 1942 onwards but this made no fundamental change in these tactics. It could be used to detect ships at night but was not as good as the radar fitted in the American submarines in the Pacific and, with their low speed, night surface attacks continued to be a question of opportunity rather than policy. This method of operating in the Mediterranean, where distances were short and traffic routes canalized, was undoubtedly the best and, if they had tried to work as submersibles like the U-boats in the Atlantic or the American submarines in the Pacific, their casualties would probably have risen to an unacceptable extent and they might have been driven out of the central Mediterranean.

The Italians employed 136 individual submarines at one time or another in the Mediterranean. They entered the war with over twice as many boats as either the British or the Germans, but in general their submarines proved to be an unimportant factor in the war in the Mediterranean. They were used princi-

156

pally as an auxiliary to the Italian Fleet for reconnaissance and to help dispute the passage of the British Fleet or convoys through the Mediterranean. A considerable proportion of their strength was, therefore, spent for long periods waiting passively for the British to enter the central Mediterranean. As the war progressed they found themselves drawn into a transport role to beleaguered outposts such as Tobruk and Leros, and they helped in the general transport of supplies to North Africa. Whilst deployed on reconnaissance they made some important sightings but also failed to guard their fleet against surprise, notably before Taranto, Matapan and the bombardment of Genoa. The sum total of their successes was the sinking of three British cruisers and the damaging of three others, half these results being achieved in August 1942 in the 'Pedestal' convoy. Nevertheless, the Italian submarines in fact sank more warships than their own aircraft or surface ships; against merchant ships in the Mediterranean their results were insignificant and they did little, with the one notable exception above, to prevent convoys from getting through the Mediterranean. The price of these somewhat meagre results was the loss of no less than sixty-six submarines. Their building programme was small and they completed only forty-one, so that the number available fell steadily from eighty-four at the beginning of the war to forty-four at the armistice.

These results could be explained by pointing out that the Italian submarines were wrongly used and that the best role for submarines has always proved to be an unrestricted attack on commerce. For most of the war, however, there were few merchant ships in the Mediterranean to attack. When after the North African landings there were plenty, they found that they were quite unable to compete with the British convoy system. On the other hand, the need to employ them on reconnaissance was urgent because of the Italian weakness in maritime aircraft and to use them for transport was essential as the outlying garrisons could not be succoured in any other way. Nevertheless the use of submarines, which are only capable of attacking unescorted merchant ships, for reconnaissance and store carrying is unlikely to exercise a decisive influence on war at sea.

The Germans ordered a total of ninety-five U-boats to the Mediterranean but five were lost in the Atlantic before they arrived, six were sunk penetrating the Straits of Gibraltar and twenty-two turned back for various reasons. Sixty-two, therefore, entered the Mediterranean but there were never more than twenty-five U-boats available at a time. For the first year their operations were almost entirely military in character and were extremely successful. They sank a battleship, two aircraft carriers, three cruisers and twelve destroyers, mostly in 1942, for the price of sixteen U-boats. The elimination of the British battle-fleet, in co-operation with the Italian human torpedoes in the eastern basin, was equivalent to a major naval victory but it did not help to solve the most pressing Axis problem of getting supplies through to Libya. Nevertheless it had a decided influence on the similar British problem of succouring Malta. The sinking of two aircraft carriers came just before the war with Japan broke out in the Far East and the shortage of this type of ship was to have serious consequences. The U-boats made their most important contribution to the land battle in North Africa not by their attack on the sea communications of the Eighth Army along the north coast of Africa, but by sinking the submarine depot ship *Medway* and so hindering the operations of the British submarines.

Against merchant shipping their total was ninety-five ships sunk of nearly half a million tons, and their presence in the Mediterranean meant that for two years the Allies had to keep ships in convoy throughout its length. Their effect on the various Allied amphibious operations and the subsequent military communications of the armies in Italy was very small. Anti-submarine measures against them were intense and all sixty-two U-boats which entered the Mediterranean were eventually destroyed. Of these twenty-eight went to ship and air patrols, fifteen to convoy escorts, while eleven were bombed in harbour and five were torpedoed by British or Allied submarines. This gave an exchange rate of one and a half merchant ships sunk for every U-boat destroyed.

Whereas the German U-boat campaign in the Mediterranean was a sideshow, the British submarine campaign absorbed their main submarine strength for three years. The British sent just over a hundred individual submarines to the Mediterranean and were assisted by twenty-four Allied boats, ten of which were French, eight Greek, four Dutch and two Polish. Until 1943 there were usually between twenty and thirty of them operating at a time.

The campaign against the communications with North Africa was a joint operation with aircraft and to a smaller extent with surface warships. The campaign was, right up to the surrender

in Tunis, never sufficient on its own to be decisive although on
occasions three-quarters of the traffic was being sunk. Without
it, however, there is no doubt that the North African campaign
on land would have gone very differently. As it was, the British
were able to supply their army in the Middle East by the long
sea route round the Cape faster than the Axis were able to supply
their army by the short route across the Mediterranean. Although
when the best results were obtained it was aircraft which sank
most, there were long periods when submarines were the only

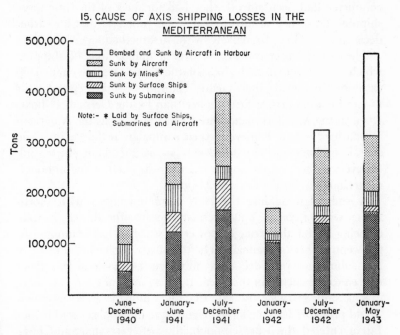

15. CAUSE OF AXIS SHIPPING LOSSES IN THE
MEDITERRANEAN

weapon achieving any success at all. Whereas the aircraft did best
in three periods when operations from Malta were at their height,
the submarine contributed a steady effort throughout the two
and a half years.

There were two ways to wage the campaign against the communications between Italy and North Africa. The first was, like
the aircraft and surface forces, to concentrate on the southbound
traffic to Libya and Cyrenaica in order to destroy the supplies
on the way and starve the Axis armies directly. The second was
to wage an unrestricted campaign against ships and so against
their carrying power all over the Mediterranean, with the aim of

reducing it to a point where there would be no ships left to supply the army in North Africa. The submarines were really used in the second way but with special attention to the North African route. At the Italian armistice in September 1943 the Axis still had 750,000 tons of shipping left, but during the year had received nearly half a million tons from France (see figure 16). The Germans themselves, however, expected that shipping resources would have been exhausted by the summer if the Tunisian surrender had not come first. Nevertheless as the Italian ocean commerce had been cut off, they had for most of the time more shipping than they needed and it seems probable that an earlier decision would have been likely by the first method.

The British submarines sank over a million tons of shipping which was approximately half of the total Axis merchant ship casualties in the Mediterranean. The rate of sinking was, as far as can be estimated, a little higher than by the German U-boats when in the Mediterranean and about the same as the American submarines were to achieve in their campaign in the Pacific. The overall exchange rate worked out at six merchant ships sunk for every submarine destroyed and this was tough going although not as tough as for the German U-boats.

A campaign against the Axis communications with North Africa was, of course, only necessary because the British, in spite of being by far the stronger power at sea, had lost command of the central Mediterranean. They realized somewhat belatedly that submarines provided a way in which they could at least deny the sea to the enemy in this area. If the submarines had been able to sink ships at twice the rate that they did, the Axis campaign would probably have collapsed eighteen months earlier and before Japan entered the war. Undoubtedly better results could have been obtained, at some sacrifice in other directions, if all the home operational submarines had been sent to the Mediterranean, if no diversions, such as store carrying, had been permitted and if the whole effort had been concentrated on the southbound routes to North Africa instead of on carrying power all over the Mediterranean. Nevertheless this would still not have been enough and what was really required was a larger fleet of submarines.

The British had only fifty-seven submarines at the beginning of the war and many of these were obsolescent. Altogether they built 170 new boats during the war but twenty of these they supplied to their allies. The real expansion of the submarine

Mediterranean, June 1940 — Sept 1943

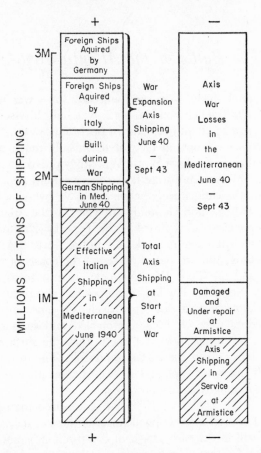

force did not occur until the Mediterranean campaign with its heavy losses was over. By the end of the war they had a fleet of 131 submarines which was only a little larger than the Italians had at the beginning. If this force had been available at the start of the campaign it would probably have been decisive. The reason that it was not was a legacy of the pre-war policy of abolition. They failed to realize that there would be parts of the sea which it was essential to deny to the enemy and which a battlefleet would not be able to command, and that submarines were now an essential weapon for the stronger power at sea as well as the weaker.

X

The Battle of the Atlantic 1939-43

The German U-boats were quite unready for a war with Great Britain in 1939. Their total strength was only fifty-seven, thirty of which were small and only fit for operations in the North Sea. The U-boats were not, in fact, of technically much better performance than in the First World War; they proved more reliable and silent, however, and were far stronger against depth charges. Radio communications were better and gave two-way traffic between the U-boats and Germany anywhere in the Atlantic. They were of three sizes (see figure 17), the Type II (250 tons), which were of sufficient range to work only in the North Sea; the Type VII (500 tons), able to patrol as far as the coasts of Spain and Portugal, and the Type IX (750 tons), able to go as far as the Azores (see Note 20). The last two types had sustained sea speeds of 16-17 knots and carried from twelve to nineteen torpedoes. The torpedoes were electrically propelled and so trackless and the system for firing them did not disturb the surface, making counter attacks down the tracks impossible. The torpedoes were fitted with magnetic exploders to fire underneath a ship and so to do more damage than a hit on the side.

Although the Z plan of 1938 had authorized the building of some two hundred more U-boats, most of these at the outbreak of war were still in the early stages of construction or not even laid down. The Germans considered that the first priority for the U-boat arm was to build up to the three hundred U-boats thought necessary to be decisive against a British convoy system. The Z plan was therefore scrapped and the building of all the heavy surface ships in it, which were not already launched, was stopped. A very large programme of U-boats was substituted, to be built eventually at the rate of twenty-nine a month and they were ordered up to *U850*. These were nearly all of the Type VII (500 tons) and Type IX (750 tons) but they also ordered a few large minelayers and supply U-boats as well as some large U-cruisers.

The problem now remained of what to do with the existing

All submerged speeds 6 – 7 Kts

Type II (250 tons)

North Sea Boats
50 built

Speed on Surface 11 Kts
6 Torpedoes

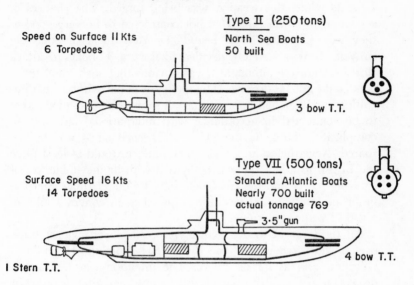

3 bow T.T.

Type VII (500 tons)

Standard Atlantic Boats
Nearly 700 built
actual tonnage 769

Surface Speed 16 Kts
14 Torpedoes

3·5" gun

1 Stern T.T.

4 bow T.T.

Type IX (750 tons)

Long Range Boats
Over 150 built
actual tonnage 1051

Surface Speed 17 Kts
19 Torpedoes

4·1" gun

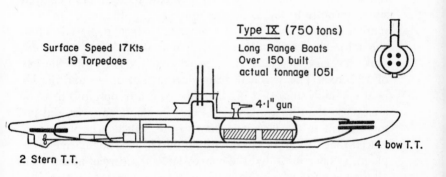

2 Stern T.T.

4 bow T.T.

Type XIV (U-tanker)

Supply U-boats
10 built
1688 tons

No Torpedo Tubes
635 tons fuel to replenish
up to a dozen other
U-boats

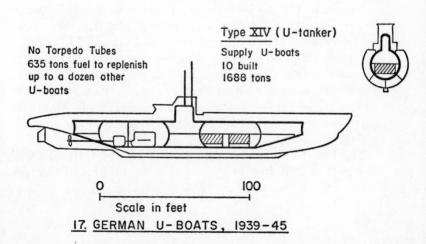

0   100

Scale in feet

17. GERMAN U-BOATS, 1939–45

U-boats whilst this weapon was being forged. The chances of success against warships were not considered to be very good as they were expected to be heavily escorted by Asdic-fitted destroyers. It was therefore decided to use the U-boats to attack British commerce although it was obvious that such small numbers could not be decisive. This policy was not without its difficulties, as Hitler had ordered that all submarine operations were to be conducted in accordance with international law and, to complicate matters further, that all French ships were to be spared. Nevertheless an attack on commerce would at least force the British to adopt the convoy system with its inevitable loss of carrying power and the advantage that, by the German interpretation of international law, the ships when in convoy could be attacked without warning.

All the larger U-boats were therefore deployed against trade over a wide area west of the British Isles from the Hebrides to Gibraltar and as far as 25°W. The intention was to cause a dispersion of the British patrols and to outrange aircraft based in the United Kingdom. The whole U-boat strength was deployed simultaneously to try to sink as much as possible before the formation of convoys. The U-boats were, in fact, deployed before the outbreak of war and on the very first day *U30* torpedoed and sank the passenger liner *Athenia* without warning with the loss of 128 lives. This was a flagrant disregard of orders and the U-boat captain's story that he thought it was a troopship is more of an excuse than an explanation. This incident, however, did far more harm to the Germans than to the British, who were convinced that they were faced with an unrestricted submarine campaign, at once instituted the convoy system and went ahead with all the measures which they had learnt to be necessary in 1917-18.

The small U-boats were deployed against traffic in the North Sea as best they could, but it was soon decided that they would be better employed laying mines. The Germans had an unsweepable magnetic mine in production and they hoped to use it in quantity before the British could devise a counter measure. Minelaying was quite within international law, provided that the mines were laid in British territorial waters. Starting in November thirty-four minefields were laid in port approaches and in navigational channels round the United Kingdom.

The London Submarine Agreement signed by both sides was as recent as 1936 but, in spite of this, the British and German interpretations of it were widely different. The British considered that their merchant ships should only be sunk after visit and search and then only if carrying contraband; the crews should in any case be put in a place of safety which did not include the open boats. The Germans agreed with much of this but held that any defensive measure at all rendered the merchant ship liable to be sunk without warning. If, therefore, the merchant ship used radio, zigzagged, mounted a defensive armament or even darkened ship at night, it, in their view, forfeited its immunity. With so wide a divergence of opinion it was only a matter of time before the campaign drifted into unrestricted submarine warfare and by November 1939 it had already become a fact.

In the Atlantic the Germans withdrew half of their U-boats a few days after the outbreak of war, in order to settle down to a routine of patrols. In this first phase up to the end of March 1940, a period of seven months, the U-boats sank 222 ships of 765,000 tons (see p. 186; fig. 19, i): half a million tons more were sunk by mines, a proportion of which had been laid by U-boats. These sinkings were ten times those achieved by the warship raiders *Graf Spee* and *Deutschland*. In this period nearly all the attacks were made in daylight on independent shipping, and only 10 per cent of the losses were sunk in convoy. Attempts were made to form the so-called wolf packs, which had been used in manœuvres in 1937, to attack the convoys but in these early stages they were still experimental. The first plan was for a senior officer in one of the U-boats to control the pack but it was soon found that it was better to control operations from the shore. Although it was only possible to keep three to five U-boats on patrol at a time, their rate of sinking of ships was high. It varied from two for each submarine on patrol in November to five in January (see p. 187; fig. 20, ii).

The British anti-submarine forces consisted initially of some sixty escorts, forty Sunderland flying-boats and a number of short-range reconnaissance landplanes. In an attempt to extend the range of air operations against U-boats, the Admiralty deployed two aircraft carriers in the western approaches. *U29* soon sank the *Courageous* employed on these duties and *U39* very nearly sank the *Ark Royal*: she was saved only by a premature torpedo explosion. *U39* was sunk in the subsequent counter attack but after this the carriers were withdrawn. In the first seven months the Germans lost eighteen U-boats, eleven to surface vessels, seven of which were escorts of warships or convoys, and four to mines, three of which were in the Straits of Dover. The mine barrage laid in the Straits of Dover was a great success; although three U-boats got through, three others were sunk and the Germans then abandoned the use of the Straits altogether. The exchange rate over the whole period worked out at 12½ ships sunk for every U-boat destroyed (see p. 187; fig. 20, ii). In this same period thirteen new U-boats were commissioned and so their total strength fell slightly (see p. 187; fig. 20, i).

This first period was brought to a close at the end of March 1940 by the withdrawal of all U-boats for the campaign in Norway. The British merchant ship losses, heavy as they were, were all made good, mostly by new construction but partly by putting into service ships captured from the enemy. In spite of the U-boat losses the Germans were well satisfied. They were pleased with their submarines, especially the Type VII (500 tons), but not with their torpedoes, the magnetic exploders of which had up to 25 per cent failures, and they reckoned 300,000 tons of shipping escaped due to this defect. They decided that with the number of U-boats available their wolf packs were not worth while and that the better course would be to continue to operate independently over a wide area to disperse the anti-submarine effort. An attempt to penetrate into the Mediterranean with some of the long-range U-boats was, however, a failure. Although eleven of the eighteen casualties had been caused by Asdics, and the Germans had learnt to respect it, they were agreeably surprised that it was not more effective. They were able to approach formations of warships and attack without detection and, with the rate of sinking of merchant ships which they had achieved, there was hope for the future.

After the Norwegian campaign the U-boats were not ready to resume the battle in the Atlantic until June 1940 a period of two months. Their strength had slightly declined since the beginning of the war and there were now only twenty-nine boats ready for operations out of a total of fifty, the balance being needed for training the crews of the new boats under construction.

On 23 June France fell and no time was lost in moving the U-boat bases to the Atlantic coast. In July Lorient was opened and *U30* arrived there on the 7th of the month. The advantages of the French bases were considerable. The U-boats were spared the long passage through the North Sea and round the north of Scotland in which they could be harried by mines and patrols. The distance to the Atlantic was much shorter and this allowed 25 per cent more boats to be kept in the operational area and the area itself to be extended to the west. French dockyards were brought into use for repairing U-boats, which greatly eased the congestion in Germany, and finally it was possible to use some of the small Type II U-boats west of the British Isles.

In the late summer all merchant ships of under 15 knots were already in convoy, but the outward convoys were dispersed at 15°W and the inward convoys did not receive their anti-submarine escort until they reached the same longitude. After the fall of France all traffic was brought in through the north-western approaches. There had been heavy casualties amongst the British destroyers and sloops in Norway and at Dunkirk and a large number of them had still to be kept on the east coast as a defence against invasion. Escorts were, therefore, very weak and often consisted of only one or two ships. Coastal Command aircraft totalled only 226 in September and they had been ordered to give priority to reconnaissance in the North Sea against invasion : air patrols in the Atlantic were, therefore, few and far between.

The U-boats had now developed new tactics. They had decided that the best counter to Asdics was to attack on the surface at night. When on the surface they were difficult to detect by Asdics and at night the U-boats had little difficulty in sighting convoys and were seldom seen by the escorts. In bad visibility they could use their hydrophones which could hear the convoys at considerable distances. As they were faster than most merchant ships, and many of the escorts as well, the U-boats were able to manœuvre into a good firing position more easily than they could do submerged. After firing their torpedoes the U-boats would do their best to remain on the surface and disengage at high speed. If they were forced to dive by an escort they were apt to be picked up by Asdics and heavily depth-charged. After disengaging they would reload, regain a firing position and attack again.

Although the Germans still had very few U-boats, they now decided to try a wolf pack again which in theory offered a better chance to find the convoys and would oppose the escort with a concentration of U-boats. The first indication of a convoy was often received in the U-boat headquarters ashore by radio intelligence. The U-boats would then be ordered to spread in a scouting line across the expected track of the convoy. On sighting the convoy the first U-boat would report by radio and shadow until the other boats arrived. Such a concentration of U-boats was sometimes made from as far away as 300 miles and this involved long periods at high speed on the surface, often in daylight. The concentration of the U-boats against a convoy was, therefore, controlled from the shore but once the attack had begun the U-boats were allowed to work individually.

The U-boats took a week or two to discover that all the traffic was coming in through the north-western approaches. The larger U-boats were then concentrated in this area against the convoys and one or two of the small U-boats patrolled independently off the entrance of the North Channel. A single large U-boat was sent to raid the Freetown area where it sank seven ships.

The U-boats began to obtain substantial successes almost at once. Between June and October they sank 274 ships of 1,400,000 tons. The rate of sinking started at three ships for every U-boat on patrol each month and rose to over five in October. Two-thirds of these ships were in fact independent, generally straggling from convoys, or the ships that had been dispersed from the outward-bound convoys. Even then one-third were actually sunk in attacks on convoys, against which the U-boats did particularly well in October. Convoy SC7 (see Note 21) started with thirty-four ships and lost twenty of them to a pack of seven U-boats. This convoy had only three slow escorts to begin with but they were later joined by two more. Immediately afterwards convoy HX79 (see Note 21), which had forty-nine ships, lost twelve of them and would have lost more if the U-boats had not run out of torpedoes. This time the pack consisted of only five U-boats and the escort of two destroyers, a minesweeper, four corvettes and three trawlers was substantial. It was found, however, that the U-boat pack had to patrol a long way to the west if it was to have time to concentrate on an inward-bound convoy before it reached the coast. This led to a westward movement which also brought them a rich harvest in dispersed ships and stragglers. However this was countered to a certain extent when the convoy dispersal point was moved, first to 17°W, and then to 19°W in October. In November a second U-boat was dispatched to the Freetown area where she sank another four ships.

In the whole of this period only two U-boats were sunk by the convoy escorts and the British anti-submarine measures scarcely worried them at all. The escorts at this time had to rely on visual lookouts and seldom even saw the U-boats. Although Coastal Command air patrols were an inconvenience to the U-boats, as they forced the U-boats to submerge and denied them their surface mobility, the large Sunderland flying boats could always be seen in time to dive and the bombs they carried went off on the surface and were not very effective. Aircraft were, however, able to drive the U-boats out of the immediate vicinity of the North Channel. The U-boats' main difficulty was, as in the First World War, to find the convoys; of these the vast majority still reached their destination without being attacked at all. In August 1940 in an attempt to solve this problem, some German reconnaissance aircraft had been allocated to work with the U-boats but there was little possibility of co-operation as they were at first of too short an endurance.

In August the Italian submarine contingent for the Battle of the Atlantic began to come out of the Mediterranean. Three boats patrolled off the Azores in August and in October six boats joined the Germans west of the North Channel. They patrolled submerged most of the time waiting for targets to appear, which in the open Atlantic was an infrequent occurrence and in a period of two months they sank only one ship. German efforts to persuade them to operate on the surface and use their mobility were unsuccessful, as were Doenitz's later plans to use them to scout for the German U-boats. These poor results were disappointing to the Axis: the Italian submarines at this time actually outnumbered the Germans in the Atlantic by twenty-five to eighteen.

Sinkings fell off during the winter partly because there were fewer U-boats on patrol but mainly because of bad weather. Rough weather not only decreased the speed of the U-boats on the surface but made lookout difficult, and bad visibility made it still harder to find the convoys; furthermore torpedoes were liable to run erratically in heavy seas. At the end of the period another attempt was made to work with the Italians but it was soon found that they were of use only for attacking independent ships, so they were allocated a separate area and all idea of direct co-operation with the Germans was given up. The poorer results during the winter indicated that it would be worth while to send more U-boats to the Freetown area, where it was hoped that a rich harvest of independents could be reaped and offset the long passage time. Preparations were therefore made to raid the central Atlantic in force.

From November 1940 to February 1941 there were between four and six U-boats at sea. By the end of February since they had renewed their attack in the Atlantic in June the U-boats had sunk just over 400 ships of over 2 million tons. They had only lost eight U-boats altogether, four to the escorts of convoys, one to a mine in the North Sea, and another to a British submarine. At the same time the Italians lost four boats, two to escorts, one to an aircraft and another to a British submarine. The rate of sinking during the winter had fallen again to three ships for each U-boat on patrol each month. The overall exchange rate for the period was, however, good for the Axis powers and was fifty ships sunk for every U-boat destroyed (see pp. 186, 187; figs. 19 and 20).

During this period a considerable number of ships was sunk by other German forces. Long range FW200 aircraft had arrived at Bordeaux in January and, although the original intention was for them to scout for the U-boats, they proved to be of little use in this role, due to navigational errors and bad communications. They could reach to 20°W and although there were thirty of them, they were not able to shadow a convoy for long enough for the U-boats to make contact. They managed, however, to sink many ships on their own. Over the whole period, aircraft sank about half a million tons in all areas, mines accounted for 300,000 tons and surface raiders and E-boats another 683,000 tons. The total loss of shipping to the Allies was well over 3 million tons in these nine months. Furthermore over 2 million tons of shipping were under repair and so out of action.

This heavy loss of shipping was at twice the rate they were being built in the United Kingdom, but with the fall of the Allied countries in Europe, over 3 million tons of their shipping had become available. Imports into the United Kingdom fell very considerably but it has been estimated that only 15 per cent of this was due to losses and the rest for other reasons. Nevertheless there was a pressing need for ships for military purposes, especially to support the army in the Middle East round the Cape.

Admiral Doenitz was now certain that night surface pack tactics were the answer to the problem of attacking convoys, but the difficulty of finding them remained. He hoped in the future to solve this with larger numbers of U-boats and improved co-operation with aircraft. He fully realized that the sinkings were at present insufficient and that he was likely to have to compete in the future with $2\frac{1}{2}$ million tons of new construction a year built in Canada and the U.S.A. as well as in Great Britain. Nevertheless, if he could achieve the present rates of sinking with a hundred U-boats on patrol instead of a dozen or so, he should be able to obtain a decision. If a total of thirty U-boats could sink 2 million tons in nine months, then three hundred U-boats could sink 20 million or the whole British merchant fleet in the same period. U-boat production, however, was not going as fast as planned. From June 1940 to January 1941 the completion rate had risen from five to ten new U-boats a month, but this was a long way short of the twenty-five boats a month to which the original plan had already been reduced.

The British were now thoroughly alarmed. Although two-thirds of the U-boats destroyed had been sunk by the aid of Asdics, it was obvious that the effectiveness of this device had been overestimated and that it was not the complete 'answer' to the submarine. It was of comparatively short range and great difficulties were being experienced with spurious echoes and in training and maintenance. Even when firm contact with a U-boat was established, the chance of success with a pattern of five depth charges was less than 10 per cent.

The British, however, reacted strongly to the threat of the U-boats and energetically set about improving their counter measures. On 6 March 1941 the Prime Minister issued a directive on the Battle of the Atlantic which gave everything connected with it a very high priority. The first and most immediate need was to reinforce the Atlantic with more escort vessels and aircraft. This was essential not only to stiffen the escort of each convoy but to extend the convoy system over the whole area in which U-boat operations were possible. Since the war began, the Admiralty had ordered over a hundred new destroyers and four hundred other escorts of various types. These were now coming into service as well as the fifty over-age destroyers obtained from the U.S.A. The first reinforcements had already been provided by the release of destroyers from anti-invasion duties on the east coast. Measures were also taken to increase the efficiency of the escort groups by

171

keeping them together and improving their communications. Coastal Command directive was now altered to make the Battle of the Atlantic their primary task and a greater proportion of their strength was turned to the west of the British Isles.

The German U-boats' method of operating involved a great many wireless signals, not only from the shore headquarters to the U-boats but from the U-boats to the shore in order to give them a picture of the situation. This obviously gave away a great deal of information in various ways, especially to the shore direction-finding network. The Admiralty tracking-room, using this and every other available source of information, soon became very efficient in predicting where the U-boats were and in routing the convoys clear of them.

By 1 March the total U-boat strength had risen to ninety-eight, but only twenty-seven of these were as yet operational. U-boats were now being completed at the rate of thirteen a month. In March, however, there was only an average of thirteen at sea and these small numbers took a little while to detect that shipping had been diverted northwards towards Iceland. In their first attacks, on convoys OB293 (see Note 22) and HX112, in this area they suffered a serious reverse and lost five boats in quick succession. These losses included *U47*, *U99* and *U100*, three of the most successful U-boats, and this was a severe blow. The reason for these losses was a mystery to the Germans and they decided to abandon the area and move to the south-west. In fact they were all sunk by escort vessels at night after being sighted on the surface at close range and forced to dive. No new techniques or secret weapons were involved and there is little doubt that the U-boat captains had become over-confident. The move to the south-west brought results: several convoys were attacked in April and May, some before their escorts had joined. In April the Germans thought of a new use for the Italians, putting them to patrol in an area west of Ireland in the hope that they would be seen and so divert traffic into the area where the German U-boats were stationed.

Three U-boats had left for the South Atlantic in February and they were followed by another five and one or two Italian boats. For the rest of the year between six and eight U-boats patrolled off Freetown, the Canary Islands, the Guinea coast and even as far south as St. Helena. They were supplied partly by German ships interned in the Canary Islands, until British protests stopped this practice in July, and partly by surface supply ships. Throughout the year they obtained substantial results.

It was obvious to the British that they must extend the convoy system farther to the westward. The British occupation of Iceland of a year before was now put to advantage. Some escort groups were refuelled there and were able to escort convoys as far as 35°W. By midsummer Canadian escort groups were able to meet them and, at the end of May 1941 convoy HX129 was the first to have continuous escort right across the Atlantic. This was made possible by the substantial increase in escort strength which in June, in all areas, had risen to 250 destroyers, 150 corvettes and sloops and 300 trawlers and yachts. There were another 300 of all types building. Coastal Command had been able to move up aircraft to Iceland in April and give air escort as far as 35°W. Air bases were also established in Canada but there was still a 300-mile gap between their limits and those of the aircraft in Iceland.

In May the U-boats occupied areas as far as south-east of Greenland, but in the western Atlantic they found a great deal of fog and bad weather and it was, of course, out of range of the FW200 aircraft so there was no possibility of air co-operation. This was serious, as the U-boat's problem was still almost entirely one of finding the convoys, the vast majority of which were never attacked at all. The sequence of operations was, as before, that the U-boat headquarters, from knowledge of convoy routes and cycles and using radio intelligence, would order the U-boats to take up a patrol line to intercept a certain convoy. But the inevitable signalling which was involved was used by the Admiralty tracking-room to assess the patrol line's position and divert the convoy clear of it. The patrol lines would then be redeployed, and so on; and this sort of shadow boxing went on all summer and autumn and it was this search problem, rather than the actual attacks on convoys, that worried the U-boat command.

The U-boat operations, which depended entirely on using their surface speed, were badly hampered by aircraft, even though the aircraft were not at this time particularly dangerous to them. Indeed, in the whole ten months from March to December 1941, aircraft sank only two U-boats and assisted surface vessels with the sinking of two others. However, the appearance of air patrols was enough for the U-boats to move on to areas where they could operate undisturbed.

During the summer, in attempts to evade the air patrols, the U-boats ranged right across the Atlantic as far as Newfoundland. By midsummer there were over thirty U-boats at sea and more than one pack was operating at a time. But the rate of sinking by each U-boat fell off sharply from three ships sunk by each U-boat on patrol each month in March to half a ship in July and August. In August the U-boats began to operate on the Gibraltar route; here they could co-operate with the FW200 aircraft and did so with some success. As the summer wore on, however, the escorts of convoys began to be much more efficient. More of the ships were being fitted with radar and a larger depth charge pattern; the aircraft were also getting a better radar set and were now armed with depth charges. The U-boats found it very much harder to close the convoys or even to shadow and were frequently driven off. In August Doenitz ordered U-boats to retaliate by attacking escorts but only four were sunk before the end of the year. In September there were at one time four groups of U-boats operating : four convoys were attacked and thirty-six ships sunk, convoy SC32, in particular, being severely mauled, until air support arrived from Iceland.

Coastal Command now took the offensive to harass the U-boats on passages and stepped up its sweeps in the Bay of Biscay and round the north of Scotland. There were many sightings, but attacks were seldom successful, in spite of the depth charge armament, but in August *U570* surrendered after being damaged by an aircraft and in November *U206* was sunk in the Bay.

In December the U-boats had a severe check in an attack on convoy HG76 (see Note 23) from Gibraltar to the United Kingdom. The convoy had a heavy and efficient radar-fitted surface escort and air support for the whole way, which was provided partly from air bases at Gibraltar and in the British Isles and partly from the auxiliary aircraft carrier *Audacity*. The U-boats sank the *Audacity* and two merchantmen but they lost five of their number.

The stiffening of the resistance was not the only problem for the U-boats at this time. In September 1941 Hitler had ordered them to the Mediterranean and this was the largest of a series of diversions from their main task of attacking shipping in the Atlantic. They had already been used as weather ships to help the Luftwaffe bomb Britain and as escorts through dangerous areas for blockade runners, supply ships and raiders. Some boats had been sent to the Arctic to attack North Russian convoys and they were also used for reconnaissance by surface raiders. In November 1941 they were ordered to produce a heavy concentration of U-boats west of Gibraltar at the entrance of the Mediterranean and all these measures absorbed so many U-boats that they brought operations in the North Atlantic virtually to a standstill for the last two months of the year and shipping losses fell accordingly (see p. 186; fig. 19, i).

In the western Atlantic operations had been made harder for the Axis naval forces in the second half of the year as the Americans with their neutrality patrols and 'short of war' policy took a progressively greater part in the Battle of the Atlantic. American warships were allowed to take defensive measures against U-boats and in September convoy HX150 was actually escorted by American destroyers. U-boat operations had to be restricted to avoid incidents with them, but in October they torpedoed the U.S. destroyer *Kearney* and sank the *Reuben James* which led to a further deterioration of relations.

Towards the end of the year, therefore, the U-boat campaign was beset by considerable difficulties. Even the U-boats in the South Atlantic had had to return because their surface supply ships had been sunk. Nevertheless, in this period of ten months, they had sunk 372 ships of 1,847,000 tons and other forces, including surface raiders, mines and aircraft, had contributed about the same amount. In the Atlantic twenty-seven U-boats had been lost, but production was now at a stage where strength was rising rapidly. By the end of the year there were 236 U-boats altogether, eighty-seven of which were operational, the balance being used for training or on trials. Convoy escorts had caused three-quarters of the U-boat losses and although one-third of the merchant ships sunk were in convoy, this gave an exchange rate in convoy battles of six merchant ships for every U-boat sunk. The rest of the sinkings were independent ships divided between the North and South Atlantic. Eighty-one ships were sunk in the South Atlantic with a rate of sinking greater than in the north, furthermore only one U-boat was lost, giving an exchange rate of eighty-one. In mid-July, however, convoy was continuous from Freetown and the long passage made it actually less profitable for U-boats than the North Atlantic. The overall exchange rate in all areas worked out at 13.7 ships sunk for every U-boat destroyed.

175

These heavy merchant ship losses were greater than the number of ships being built and the total size of the British Merchant Navy declined again in 1941 : it was now 3 million tons smaller than at the beginning of the war. Neutral shipping on charter and American assistance, however, had more than made up the deficiency and although both civil and military belts had had to be tightened, all essential demands on shipping were still being met.

The most serious feature of the campaign from the German point of view was that the overall rate of sinking had fallen by the end of 1941 to less than one ship for each U-boat each month. This meant that although the number of U-boats had trebled, the capacity of the U-boat force for sinking ships had not improved during the year. There was the gnawing fear that anti-submarine measures were developing faster than the U-boat force was being expanded and they had still not reached the twenty-five boats a month of the programme started at the beginning of the war. Nevertheless Admiral Doenitz was reasonably confident. The U-boat force was expanding fast but he still had nothing like the three hundred operational U-boats which he had always said were necessary; but when he had as many as that, he hoped that he would be able to solve the problem of finding the convoys. He had a homing torpedo under development with which to attack the escorts and expected much from various radio counter measures.

The Japanese attack on Pearl Harbor came as a surprise to the Germans, but the German declaration of war on the United States on 11 December 1941 was received with relief by the U-boats. Whilst they had been forbidden to attack ships in the Pan-American Security Zone, American forces had been free to retaliate against them. At least the war in the Atlantic would now be regularized. But now there was a pressing need to sink ships faster than ever before to compete with the American shipbuilding programme which was known to be very large.

Shipping off the American coast was unescorted and very dense with many focal points and was a most promising target. The distance from the U-boat bases was about as far as Freetown, and the main body of the U-boat fleet, consisting of Type VII

(500 tons), could only reach the vicinity of Nova Scotia. The Type IX (750 tons) U-boats could, however, get to the coast of Florida and the latest Type IXC could reach the Trinidad area. There was a need to strike swiftly before convoy could be instituted or anti-submarine measures perfected, and Admiral Doenitz at once proposed to send twelve Type IX U-boats. The German High Command, however, still considered the Mediterranean of higher priority and would permit only five to go, but some Type VII U-boats had enough fuel to be diverted at sea to the Nova Scotia area. These boats did not arrive until the middle of January 1942 and were then disposed individually between the St. Lawrence and Cape Hatteras.

Success was immediate. Attack was entirely unrestricted and on unescorted ships and the U-boats had not had such a chance since 1917. *U123* sank eight ships off Cape Hatteras in twenty-four hours (see Note 24). Most of the attacks were made at night, the U-boats resting on the bottom by day. Shipping was so plentiful that they were able to choose their targets and their torpedoes were expended well before they reached the limit of their endurance. In January, fifty-eight ships of over 300,000 tons were sunk in the western Atlantic, half of them valuable tankers.

The Germans at once decided to reinforce the area and the transfer of a large number of U-boats to the Mediterranean was cancelled. It was soon found that the range of the Type VII U-boats, which had been having difficulty with fog and bad weather off Nova Scotia, had been underestimated and that they could reach New York. In February a new wave of the long-range Type IXC boats was sent to the Caribbean and with these moves the shipping casualties rose to nearly half a million tons. The American opposition was very weak : most of the anti-submarine vessels were small Coastguard cutters and initially they had no naval planes of any range.

At the end of January, Hitler became nervous about a British invasion of Norway and ordered six U-boats to be diverted there and another eight to be retained in the Iceland-Hebrides area. By mid-February the total number diverted in this way and so held back from the American coast was twenty. Although, therefore, at the beginning of the year there were ninety-one operational U-boats, half of these were employed in the Arctic and Mediterranean and it was not possible to keep more than twelve boats on station at a time off the U.S. coast.

Over half a million tons were sunk in March and nearly half a million in April and so far only one U-boat had been lost in the western Atlantic. The exchange rate, therefore, soared to 198. Towards the end of April, the sinkings off the U.S. coast declined as the Americans began to form convoys. At the same time *U459*, the first of the U-tankers (see p. 163; fig. 17), came into service and it became possible to extend the operations of all types of U-boats. Excellent results were obtained in the Caribbean and the Gulf of Mexico. In May and June, sinkings rose still higher and in the latter month were very nearly as large as in April 1917. In the first seven months of 1942, 681 ships of $3\frac{1}{2}$ million tons were sunk, mostly in the western hemisphere where only eleven U-boats were destroyed in the same period. General Marshall, the U.S. Army Chief of Staff, seriously alarmed by the losses, considered that, if they continued, America would be unable to deploy her armies overseas in sufficient force to be decisive and the whole war effort would be jeopardized. In June, however, convoy was extended to the Caribbean, and anti-submarine measures everywhere became stiffer. In July, three U-boats were sunk and two were damaged and forced to return to base and the U-boats were driven from the U.S. coast.

Whilst the main U-boat force was on the American coast, some had been held back to continue to work against convoys off Iceland and on the Gibraltar route. This was partly with the aim of preventing anti-submarine forces from being transferred to the other side of the Atlantic and partly to keep up to date on the opposition which they found was stiffening. Results were only moderate but this was attributed to the inexperience of the crews of the new U-boats. In June three U-boats were damaged by aircraft in the Bay of Biscay and the U-boats were ordered to stay submerged by day and night as much as possible. Whilst the U-boats had been reaping their harvest on the American coast, the opposition elsewhere had indeed greatly improved. Thirty-two U-boats were sunk in all areas, nine of which were in the Mediterranean or Arctic and twelve in the Atlantic. Convoy escorts continued to be the main U-boat killers, scoring thirteen, but aircraft had done much better, sinking eight in the period.

In these seven months from January to July 1942, German U-boat strength rose to 331, 140 of which were operational with another 191 doing trials and being used for training. Operational strength in the Atlantic, however, increased by only twenty-nine boats, as trials in the Baltic had been much delayed by ice during the previous winter and the diversions to the Mediterranean and the Arctic took most of the increased strength.

In the campaign in the western Atlantic, although the Americans lost heavily, many of the ships sunk were British, either before they had joined their convoys or after they had been successfully escorted across the Atlantic. By the end of the period, in spite of considerable help from America, British shipping declined another half a million tons. The enormous American shipbuilding effort was, however, beginning to materialize and the U.S. shipping losses were not only replaced but their merchant fleet slightly increased during this period. Nevertheless the Allies' need for shipping was immense, especially to transport the U.S. troops to Europe and to reinforce the Middle and Far East, and the losses could be ill afforded.

The German U-boat campaign on the American coast and in the Caribbean in the first half of 1942 was an outstanding success. It was an astute strategic move executed with skill over vast distances. The slowness of the Americans to adopt convoy led to greater losses than necessary, but the results might have been greater still if Hitler had not held back half the U-boats in Norway and the Mediterranean.

With the institution of convoys off the American coast and in the Caribbean, there was little point in sending the U-boats so far to make their attacks. It was clearly better to concentrate them in packs against the Atlantic convoys, where three U-boats could be kept on patrol for every one in the Caribbean. Moreover the increase in the numbers of U-boats now afforded a greater chance of success against the Atlantic convoys, but the Germans decided to exploit all the weak places in the western hemisphere and South Atlantic as well and approximately a third of the U-boats continued to work in these distant areas.

In August 1942 there were fifty U-boats on patrol and another twenty on passage out of the 140 which were now operational. Of the boats on patrol, about thirty were in the North Atlantic and twenty in the Caribbean and off Brazil. With several packs operating at a time, a fresh trial of strength between the U-boats and the convoy escorts now began. The Germans continued to receive considerable intelligence of convoy movements, especially from radio messages which they were often able to decode, the wolf packs would wait on both sides of the Atlantic at the limit of the range of shore-based aircraft so as to concentrate and attack in the gap in the central Atlantic where no air cover was possible. There was little change in the tactics of the wolf packs which were spread at twice visibility distance apart to try to intercept the convoys in daylight. To avoid their slipping through the patrol lines at night, the U-boats would turn and proceed on a similar course until daylight. The high speed often necessary led to increased fuel consumption, but this was made good by U-tankers which replenished them at sea.

The British escorts now numbered over 400 in the Atlantic and Coastal Command had over 500 aircraft. The escorts not only had efficient radar, which revealed to them the position of the U-boats on the surface at night, but also a radio direction finding apparatus which indicated the presence of a U-boat when it transmitted a report. They were, therefore, often able to drive off shadowing U-boats and so prevent the concentration of the wolf packs. The results also depended much on the strength and efficiency of the escorts and on the weather, but above all on the presence of air cover.

Eighteen U-boats attacked convoy SC94 in August and sank eleven ships for the loss of two of their number : in September, twenty-nine ships in all were sunk in convoy. In October, convoy SC104 lost eight ships, but three U-boats were sunk, and in November SC107 lost fifteen ships for three U-boats. However, at the end of the year convoy HX217 lost only two ships for two U-boats out of a pack of twenty-two which attacked. The vast majority of the U-boat losses were caused by the sea and air escorts of convoys.

Although in this period the Germans had greater success in locating convoys, the British were still able to divert the majority of them clear of the concentration of U-boats. The efficiency of aircraft was now greatly improved and they were able to find the U-boats by radar and attack them effectively with depth charges when they caught them on the surface both by day and by night. At night they used the Leigh light, which was a searchlight switched on at the last moment to give them a point of aim. In October, however, the Germans had produced a search receiver for the U-boats which warned them of the approach of

180

radar-fitted aircraft in time to dive, which gave them considerable protection.

The U-tankers made it possible for the Germans to operate their larger U-boats as far south as the Cape of Good Hope and even round into the Indian Ocean in their search for independent shipping. Not only did they find plenty of independent ships in these areas but they caused a dispersion of the anti-submarine effort from the North Atlantic which could be ill afforded.

Throughout these five months, from August to December 1942, the U-boats were able to sink an average of a hundred ships totalling half a million tons for the loss of roughly ten U-boats every month. The exchange rate was therefore about ten merchant ships sunk for every U-boat destroyed. These U-boat losses were considerably less than the numbers being built and so did not cause the Germans undue concern. The rate of sinking merchant ships, on the other hand, was still only one ship by each U-boat at sea each month, although in November, with the withdrawal of a hundred escorts for the North African landings, the U-boats did particularly well and sank 119 ships of 729,000 tons.

At the end of the year, although the Allies had been able to support all their military operations and to mount the North African invasion successfully, there was something akin to a shipping crisis. In 1942 they had lost the huge total of $7\frac{3}{4}$ million tons of shipping, mostly to the U-boats. But by now the American shipyards were well into their stride and building on both sides of the Atlantic had already replaced 7 million tons. The employment of British merchant ships was extremely efficient and, although imports to the United Kingdom were a third less than before the war, the shipping shortage did not threaten starvation or the output of the war industries: the problem was to find sufficient shipping for the future offensive to defeat Germany and Japan.

At the beginning of 1943 there were over two hundred U-boats available for operations out of a total of nearly four hundred. Not only was the total number much greater, but Admiral Doenitz had managed to obtain the return of most of the U-boats from Norway for the Atlantic. In January the results were poor, mainly because of the very bad weather, but convoy TM1 of nine tankers escorted by a destroyer and three corvettes lost seven ships. This convoy had no air cover and the radar in all of the escorts happened to be out of action. This incident, as well as showing what would happen to convoys without radar-fitted escorts, illustrated a fact well known to operational research, that a higher proportion of the ships would be lost in small convoys than in large ones.

In February there were over a hundred U-boats at sea, those in the Atlantic being in four groups. The U-boats left their bases in western France in a steady stream to join the wolf packs piecemeal as ordered by the shore headquarters. The packs were, as usual, closely controlled from the shore until contact with a convoy was made. Although the Germans were perfectly aware that the Allies could intercept the radio signals from the U-boats, a considerable amount of traffic was inevitable. The shore control had to assess results and know which U-boats had expended their torpedoes and which were short of fuel. Shipping casualties rose again but results varied considerably. Convoy ON116 (see Note 25) lost fourteen ships for one U-boat sunk, but convoy ONS165 lost only two ships for two U-boats sunk. In general, however, attacks on convoys were expensive. In this month, thirty-four ships were sunk in convoy but thirteen U-boats were lost to the escorts giving an exchange rate in convoy actions of two and a half ships for each U-boat destroyed.

In March in the largest convoy action of the war, forty U-boats fell upon convoys HX229 and SC122 and sank twenty-one ships, losing only one U-boat. In this month the U-boats sank 108 ships of 627,000 tons, seventy-two of which were in convoy: furthermore they lost only six U-boats attacking the convoys. The U-boats were now achieving results nearly as great as in April 1917 but against convoys, not independent ships: moreover the Allies were in great strength having some 500 escorts and 1,100 aircraft in the Atlantic. German hopes rose and it seemed as though numbers might yet master the convoy system. The Allies' anxiety was such that convoy itself was challenged as a principle. Nevertheless the overall exchange rate for the month in all areas was only seven merchant ships sunk for every U-boat destroyed and the U-boats were still sinking only one ship for each U-boat on patrol each month.

The German success was, however, short-lived. A number of

very effective anti-submarine measures came to the Allies' aid in the next month or two. The first and most important of these was the bridging of the gap in the air escort of convoys to give them continuous air cover. This was done by increasing the number of very long-range aircraft and using aircraft from escort carriers which accompanied the convoys. The second measure was that, by the use of larger convoys, they were able to economize in escort vessels and so form support groups to reinforce convoys which were directly threatened. At the same time new radar sets, which the German search receivers could not pick up, were being fitted in aircraft and the offensive in the Bay of Biscay really began to take effect. In April shipping losses were halved and the exchange rate fell to four ships sunk for every U-boat destroyed. Convoy HX233 when attacked by a wolf pack lost only one ship and the escort succeeded in sinking a U-boat into the bargain. Convoy ONS5 lost twelve ships but seven U-boats were sunk. In both these cases the U-boat failure was due to the presence of a support group.

The crisis for the U-boats came in May, when there were sixty of them disposed in four groups in the North Atlantic alone. Convoy SC130 was attacked by all four groups of U-boats but they sank no ships at all and lost five of their number. A support group and continuous air cover were mainly responsible for this serious defeat. Aircraft from an escort carrier successfully beat off attack on HX239 and the U-boats now found it difficult to close the convoys at all. In May the U-boats succeeded in sinking only twenty-six merchant ships in convoy and lost twenty-seven U-boats whilst doing so. The exchange rate against convoys therefore fell to one and, although there were 118 U-boats at sea, they were sinking less than half a ship each in all areas each month. But the most significant fact was the very rapid rise in the total U-boat losses for the month. Forty-one U-boats were lost, six in a new offensive by aircraft in the Bay of Biscay. These casualties were at nearly double the rate at which U-boats were being built; Admiral Doenitz therefore ordered the withdrawal of U-boats from the North Atlantic and the campaign against shipping collapsed.

It had been doubtful for some time whether the shipping losses could ever be forced up enough to exceed the gigantic American shipbuilding programme, the output of which was doubled in 1943. The Germans had hoped that if they had enough U-boats

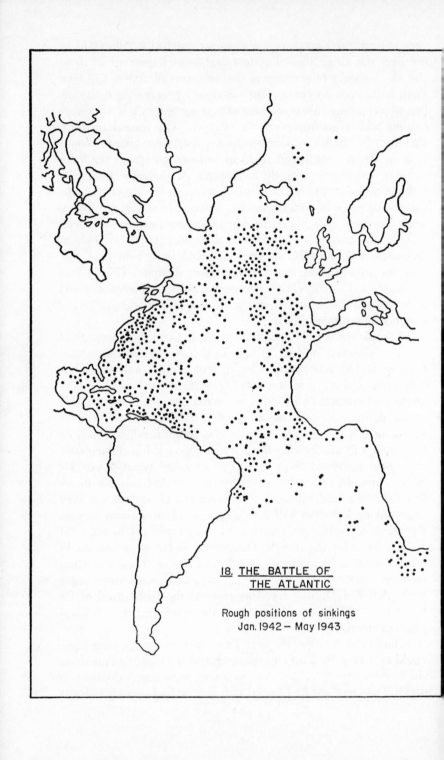

18. **THE BATTLE OF
THE ATLANTIC**

Rough positions of sinkings
Jan. 1942 — May 1943

they would still have a chance. As the number of U-boats increased, however, the rate of sinking by each boat fell off and the total tonnage sunk did not increase. When the U-boats began to be destroyed faster than they were being built, the last hope was gone and there was no point in continuing the campaign. In the period of ten months, from August 1942 to May 1943, of the final attack on the Atlantic convoys, the Germans had lost 151 U-boats, eighty of which had been sunk by aircraft, fifty-one by ships and twenty by other measures. Ninety-five had been sunk in the vicinity of the convoys by air and surface escorts. Anti-submarine blockade measures such as minefields, British submarines on patrol on the submarine passage routes, and aircraft in the Bay Offensive, although they sank an acceptable bonus, were of minor importance. It was in the battles round the convoys where the Battle of the Atlantic was won. The convoys, however, were not only being used as an anvil on which to kill U-boats but with continuous air cover they were really being defended by the sea and air escorts. The U-boats were driven from the surface of the sea by radar in aircraft and so could not get into position to attack. The whole basis of the German wolf pack system was therefore countered and the U-boat fleet was defeated decisively and in a way they had never suffered during the First World War.

From the beginning of the war until May 1943, when the campaign against shipping was defeated, the Germans had thrown over 650 U-boats into the battle and had lost 250 of them. Their strength, therefore, rose from the fifty-seven they had in 1939 to over 400 (see pp. 186, 187; figs. 19, ii and 20, i). Nevertheless they never had more than 240 operational and so Admiral Doenitz never achieved the 300 operational U-boats which he estimated to be necessary to defeat the convoy system. The Germans fell short in their plans to build U-boats, which were originally to complete twenty-nine each month from about the middle of 1941. This plan was clearly well within their capacity and their failure to achieve it was simply a matter of priorities. If they had fulfilled it they would have built over 900 U-boats in this period, or half as many again, but above all they would have been far stronger in the critical year 1942. They would of course have

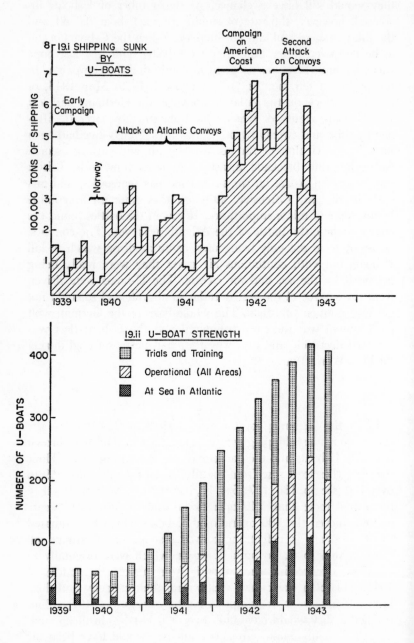

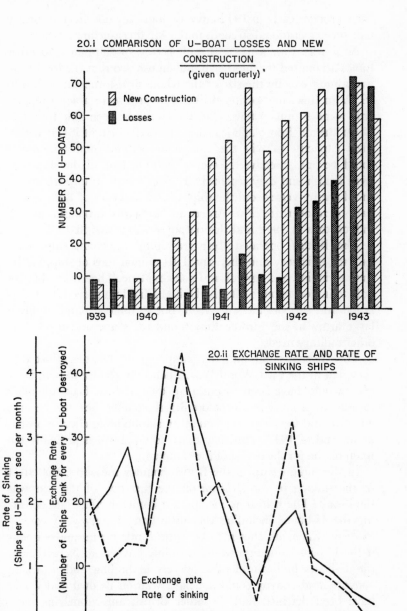

20.i COMPARISON OF U-BOAT LOSSES AND NEW CONSTRUCTION
(given quarterly)

New Construction
Losses

NUMBER OF U-BOATS

20.ii EXCHANGE RATE AND RATE OF SINKING SHIPS

Rate of Sinking
(Ships per U-boat at sea per month)

Exchange Rate
(Number of Ships Sunk for every U-boat Destroyed)

Exchange rate
Rate of sinking

been stronger early in 1942 anyway, had they not diverted nearly half their operational strength to the Mediterranean and Norway.

As it was, they sank 12.8 million tons of shipping and other forces accounted for another 6 million tons, so that the total sunk was almost exactly the size of the whole British merchant fleet in 1939. In this same period British shipyards were able to replace only some 4 million tons. Had the Germans been able to isolate Great Britain from America, there is no doubt that it was within their capacity to win the campaign before counter measures could become effective. However, nothing like all the ships lost were British and they replaced well over 4 million tons from captured enemy vessels and the ships of the countries of Europe that had been overrun. The American shipyards produced over 5 million tons in 1942 and this output was doubled in 1943.

The British operated their remaining merchant ships with extreme efficiency and they saved 10 million tons of shipping by their rationing and agricultural policies alone. They were able not only to import enough into the United Kingdom to feed the population and support the war effort, but to build up and supply a large army in the Middle East round the Cape and meet their other military needs.

The Germans put into the campaign double the effort that they had in the First World War. Their only chance to win, however, would have been to build up their U-boat fleet still more rapidly, to produce results before British counter measures became effective and the enormous American shipbuilding effort matured at the end of 1942. This they failed to do and it is probably the main reason for the defeat of the campaign.

In the building up of the British counter measures, the effect of the sinking of the *Athenia* on the first day of the war was significant. The British at once put an immense effort into defeating the U-boats, including the institution of convoy. A convoy strategy was again shown to be quite fundamental and without it the U-boat campaign would certainly have won. Nevertheless, the U-boats had considerable success in finding and attacking convoys, and convoy could not have won on its own and would have been defeated had the other British anti-submarine measures not been successful. It was only because the British anti-submarine measures were able in the end to triumph round the convoys that the victory was won.

The convoy system needed very large forces to support it. All convoys had to have escorts whether they were attacked or not. The Allies put an immense effort into building up their strength in escort vessels and aircraft. It was of the order of three times as much as the Germans put into the U-boats. Unless the Allies had been prepared to do this, they would probably also have lost the campaign.

Of very great importance was the way the British brought science and new equipment to bear, or what might be called their technical superiority. At the time of the defeat of the German U-boats, they were fundamentally of the same performance with the same equipment as in 1939. Some of the newer boats could dive deeper and they had a search receiver which temporarily gave them warning of the approach of the radar-fitted aircraft, but otherwise they had not advanced at all. On the other hand the British advanced immeasurably and were always able to hold the technical initiative and keep a lap ahead. Although the value of the Asdic had been overestimated before the war and it did not prove to be the complete answer to the submarine, it was responsible for sinking over a hundred U-boats and for driving them out of the focal areas where they could do most damage. Undoubtedly the most important of all the anti-submarine devices was radar, which in the end completely countered the German surface attacks by U-boats at night and turned aircraft from minor harassing agents into lethal U-boat killers. Radio warfare, especially the use of direction-finding apparatus both ashore and afloat, was also of very great importance to both sides. But the British were well ahead and the Germans lost more than they gained from it.

Not only were the British technically superior but, using operational research, were in the end tactically superior as well. They used all their new devices and ships and aircraft in the closest co-operation and with great skill. The German U-boats, after their invention of the wolf pack which made it possible to find and attack convoys in the open ocean, were unable to advance any further. They could not produce any solution to its fundamental weakness which was that when using it, U-boats ceased to be submarines and became surface torpedo boats. It was the British exploitation of these weaknesses which was the key to the Allies' success.

It would be easy to conclude that the German U-boat campaign in the Second World War was easily countered and merely

189

confirmed the past history of the *guerre de course*, which showed that it could always be defeated by convoy. This would be a far too facile assumption. It failed only by a very narrow margin. Had the Germans built up their U-boat fleet quicker, or the British failed to adopt convoy or develop Asdics and radar, or the Americans failed in their shipbuilding programme, the results could have been very different. The Battle of the Atlantic was won only because the Allies again put an immense military, civil and scientific effort into it. They had to do this for the very reason that the submarine, as a commerce raider, was a potentially decisive weapon of seapower and, if they had not, they would have lost the war.

XI

The Submarine as a Warship in the Pacific in the Second World War
(December 1941–August 1945)

At the outbreak of war in the Pacific in December 1941 Japan had a fleet of just over sixty submarines. Forty-two of them were large, with a trans-Pacific endurance. They were fast on the surface and carried a heavy torpedo armament, but took a long time to dive and were unhandy when submerged. Eleven of these submarines carried a small seaplane, five others a midget submarine, whilst four more were fitted with special communication equipment so that they could be used as flagships. These large submarines were organized as the Sixth Fleet which was an integral part of the Japanese Combined Fleet. Its function was to operate against enemy warships and its whole training was devoted to this end : attack on merchant shipping was of low priority, only to be embarked upon if military operations permitted.

The Japanese concept of submarines as a powerful arm of the main fleet was not new : it had its origins in the British fleet submarines of the K class of the Great War of 1914-18. They did not, however, intend to use their submarines in such close co-operation with the fleet as the British, but in more distant screens and patrol lines controlled by a senior officer in one of the submarines fitted as a flagship. Many of the later Japanese submarines were very nearly as fast as the K class on the surface, carried a heavier armament and were of much greater endurance. The Japanese had had very successful results in exercises with this powerful submarine force and relied on it to compensate for the smaller size of their battlefleet. The idea of the submarine seaplane carrier for reconnaissance was copied from the British *M2*, but their use was limited as it took an hour to assemble and fly off the aircraft. The midget submarines were to penetrate harbours and hoped to destroy some of the enemy fleet before it ever put to sea.

In the plans to attack Pearl Harbor on 7 December 1941, great things were expected of the Japanese Sixth Fleet. Twenty-seven submarines were disposed around the Hawaiian Islands and on the lines of communication with the continental United States. Their purpose was to launch five midget submarines to attack the American Fleet in harbour at the same time as the carrier-borne aircraft and subsequently to use the large submarines in the force to destroy any ships which escaped. The Japanese, in fact, expected more from the submarines than from the carrier-borne air attack itself. In this they were to be disappointed: the midget submarines achieved nothing; only one managing to penetrate into the harbour and all of them being destroyed by the defences. Although there were many movements of American warships both in and out of Pearl Harbor after the raid, only one Japanese submarine managed to make an attack and that was unsuccessful. Much of the credit for this failure must go to the American patrols which harassed the Japanese submarines, one of which was sunk by a carrier-borne aircraft.

Three days after the attack on Pearl Harbor, an American aircraft carrier was reported by Japanese air reconnaissance north-west of the Hawaiian Islands and the seven Japanese submarines stationed to the north of Oahu set off at high speed on the surface to intercept. They failed to make contact, but their pursuit took them to the American coast where they operated against commerce for two weeks before returning. In a second sortie by submarines of the Sixth Fleet towards Pearl Harbor in January, they had better luck and one of them torpedoed the aircraft carrier *Saratoga* and put her out of action at a very critical time.

Other Japanese submarines accompanied their forces for the invasion of Malaya. Their purpose was to watch for sorties by the British Eastern Fleet and to cut the lines of communication to Singapore. It was the submarine *I.165* which sighted the *Prince of Wales* and *Repulse* on their way north to counter attack the Japanese landings on the coast of Malaya, and her report which led to the fatal air attacks on the two ships. Before the fall of Singapore a force of Japanese submarines pushed through into the Indian Ocean and began to operate from Penang.

The Allies had a total of seventy submarines in the Pacific on the outbreak of war. Fifty-five of these were American and they were divided equally between the Pacific Fleet based at Pearl Harbor and the Asiatic Fleet in the Philippines. The remaining fifteen submarines belonged to the Royal Netherlands Navy and were based in Sourabaya in the Dutch East Indies. The British, who had kept some eighteen submarines in the Far East for nearly twenty years in case of war with Japan, had withdrawn all of them to the Mediterranean. Three-quarters of the American boats were of the new long-range fleet type but the rest, and all of the Dutch boats, were much smaller and some were obsolete. Of the two American submarine forces, the one based in the Philippines was the more modern and powerful. It constituted the main naval defence of the Philippines in the same way as the Netherlands submarines were the main naval defence for the East Indies. More was expected from these submarines than from the weak Allied surface forces stationed in the area, which were bound to be overwhelmed by the superior Japanese fleet.

When the Japanese attacked Pearl Harbor there were only five American submarines there. Four others were at sea on patrol off Midway and Wake Islands, five were at sea on passage or exercising and the rest were on the U.S. Pacific coast. The five submarines in Pearl Harbor and the submarine base itself were undamaged in the attack. The submarines off Midway and Wake brushed with the Japanese and one made the first submarine torpedo attack of the Pacific war, but without result. The American Pacific Fleet submarine force therefore survived Pearl Harbor intact; furthermore there were another sixty American submarines in the Atlantic. Although most of the Atlantic Fleet boats were small and obsolete, there were seventy-three modern fleet submarines building in the United States.

In south-east Asia, it had been decided in Anglo-Dutch staff talks to place some of the Netherlands submarines under the British at Singapore. Seven of the Dutch submarines were used to patrol in the South China Sea and in the Gulf of Siam and were in position before war broke out. When the Japanese invaded Malaya, these submarines sank three transports and damaged four others for the loss of three of their number. The Dutch submarines which had remained under Netherlands control operated in the Makassar Straits and off North Borneo. Here they sank a destroyer and two transports and damaged two other transports. The British Commander-in-Chief pleaded for British submarines to be sent out as soon as possible. The only two that could be spared were sailed at once from the eastern Mediterranean, but only the *Trusty* arrived before the fall of Singapore on 15 February 1942.

The twenty-nine American submarines of the Asiatic Fleet were deployed partly for defence off likely landing places in the Philippines and partly on offensive patrols off Formosa, Hainan and the coast of Indo-China. The submarines attempted to intercept the Japanese landings in the Philippines but generally arrived too late and were then much hampered by shallow water. Many attacks were made but only three enemy ships were hit and there is little doubt that defective torpedoes were mainly responsible for these poor results. The submarine base at Cavite was destroyed very early in the war by a Japanese air attack and they lost most of their reserve torpedoes and spare parts. Two of the three submarine tenders were at once moved south to the East Indies, leaving one behind, but she found it almost impossible to service the submarines because of the continuous air attacks. At the end of December, Manila fell and, on completion of their patrols, the submarines had to be ordered south to Sourabaya and Darwin.

The surviving twenty-seven American, eight Dutch and two British submarines assisted as best they could in the defence of the Netherlands East Indies, losing three more boats and sinking a few Japanese ships. In March, when the East Indies fell, the American submarines withdrew to Western Australia and the British to Ceylon. Of the Dutch submarines, five had been lost, three more had to be destroyed in Sourabaya when it was evacuated and the remaining seven accompanied the Americans or British to western Australia or Ceylon.

The forty-six Allied submarines in South-East Asia had therefore failed even to impede the Japanese advance. They were very greatly hampered by the early loss of their bases and the Americans by torpedo failures and shortages, furthermore they had difficulty in getting at the enemy in the shallow water. Nevertheless the fact remains that, as a defence, they proved of very little value. They would have fared better if they had operated from secure bases with a plentiful supply of efficient torpedoes. Even if all their attacks had succeeded, however, it is doubtful whether they would have done more than impose a slight delay on the Japanese advance. This was, of course, confirmation of the experience of the past. Submarines have never proved a good weapon in defence : it is always extremely difficult to put them in the right place and their strategic redeployment to meet enemy moves is invariably too slow.

After the first wave of the Japanese advance, Japanese submarines of the Sixth Fleet made a number of offensive reconnaissances deep into Allied waters. In April a squadron of five large submarines crossed the Indian Ocean to the African coast. With their seaplanes they found the battleship *Ramillies* lying in Diego Suarez and two of the submarines then launched midgets which penetrated into the harbour and torpedoed her. A similar sortie was made by another squadron of five submarines down the east coast of Australia. After a seaplane reconnaissance of Sydney, another midget submarine attack was launched. Although one of the midgets penetrated the harbour where two cruisers were lying, this time the attack was unsuccessful. A number of similar reconnaissances were made, using submarine-launched seaplanes, notably one against Seattle. Japanese submarines were also active in other ways : minefields were laid; large flying-boats were refuelled to extend their range and they made diversions by bombarding Midway and Johnstone Islands. These operations caused the Allies more embarrassment than anxiety, but were nonetheless a demonstration of the flexibility and endurance of the Japanese submarines.

After the retreat of the Allied forces from the East Indies to Ceylon, they could muster only two British and four Dutch submarines at Colombo. This was too few to meet the pressing need for a continuous submarine patrol in the Malacca Straits to give warning of the approach of Japanese forces. The British submarine *Truant*, however, happened to be on patrol when the Japanese carriers sortied for their attack on Ceylon. Unfortunately they came out by the Sunda Straits and, although they returned through the Malacca Straits, the *Truant* had by then started on her way home and did not see them. For over a year three additional Dutch submarines from the Mediterranean were all that could be spared for the Far East and it was not until July 1943 that more British submarines began to arrive.

The Japanese advance was finally halted at the decisive naval battle of Midway and a number of submarines on both sides took part in this famous action (see figure 21). When the Japanese planned their attack on Midway, they sent twelve submarines to take up positions between Midway Island itself and Pearl Harbor to intercept any American forces that might make a counter attack. The Americans, however, had warning of the impending attack and the U.S. Task Forces passed the area before the Japanese submarines were in position, and in their subsequent pursuit they were left well astern. At the same time almost the whole American Pacific Fleet submarine force was deployed to intercept the Japanese. Twelve submarines were positioned to the north and west of Midway itself, between sixty and one hundred and fifty miles from the island. Seven were placed in two defensive patrol lines in case the Japanese repeated their attack on Pearl Harbor. All these submarines were in position before the Japanese attacked and six other submarines were already at sea farther west on passage to or from their patrol areas.

Three U.S. submarines made contact with the enemy. The *Cuttlefish*, which was 700 miles west of Midway, sighted a tanker of the Japanese supporting forces and made a reconnaissance report. The Japanese aircraft carriers were then sighted by air reconnaissance and nine submarines of the Midway group were ordered to intercept them. One of this group, the *Nautilus*, found herself in the middle of the battle and succeeded in sinking the aircraft carrier *Soryu* which had already been heavily damaged by air attack. The *Tambor* sighted four heavy cruisers on their way to bombard Midway Island. They also saw her and, in the ensuing confusion, two of the heavy cruisers collided, had to give up their attempt to bombard Midway and were later intercepted by an air attack. Only one Japanese submarine made contact and this was *I.168*, which was able to proceed at high speed to the position of the damaged aircraft carrier *Yorktown* and to sink her, as well as the destroyer *Hammann* which was alongside.

The performance of submarines on both sides at the Battle of Midway did not do much to enhance their reputation as units of a fleet in action. They were there in force on both sides and succeeded only in 'mopping up' after the carrier-borne aircraft had decided the action. They could, however, take some comfort from the fact that they had taken part in this great and decisive naval

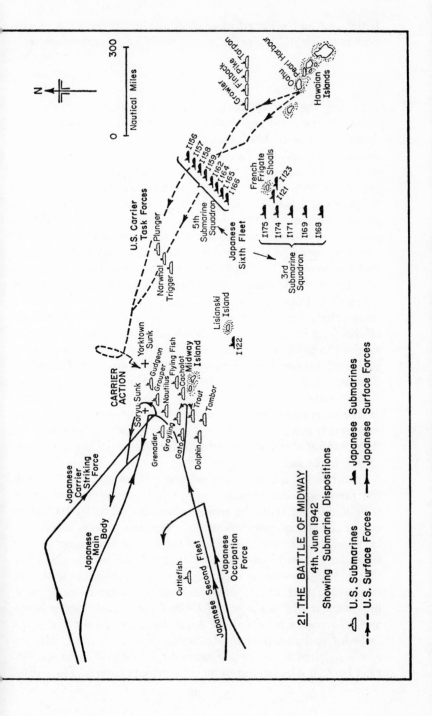

N

0   300
Nautical Miles

Oahu
Pearl Harbour
Hawaiian Islands

Growler
Finback
Pike
Tarpon

I156
I157
I158
I159
I162
I164
I165
I166

French Frigate Shoals
I123
I121
I175
I174
I171
I169
I168

U.S. Carrier Task Forces

5th Submarine Squadron

Japanese Sixth Fleet

3rd Submarine Squadron

Narwhal   Plunger
Trigger

Lisianski Island
I 122

Yorktown Sunk

CARRIER ACTION

Soryu Sunk

Gudgeon
Grouper
Nautilus   Flying Fish
Cachalot
Midway Island
Trout

Grenadier
Grayling
Gato
Dolphin   Tambor

Japanese Carrier Striking Force

Japanese Main Body

Cuttlefish

Japanese Second Fleet

Japanese Occupation Force

21. THE BATTLE OF MIDWAY
4th. June 1942
Showing Submarine Dispositions

◁   U.S. Submarines
- - -   U.S. Surface Forces

▲   Japanese Submarines
→   Japanese Surface Forces

battle and had achieved more than all the surface ships put together, which did not fire a single shot at each other in anger.

During the second half of 1942, submarines on both sides found themselves drawn into the struggles for the Solomon and Aleutian Islands. After the U.S. landing on Guadalcanal in August, most of the Japanese submarines in the Pacific were deployed in support of the forces in that area. In their early operations they tried to cut off American reinforcements to the Solomons and New Guinea as well as watching for opportunities to attack warships. They worked down the eastern Australian coast but sank few ships and lost several submarines. The Americans also attacked the Japanese communications with the area and had moved all the old S class submarines from the southwest Pacific to Brisbane, where they were joined by more S class submarines from the Panama Canal Zone. It was *S44*, one of these elderly submarines, which sank the Japanese cruiser *Kako* off Kavieng in August. The *Albacore*, one of the new Fleet submarines from the central Pacific, which reinforced the area, sank the small cruiser *Tenryu* north of New Guinea in December. The Americans then established a blockade of the main Japanese base at Truk from where the Solomons campaign was supported. In the operations against sea communications, the Americans were much more successful than the Japanese and sank twenty-three supply ships, contributing substantially to the American victory in the area.

In the naval actions which were waged around Guadalcanal, the Japanese submarines were employed as an advanced screen with their fleet, with the senior submarine officer embarked in one of the special command submarines. It was soon found that he was in a very poor position to know what was going on and his radio transmissions gave away not only his own position but that a fleet movement was in progress. Nevertheless it was in this period that the Japanese submarines achieved their most important results of the war. *I.19* sank the aircraft carrier *Wasp* and *I.15* narrowly missed the aircraft carrier *Hornet* but a torpedo hit and damaged the battleship *North Carolina*. The recently repaired *Saratoga* was again torpedoed and damaged, this time by *I.26* who later sank the light cruiser *Juneau*. The battleship *Washington* was also missed by *I.15* and finally *I.21* sank the destroyer *Porter* and *I.176* damaged the cruiser *Chester*. All these results were achieved against heavily escorted task forces and helped to reduce American carrier strength to a dangerously low level. Furthermore they were made without loss to the Japanese submarines.

The desperate situation of the Japanese forces on Guadalcanal very soon drew most of their submarines into a transport role. The American local command of the sea and air made it very difficult for any other type of ship to get through. By landing all except one gun and two torpedoes, the submarines were able to carry as much as seventy tons of cargo, which was enough to support 13,000 men for two days. From November 1942 to February 1943, a submarine delivered supplies nearly every day, eleven submarines being initially employed on this duty, rising to twenty towards the end of the campaign. Without their support the garrison of Guadalcanal undoubtedly would have collapsed much sooner. These operations in the South Pacific cost the Japanese ten submarines. They were sunk mostly by surface ships, which initially detected the submarines by radar when they were on the surface and subsequently relocated them by sonar (see Note 26) and destroyed them with depth charges.

In June, when the Japanese attacked the Aleutians, the few old American S class submarines which had been sent there for defence were reinforced from the central Pacific. In this area they operated on the supply lines from Japan under appalling weather conditions. They managed to sink six ships which was a contribution towards the American victory in the area. Japanese submarines also took part in some strength in the Aleutians and were used for reconnaissance, to transport supplies to beleaguered Kiska and Attu and finally to help in the evacuation of Kiska.

Up to the end of 1942, American submarines had, therefore, been employed a great deal on military operations and had sunk two cruisers, a seaplane carrier, four destroyers and six submarines of the Imperial Navy, as well as finishing off a damaged aircraft carrier. They had also made a number of reconnaissances and the south-west Pacific submarines had made many rescues from and supply trips to the Philippines and East Indies. In June the very large submarines *Argonaut* and *Nautilus* landed 211 U.S. Marines to raid Makin Island and this was by far the largest landing from submarines that had been attempted at any time.

In spite of these successes, however, the U.S. submarines could not claim to be more than valuable auxiliaries and no rival to carrier-borne aircraft or even surface ships on which seapower depended. The Japanese submarines had, in fact, sunk and damaged more warships than the Americans although their losses were much higher. But the same general observation applied to them. This was, however, to be the highest point of Japanese success, whereas the Americans had not yet really started.

During 1943 the American forces in the Pacific began to take the offensive and, in addition to their main function which was a general attack on merchant shipping, submarines assisted in the offensive operations. In the advance up the Solomon Islands, their most important function, as before, was the isolation of the fighting area by attacking the Japanese supplies. In the second half of 1943, the U.S. submarines, mainly based on Brisbane, sank fifty-two ships of 240,000 tons in the South Pacific, so virtually strangling the Japanese before they were ejected by the American amphibious forces. Submarines were also used for beach reconnaissance before the landings, for landing agents and, in one case, as a beacon to lead in the amphibious forces. Patrols were maintained during the actual operations off the Japanese bases in Truk and the Marshall Islands, with the aim of sinking any ships which sortied to interfere. Whilst thus engaged, the *Skate* succeeded in torpedoing the giant battleship *Yamato*, but without sinking her. In the South Pacific only one warship, a Japanese submarine, was sunk but the *Sailfish*, on an ordinary offensive patrol against shipping off Japan, sank the escort carrier *Chuyo*.

In the American attack on the Gilbert Islands in November, ten submarines were deployed in support of the operation and these also carried out weather reporting duties and others were positioned for 'lifeguard' duties to pick up pilots of aircraft which fell in the sea. During 1943 also the American submarines were diverted from their general offensive against Japanese shipping to assist the amphibious and other offensive operations in various ways. They did not achieve very much against the Japanese Navy and by far their most important military effect was to cut off supplies to the areas under attack.

After the armistice with Italy in September 1943, the expansion of British submarine strength in the Indian Ocean was steady; by the end of the year, there were nineteen operating in the Malacca Straits where their main function was to cut the sea communications of the Japanese Army in Burma. Targets were, however, scarce and they succeeded in sinking only one ship and a Japanese submarine before the end of the year.

Throughout 1943 the main strength of the Japanese submarine force was drawn into operations wherever the Americans attacked. By the end of 1943 there was a very marked increase in the Japanese submarine losses: they were quite unable to compete with radar and sonar and their strength steadily declined. Twenty-three of them were sunk during the year and they had the sole success to their credit of the sinking of the auxiliary aircraft carrier *Liscombe Bay* during the Gilbert operations.

During 1944, as the American counter offensive gained momentum, a proportion of their submarines continued to be used in co-operation with the major amphibious operations and carrier strikes. An average of seven boats was used in the assaults on Kwajalein, Majuro and Eniwetok in the Marshall Islands. The principal function of these submarines was to patrol off the enemy bases, where their instructions were to attack any isolated units that emerged but to report any major movements of the enemy fleet. They were not allowed to attack until this had been done, unless the enemy fleet had been previously sighted. This was good strategy but frustrating for the submarines, who might thereby lose the chance of a lifetime. Fortunately there were no lost opportunities and, during the carrier raid on Truk in February, the submarine *Skate* sank the Japanese light cruiser *Agano*.

In April the Commander-in-Chief of the American Pacific Fleet raised the target priority of destroyers to the next place after aircraft carriers, battleships and heavy cruisers (see Note 27). Five destroyers had already been sunk since January and during the rest of the year twenty-five more were disposed of. The submarine *Harder* alone sank four destroyers during the summer, mostly by using the 'down the throat' technique in which a spread of torpedoes was fired directly at a counter attacking destroyer from right ahead. This type of attack, although nearly always success-ful, needed a very steady nerve as, if it failed, it could be fatal to the submarine. The *Harder* was in fact sunk in August by two Japanese anti-submarine vessels. In the past, the destroyer had always been the submarine's greatest enemy but, during 1944, Japanese destroyers sank only six U.S. submarines and assisted aircraft to dispose of two more. Now, in an encounter between a Japanese destroyer and an American submarine, the odds worked out at over three to one on the submarine winning.

In June the American attack on Saipan led to the Battle of the Philippine Sea. During this operation twenty-eight American sub-marines were deployed in support in the usual ways. Three American submarines were on patrol off Tawi Tawi in the Philip-pines, where the base of the Japanese main fleet had been moved as a result of the campaign against oil tankers, since it was closer to the oil ports.

When the Japanese sortied to oppose the Saipan landings they were at once reported by the submarines *Harder* and *Redfin*, and this was the first information received by the American Fleet that the Japanese were coming out. Other Japanese units were sighted by the *Flying Fish* and *Seahorse* and accurately reported. A number of other American submarines on their way to and from patrol were then diverted to intercept the enemy. One of these was the *Cavalla*, which sighted a Japanese replenishment group of tankers but lost contact. Four more submarines were then placed to try to intercept the Japanese Fleet whilst it was refuelling. The *Cavalla* again made contact, but this time sighted the main Japanese carrier force and torpedoed and sank the air-craft carrier *Shokakku*. Shortly afterwards the *Albacore* also sighted this force and sank the new aircraft carrier *Taiho*.

In this major fleet action the Japanese lost three aircraft car-riers, two to submarines and one to carrier-borne air attack. Submarine reconnaissance gave an excellent picture of the situa-tion and this information could not, because of the distances in-volved, have been obtained in any other way. For the first time submarines participating in a fleet action sank as much as ships and aircraft put together. They shared with the carrier-borne aircraft, which cut the Japanese air groups to pieces, the laurels for this victory.

Four months later, when the American amphibious operation against Leyte Island in the Philippines was launched, most of the

202

Japanese Fleet had had to move even further south to Lingga in the East Indies, where it was right alongside the oilfields in Sumatra. Thirty-six American submarines were at sea, many carrying out the normal patrols against commerce, but others were specially disposed to cover the operation against the Japanese Fleet.

The Japanese Combined Fleet put to sea to counter attack the Leyte landings in three main groups. All three were detected leaving their bases by American submarines. *Besugo* and *Skate* sighted Admiral Ozawa's carrier force leaving Japan and the *Shark* and *Blackfish* made amplifying reports of the same force further to the south. *Icefish* and *Seadragon* reported Admiral Shima's cruiser force south of Formosa and the submarine *Bream* hit and damaged the heavy cruiser *Aoba*. Admiral Kurita's battle force coming up from the south was intercepted west of Palawan Island by the submarines *Dace* and *Darter*, which succeeded in sinking the heavy cruisers *Atago* and *Maya* and heavily damaged the *Takao*. The *Atago* was Admiral Kurita's flagship and the transfer of his flag, with the loss of half of his communication staff, considerably confused the control of the operation. Submarines took no part in the main carrier and surface action, but were well placed to intercept the retiring Japanese forces. The submarine *Halibut* sank the destroyer *Akitsuki* and the *Jallao* the light cruiser *Tama*. Two other submarines intercepted, but missed, the battleships *Ise* and *Hyuga* retiring towards Japan.

Although the submarines in this action did not sink as many ships as air or surface forces, the torpedoing of five cruisers and a destroyer was still a considerable achievement. Submarine reconnaissance was again excellent and all the main Japanese movements were reported well outside the range of reconnaissance aircraft. Submarines, therefore, confirmed that their high performance in the Battle of the Philippines Sea was not just luck and that they must be considered a formidable factor in any fleet action in the future.

In the subsequent retirement of the Japanese forces from the South China Sea to Japan, the *Sealion* sank the Japanese battleship *Kongo* and her escort, the destroyer *Yurakaze*. Four submarines fired twenty-three torpedoes at the heavy cruiser *Kumano* finally hitting and driving her ashore in the Philippines where she was later finished off by carrier-borne aircraft. Lastly the *Bergall* damaged the heavy cruiser *Myoko* off the coast of Indo-China.

203

These sinkings in the Battles of Leyte Gulf and the Philippine Sea were made by submarines deployed with the aim of intercepting enemy naval forces, but during 1944 submarines sank many warships in the ordinary course of their patrols against commerce. The very large and brand-new aircraft carrier *Shinamo* was sunk off Japan by the *Archerfish* in November and the smaller aircraft carriers *Unryu, Otaka, Unyo* and *Jinyo* were dispatched by the *Redfin, Rasher, Barb* and *Spadefish*. Six other light cruisers were sunk, including the *Kuma* by the British submarine *Tally Ho* in the Malacca Straits. These successes were in addition to the thirty destroyers already mentioned. The total successes by submarines against the Japanese Navy during the year 1944 compared favourably with the sinkings by all other types of ship and aircraft (see Note 28).

It was in this critical year that the Japanese Navy was really defeated, in addition to their contributions in the two great naval battles of Leyte Gulf and the Philippines Sea the submarines won what amounted to a third major naval victory by themselves.

Whilst these great events were taking place in the Pacific the British had built up their submarine force in the Malacca Straits. For some time they were the only part of the British Eastern Fleet able to take the offensive but suffered from a dearth of targets. As has already been told, the *Tally Ho* sank the light cruiser *Kuma* in January and the *Templar* damaged the *Kitagami* in the same month. They succeeded in sinking three U-boats, two German and one Japanese, and conducted a vigorous campaign by gun and mine, as well as torpedo, against the supply line to the Japanese army in Burma. The sea route to Burma through the Malacca Straits was abandoned by the Japanese in the autumn, a success which the submarines shared with aircraft.

In contrast to the great success of the American submarines against warships during 1944, the Japanese submarines suffered a severe and decisive defeat. Strategically they had the disadvantage that they were operating on the defensive. Tactically they were no match for the American surface anti-submarine vessels. In May 1944, eight Japanese submarines tried to intercept U.S. forces advancing to Biak and Palau and their whole patrol line was rolled up by a few American destroyer escorts and five submarines were sunk. The only ones to escape were two which left the patrol line on their own initiative and a third which was one of the early Japanese submarines to be fitted with radar. When the Americans attacked Saipan, twenty-two Japanese submarines were sent to the area to oppose the landings and no less than thirteen of them were lost. By the time of the Leyte landings in October 1944, there were only eleven submarines available to oppose them.

During the year the Japanese lost fifty-seven boats, thirty-eight of which were sunk by surface anti-submarine vessels, eight by other submarines and four by aircraft. Although the huge American carrier and amphibious forces with their replenishment groups and supply convoys presented unlimited opportunities, the Japanese submarine force was no longer even a threat to them.

In 1945 there was a dearth of merchant ship targets and the American submarines were used in greater numbers for military purposes. For the assault on Iwojima thirty-two submarines were disposed in covering positions during the operation. Some of these were used to make photographic reconnaissances of the island before the landings, others to make a sweep to clear Japanese picket boats from the area and to act as weather reporting stations. In the Okinawa operation in March and April, most of the U.S. submarines at sea were involved in some way. In this phase of the war there was not much of the Japanese Navy left afloat and the submarines had little chance to sink worthwhile targets. In April, however, *Threadfin* and *Hackleback* sighted and reported the giant battleship *Yamato* as she came out of the Bungo Suido to meet her end at the hands of the aircraft of the Third Fleet. The submarine *Charr*, one of a wolf pack on an ordinary offensive patrol, sank the light cruiser *Izuzu* in the East Indies. Other submarines sank half a dozen or so smaller warships and these were in addition to a number of convoy escort vessels the sinking of which will be described in the next chapter. Since it was expected that the Japanese submarines would become more troublesome as the Americans closed in towards Japan, the American submarines gave more attention to their destruction and sank nine of them during the year. An immense effort was also put into 'lifeguard' duties and no less than 380 aviators were rescued from the sea. But in general the task of the American submarines was over, the war at sea was already won and it was the day of the forces more suited for the mopping-up operations which were now required.

By the time two British submarine flotillas had been transferred from the East Indies to the Pacific to work with the Americans, the war was virtually over and there was little for them to do. Nevertheless the *Trenchant* sank the heavy Japanese cruiser *Ashigara* in the Banka Straits in June, and British midget submarines entered Singapore and further damaged the Japanese cruiser *Takao* which had been there since the Battle of Leyte Gulf.

By the beginning of 1945 the Japanese had lost 102 submarines, but had built 97 and so still had a considerable force. They were, however, of very little use as it was suicide for them to approach American anti-submarine forces. They realized that the reason for this was their technical inferiority and the very great superiority of the American radar and sonar against which they had no counter measure. Radar was also the key to the success of the American submarines against them. Even the Japanese submarines employed on transport suffered casualties. At the time of the evacuation of Luzon three Japanese submarines were employed on a shuttle service to Formosa and all were lost : they were sunk by the American submarine *Batfish* over a period of a few days. She was able to pick them up by radar at night and to torpedo them.

The Japanese made strenuous efforts to recapture the technical initiative so that their submarines could regain their effectiveness. They had acquired two German U-boats for experiments in 1943 and began to fit radar in their submarines from the middle of 1944. It was, however, much inferior to the American radar and did not help them very much. In January 1943, in common with the development of other suicide weapons, they started the design of a human torpedo. These Kaitens, as they were called, were fast and powerful torpedoes launched from a submarine and steered by a man inside them using a periscope. They were first used in 1945 against stationary targets but later were employed against ships under way. Attempts were made against American shipping at Ulithi, Okinawa and Iwojima but with extremely poor results and many of the parent submarines were lost as well.

At the end of 1942 it had been decided to build eighteen very large submarines, each to carry three torpedo bomber aircraft. Only three of these submarines were completed before the end of the war, nevertheless a force of them actually left Japan to make an attack on the locks of the Panama Canal but the surrender came before they could get there.

The Japanese, in the same way as the Germans, tried to produce submarines of high underwater speed, but these were only just completing at the end of the war. The Japanese submarines were, therefore, unable to regain their effectiveness and in March 1945 their operational strength had fallen to forty-one boats. Right at the end of the war, *I.58* sank the U.S. cruiser *Indianapolis* and, as she was unescorted, the submarine survived: but this was their only success. Nevertheless, at the time of the surrender, a Japanese submarine force was still 'in being' when the rest of their navy was at the bottom of the sea.

The performance of submarines against warships in the Far East is the story of a brilliant victory on the one hand and of abject defeat on the other. Both the main submarine forces were built and trained for attack on warships; both were composed of large, fast and powerful submarines of the trans-Pacific endurance and the reason for this discrepancy is at first hard to discern. This is especially so as the side which was dedicated to a military role was the one that failed and the side which concentrated on attacking commerce did best against warships.

The American submarines destroyed just under a third of the Japanese Navy. The results compared with the achievements by other types of ship and aircraft can be seen in the table below. The efficacy of various types of warship cannot, of course, be judged solely by the ships they sink any more than the value of

Type of Ship Sunk	Ships sunk by				
	Surface Warships	Shore-based Aircraft	Carrier-borne Aircraft	Submarines	Other Causes
Battleships	3½	1	4½	1	1
Aircraft Carriers	–	–	11½	8½	–
Cruisers	6	1½	16	14½	–
Destroyers	28	19½	33	45½	8
Submarines	73	6	8½	25	15

various positions of members of a football team by the goals they score. Nevertheless the destruction of the enemy's fleet has always been the principal aim of naval battles and the best way to command the sea.

The total Japanese achievements, which included the sinking of three aircraft carriers, one of which was heavily damaged already by aircraft, and the damaging of another one on two separate occasions, were small when compared with the American successes. Furthermore, these results cost them 130 submarines during the war. Although they did just as well as any other type of Japanese warship, as a warwinning factor they were insignificant.

It is often assumed that the Japanese submarines would have been far better employed in an unrestricted attack on commerce. The United States, however, could not be defeated by an attack on their oceanic trade in the same way as Great Britain or, indeed, Japan: they were not sufficiently dependent on the sea. In any case the most important American traffic was in the Atlantic and only a small proportion of British trade, which the Japanese did try to attack, passed through the Indian Ocean. The Japanese were not, therefore, strategically within reach of their enemy's lifeline; their submarines did, in fact, try to interrupt the American military communications in the South Pacific during and after the Solomons campaign, but they managed to sink only twenty merchant vessels for the loss of seven submarines. This gives an exchange rate of just under three and operations could not have been continued at this pace for long. They probably achieved as much as they were able by forcing all the American military traffic in the Pacific to proceed in convoy, and an attack on commerce was unlikely to have had much effect even if they had concentrated everything upon it.

The comparative failure of the Japanese submarines is not, therefore, to be accounted for in a mistaken strategy alone. They hoped to achieve the results which were certainly shown by the Americans to be possible at the Battles of Leyte Gulf and the Philippine Sea or indeed, that they themselves achieved in the Solomons campaign. They might well have exercised a decisive influence in fleet operations had they not been technically outclassed and quite unable to compete with the American antisubmarine measures.

One thing that was common to both sides was the failure of

the submarine in defence. This was not only when they were deployed defensively, but seemed to apply when they were operating offensively in a tactical sense, yet were strategically on the defensive. The large American and Dutch submarine forces in the early part of the war did not, as the official American historian has said, delay the Japanese advance more than did the weather. In the second half of the war, in attempting to resist the advance of the Americans across the Pacific, the Japanese submarines were rushed from landing to landing, suffering very heavy casualties and achieving practically nothing. It leads to the conclusion that the British made a sound strategic decision when they refused to transfer more than two submarines from the Mediterranean to the Far East after Pearl Harbor. They would have taken them from offensive operations, where they were doing very well, in order to use them for defence.

In co-operation with surface fleets, submarines in the Far East achieved greater success than in the past, notably by the Americans in the Battles of the Philippine Sea and Leyte Gulf and by the Japanese during the Solomons campaign. The successes were both in reconnaissance and in the sinking of warships, but most of the results were obtained at a distance rather than in the battle area itself. Substantial results were also obtained in enemy waters independently in the course of normal offensive patrols. As ever, the submarine did best when used as a weapon of attrition and when making a sustained effort in enemy waters where other forces could not operate. Destruction over a long period by attrition has never had quite the same impact as a naval battle, but it can deny the sea to an enemy just as effectively in the end. These results are sufficient to show that the American submarines in the Pacific in World War II were one of the most important factors in the defeat of the Japanese Navy. They were of more value than a battlefleet and in the same class as carrier-borne aircraft, even when employed part-time against warships. It was clear that the submarine had now become a potentially decisive weapon against warships as well as against commerce.

XII

The American Campaign against Commerce in the Pacific
(December 1941–August 1945)

On the afternoon that the Japanese attacked Pearl Harbor on 7 December 1941, the U.S. Chief of Naval Operations directed unrestricted air and submarine warfare to be executed against Japan. No such trenchant order had ever before been issued to a submarine force at the outset of hostilities. The Germans and the British were by now both virtually waging unrestricted submarine warfare but without admitting it. They had come about it gradually, partly in retaliation and partly because it was obviously the only effective way to use submarines. American anger at the Pearl Harbor attack was such that this step was taken as a matter of course. The fact that it was the German unrestricted submarine campaign which had brought the U.S.A. into the First World War was forgotten.

Soon after the Pearl Harbor attack, half a dozen submarines of the Pacific Fleet left for patrols off Japan to implement this directive. The Asiatic Fleet submarines, in their retreat southwards to Australia, had been almost entirely engaged in military operations. It was not until they had established their bases in Western Australia that they were able to turn their attention to an attack on commerce. Their mission was then to attack the enemy supply lines linking Japan to the Netherlands East Indies and Malaya.

Japan was very nearly as dependent upon the sea as Great Britain. Thirty per cent of her raw materials and twenty per cent of her food had to come from abroad. Furthermore, the internal sea communications between the islands of Japan herself were essential to her economy. Roughly half her trade before the war had been carried by neutrals, now the whole load fell upon her own merchant marine. The shipping available to her was, moreover, only a third of that available to the British. At the outbreak of war her shipping pattern changed considerably : trade was now restricted to the Far East and to the so-called Greater East Asia Co-prosperity Sphere. To exploit the captured territories, to make up for the loss of her world trade and to support the military forces in the Philippines, the East Indies, Malaya and Burma, made the demand for tonnage insatiable. An attack on shipping in general promised, therefore, to be a decisive way to defeat Japan.

The Japanese expected to lose ships to American submarines but had hoped to seal off the passages between the outer islands of the Co-prosperity Sphere and sail their ships in safety behind a perimeter defence. Some of the important military traffic was in convoy but most shipping sailed independently in the open sea and was escorted by local anti-submarine vessels at each end of the voyage. The distances in the Pacific are enormous and it took a very long time for the U.S. submarines to reach their patrol areas. From Pearl Harbor to Japan was roughly the same distance as from Lorient to the West Indies. Out of an average force of sixty-seven American submarines available in 1942, only thirteen could be kept on patrol at a time in the operational areas. The average length of patrol was between six and seven weeks, over half of which was spent on passage.

During 1942, as already told, a proportion of the American submarines were busy with military tasks at Guadalcanal and the Aleutians. Other submarines, particularly in the south-west Pacific, were frequently diverted to pick up aviators, rescue survivors and make transport trips to supply guerilla forces in the Philippines. Nevertheless, submarines positioned for military purposes were often able to sink merchant vessels and, during the Guadalcanal and Aleutian campaigns, some thirty ships of about 100,000 tons were sunk. Altogether some 500 attacks were made on merchant ships by American submarines during the year, in which they sank approximately 140 ships of well over half a million tons. Half of these ships were attacked in Japanese waters by about sixteen American submarines from Pearl Harbor without losing a single boat. In April and May the submarine *Triton* working in the East China Sea sank four ships of over 14,000 tons. She also sank two small craft with her gun but missed four other ships with torpedoes. This patrol illustrates how the submarines fared; some of the attacks were by day and others at night and included both submerged and surface torpedo attacks.

The average rate of sinking was less than a ship a month for each submarine in an operational area. This was much less than the German U-boats were achieving during the same period off the American coast. The principal reason was that the Japanese merchant marine was about a quarter of the size of that of the Allies, thus far fewer ships presented themselves as targets. To a certain extent it was because only one attack in four was successful. This was partly because the American torpedoes were scarce and unreliable and partly because pre-war training had been against warships rather than merchant ships. The training had also expected a tougher opposition and so proved somewhat too cautious.

The Japanese anti-submarine measures were not very effective and only eight U.S. submarines were lost during 1942, four of these being of the obsolescent S class and only three lost definitely because of Japanese anti-submarine measures. The exchange rate was, therefore, forty-six merchant ships sunk for each submarine destroyed by the enemy. With such small losses and the commissioning of thirty-five new submarines, American strength in the Pacific rose to eighty submarines by the end of the year.

Submarines were joined by aircraft in the campaign against shipping and these, as well as some casualties from ships and mines, swelled the total Japanese merchant ship losses to about a million tons. The Japanese were able to replace only a quarter of these ships and their total tonnage declined during the year. The Japanese civilian standard of living began to suffer, but these sinkings were about what they had expected. At the end of 1942, the unrestricted campaign against Japanese shipping did not promise to be more than an irritation to them.

The Japanese submarines made their only serious attack on trade in the Indian Ocean. In 1942 a squadron of submarines was stationed at Penang throughout the year. The campaign was conducted in a series of forays, the most successful being by the force which had damaged H.M.S. *Ramillies*, which also sank twenty-two merchant ships in the Mozambique Channel. Altogether some fifty unescorted ships were sunk without the Japanese losing a submarine. Just before the landings on Guadalcanal in August, the Japanese had decided to extend the campaign against commerce by making large-scale raids with their main strength, but Guadalcanal and the Aleutians drew nearly all of them into military operations.

In November 1942, a group of German U-boats, using U-tankers to refuel, had rounded the Cape and worked in the Mozambique Channel where they sank thirty ships before they returned to Europe. In December the Japanese proposed that the Germans should base some U-boats in the Indian Ocean at Penang. Preparations were made with the base but the Germans were reluctant to send U-boats so far afield when they were doing well in the Atlantic.

In April 1943 one of the large German U-cruisers of a group which had been operating south of Madagascar was sent to Penang to test the base facilities. Another of this group, *U196*, had been thirty-one and a half weeks at sea by the time she returned to Bordeaux, so making the record cruise by any submarine in the Second World War. By May 1943 the German U-boats had lost the initiative in the Atlantic and Admiral Doenitz decided that the time had come to extend their operations to the Indian Ocean where shipping was not even in convoy. At the end of June, eleven large U-boats sailed from Europe. The plan was to refuel them with a U-tanker in mid-Atlantic and with a surface tanker near Mauritius. Opposition in the Atlantic was so intense that they had great difficulty in refuelling. Several U-boats were sunk and some had to be used to refuel the others. It was not until November that four U-boats, which were all that survived, entered Penang. German U-boats sank some forty ships during the year in the Indian Ocean, which was better than the results being obtained in the Atlantic at the time. (During 1943 a few Japanese submarines from Penang continued to operate against commerce in the Indian Ocean and sank some twenty ships.) Seven more U-cruisers left French and German bases during the second half of 1943, but all were sunk in the Atlantic and not a single one of them reached the Indian Ocean.

Throughout 1944 the Germans maintained some half a dozen U-boats at Penang, but they returned to Germany after a patrol or two with cargoes of tin and rubber and were relieved by new U-boats. The large U-cruisers were able to reach Penang from Germany without refuelling and so no longer needed to use surface or U-tankers. In 1944 the Germans sank thirty-six ships, but they lost another five U-cruisers either on their way to, or in, the

213

Indian Ocean, which did not give a very satisfactory exchange rate. In the autumn the British had been forced to adopt convoy in the Indian Ocean and the campaign collapsed. Japanese submarine strength in the Indian Ocean had been decreasing steadily to meet urgent calls nearer home. They were in any case quite unable to compete with convoys and in August were withdrawn altogether from the Indian Ocean. The remaining German U-boats were all ordered to leave the Indian Ocean by January 1945 with cargoes, and their operations came to an end.

The German U-boats sank 118 ships in two years in the Indian Ocean, whereas the Japanese sank only seventy ships in three years. It was the Germans who forced the British to adopt convoy, but their campaign was really defeated in the Atlantic where nineteen U-boats were sunk on their way to or from the Indian Ocean. The campaign is mainly remarkable for the incredible distances involved which were far greater even than in the Pacific.

In 1943 the American attack on commerce began in earnest. At the beginning of the year the Japanese, in spite of their losses, still had over half a million tons of shipping more than the minimum required to support their war economy. Many more American submarines were now available and new boats were coming forward at the rate of about five a month. Furthermore, the military diversions at Guadalcanal and the Aleutians were practically over. A few submarines were kept to watch the Japanese naval bases in the Marshall Islands and at Truk and Palau, but the rest were released against commerce and the average number of submarines on patrol rose to over eighteen.

During 1943 the majority of the U.S. submarines worked individually, but they were fitted progressively with the new SJ radar. This set, which was for use on the surface, meant that at night they could find ships over a wide area. With their high speed of 20 knots they could manœuvre into position to attack, either on the surface at night or submerged next day. The silhouette of the American submarines had been cut down so that they were very much harder to see and even the Japanese, justly famous for the efficiency of their night lookouts, had difficulty in detecting them. In January the U.S. submarine *Wahoo* attacked a convoy off New Guinea and, in a ten-hour running battle, sank

214

Coastal Command Air attacks on U-boats

Convoy

THE DEFEAT OF
THE U-BOATS
1943

*Imperial War Museum
photographs*

U.S.S. *Nautilus*—the first nuclear propelled submarine in the world

U.S.S. *Grayback*—a Fleet submarine converted to carry Regulus II missiles

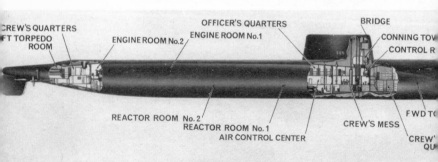

U.S.S. *Triton*—a very large nuclear propelled radar picket

three ships of about 12,000 tons, damaging a fourth, and in a patrol in March, in the Yellow Sea, the same submarine sank nine ships of nearly 20,000 tons.

Early in the war the U.S. Chief of Naval Operations had directed the American submarines to work in wolf packs, but it was not until September 1943 that they were numerous enough even to make experiments. The American wolf packs were organized in a different way from the Germans. Three or four submarines would leave harbour in company and were controlled by the senior officer using high frequency voice radio which at that time the Japanese could not intercept. The first wolf pack consisted of the submarines *Cero*, *Shad* and *Grayback* and operated in the East China Sea in October, sinking three ships of nearly 24,000 tons. In the second group in November the *Snook*, *Harder* and *Pargo* sank seven ships of 32,000 tons in the Marianas area. Opinion was by no means unanimous on the efficacy of wolf packs. Indeed, in September, the submarine *Trigger* by herself sank four ships of 26,000 tons in the East China Sea, which was comparable with the total score of a wolf pack. These early operations confirmed that wolf packs were of more use for finding ships than in attacking.

Many of the American torpedo troubles were by now overcome but others, notably with a magnetic exploder, continued. Torpedoes were still scarce and in March submarines had to be ordered to lay mines instead in order to conserve them. Only thirteen minefields were, however, laid during the rest of the year and these seem to have sunk only two ships. Nevertheless there were enough torpedoes for nearly four thousand of them to be fired during the year in over a thousand attacks on merchant ships.

Japanese shipping now moved in relatively small convoys of four or five ships with an escort of up to the same number of destroyers or frigates. They sailed close inshore in shallow water whenever possible and made the passages in the open sea at night. The Japanese had a good network of radio direction finding stations on shore, but the U.S. submarines very seldom used frequencies which were susceptible to interception, and so it was not of much use to them. The Japanese had no radar in their ships or aircraft during 1943, but the escort vessels had an echo detection system similar to sonar, although it was not as good as equivalent British or American equipment. Tactically they lacked persistence and often gave up well before they had sunk a submarine which was then able to escape.

The Japanese laid a great many mines as an anti-submarine measure, but they spread them too thinly over large areas and they probably sank only two submarines during 1943. For instance, they tried to block the complete area from the northernmost tip of Formosa to Japan. Nevertheless, the mine barriers which guarded the Sea of Japan generally achieved the aim of keeping the American submarines out and only one incursion, by three boats, took place during the year.

In 1943 the Japanese shipping losses caused by submarines averaged well over 100,000 tons a month, rising to 231,000 tons in November (see p. 222; fig. 22). Just over 300 ships were sunk, one out of three attacks now proving successful. In November, the best month of the year, only just over two ships were sunk for each submarine in the operational area. The average rate of sinking, at just under one and a half ships per submarine on patrol each month, was, however, twice as good as in 1942.

The Japanese realized during the year that they must do more about anti-submarine measures and organized the so-called Grand Escort Fleet. This started work with forty escorts, rising late in the year to nearly one hundred and fifty. It included aircraft with a magnetic detector which, however, had only a very limited range. Nevertheless, during the year the Japanese succeeded in sinking fifteen American submarines. Of these six were sunk by surface anti-submarine vessels, three of which were escorting convoys at the time, four were sunk by aircraft and one by a Japanese submarine. The exchange rate was, therefore, twenty merchant ships sunk for every U.S. submarine destroyed. The American submarines had, as already told, developed an effective method of dealing with escorts with the 'down the throat' shot, and during the year they sank seventeen anti-submarine vessels of various types from destroyers to submarine chasers.

The Japanese made immense efforts to replace their shipping and in fact built nearly 800,000 tons during 1943. But their total losses, which were mainly caused by submarines, were 1,800,000 tons and so their tonnage steadily declined until, at the end of the year, it was $7\frac{1}{2}$ per cent below what it had been at the beginning of the war. The situation was, therefore, very similar to that of the British in 1917. Although the tonnage available to the Japanese was still able to compete, their shipping was being sunk faster than it could be replaced, their anti-submarine measures were quite unable to compete with the American submarines, and it was clearly only a matter of time before the shipping losses would become crippling.

At the beginning of 1944, the Americans had 123 submarines operating in the Pacific: sixty-six new boats having been delivered during the previous year. Their torpedo troubles had been overcome and they now had a lavish supply of these weapons. All submarines now had the SJ radar, which proved a magnificent piece of equipment and enabled them to find the Japanese at night without being seen by them. By January 1944 the Japanese Grand Escort Fleet was fully organized and the convoy system was largely established. The convoys, consisting of half a dozen ships or so, were small by British standards. The escort groups, although smaller than in the Atlantic, were large compared with the number of ships escorted. The convoys still hugged the coast in shallow water whenever possible but, because of the heavy casualties suffered in night attacks, had often reverted to daylight passages in the open sea.

In January there were twenty-seven U.S. submarines on patrol and their operational areas were spread all over the western Pacific: they sank fifty ships of close on a quarter of a million tons, which was more than in any month to date. In February there were fewer submarines at sea, but they did better still and, with the casualties caused by air and other forces, the total topped the half million mark. The five submarines *Snook*, *Pogy*, *Rasher*, *Puffer* and *Grayback*, acting independently of each other, sank more than 100,000 tons. In March and April sinkings declined sharply to about half the January and February figures. This was almost entirely because the Japanese held ships in port to reorganize the convoy system. Japanese shipbuilding was now at its zenith and in March they completed eighty-nine ships of over a quarter of a million tons. In spite of this immense effort, their total casualties were so high that, at the end of the first quarter of 1944, their shipping had declined by over half a million tons since the beginning of the year.

In April and May, advanced submarine bases were set up on Manus, in the Admiralty Islands, and at Majura, in the Marshalls, which greatly decreased the time submarines had to spend on passage. In May also, a new operational plan was devised for the U.S. submarines with the aim of concentrating them against the convoy system where shipping was densest. In this month the number of submarines on patrol had risen to thirty-five: they again reached the February figures and sank over a quarter of a million tons. It was in this month that the submarine *Gurnard* created a record by sinking four ships of nearly 30,000 tons. In June and July the total figures were not quite as high as in May, but the submarine *Tang* in the East China and Yellow Seas broke the record again and sank ten ships of nearly 40,000 tons.

Oil was the lifeblood of the Japanese war effort and a steady flow from Sumatra, Java and Borneo, north to Japan and then out again to the fighting fronts was absolutely essential to them. As early as mid-1943, oil tankers had been given a target priority immediately after aircraft carriers and battleships, but only fifteen of them were sunk in the last four months of the year. By the end of 1943 the Japanese tanker fleet was, in fact, larger than it had ever been before. In January and February the target prority began to take effect: twenty-one tankers were sunk, which was at three times the rate at which they were being built. In April and May their shipbuilding again caught up and all tankers, many of which had been sailing independently, were put in convoy. The cumulative effect of the losses and the consequent delays was that, in May, the oil imports into Japan were only just over half the January figures. Most of the success against tankers was the work of the submarines based in Western Australia, whose numbers had now been raised to thirty boats. The consumption of oil was now three times as much as in peacetime, which was much greater than had been estimated, and reserves in Japan were already falling.

Only two experimental wolf packs had put to sea in 1943 and during the spring of 1944 less than half a dozen more were employed with no very significant results. With the re-organization and spread of the Japanese convoy system, the number of wolf packs was increased. In May and June a pack consisting of the submarines *Shark*, *Pilotfish* and *Pintado*, under the nickname of 'Blair's Blasters' after their senior officer, sank 35,000 tons in convoy in the Marianas area. Although the original doctrine for wolf packs had visualized the close co-ordination of an attack by the senior officer, it was found best to allow the submarines to attack individually. Only the broadest directions were given, such as detailing 'flankers' and 'trailers', and the submarines then worked together like a football team. The search was, however, closely controlled and was mainly conducted on the surface at night when they could best exploit their radar and high speed. A submarine sighting the enemy would call up her colleagues and either attack at once or shadow until they had made contact. After attacking, a submarine would use her surface speed to make what was known as an 'end around' to get ahead again and make another attack. Such tactics proved very effective and the Japanese, having no radar, had practically no answer to them.

In July and August 'Donk's Devils', consisting of *Picuda*, *Redfish* and *Spadefish,* operating north of Luzon, sank thirteen ships of over 64,000 tons which was the highest wolf pack score to date. The casualties included a destroyer and were nearly all in convoy. In August the submarines *Ray*, *Haddow*, *Harder*, *Guitarro* and *Raton* engaged a convoy of twelve ships with five escorts in a running fight which continued the length of the South China Sea. They sank five ships of 28,000 tons, despite the fact that the convoy had air cover throughout and hugged the coast wherever possible.

Japanese losses from submarines during the summer averaged well over 200,000 tons a month, as the wolf packs gained the upper hand over the convoys (see p. 222; fig. 22). Carrier-borne aircraft in attacks on the Pacific islands also destroyed a great deal. The Japanese were unable to increase their shipbuilding any more and the size of their merchant marine began to decline rapidly. Food was short in Japan and a lack of raw materials was seriously hampering production : by the end of the summer defeat was in sight.

The last three months of 1944 sealed the doom of the Japanese merchant service. In October there were forty-three U.S. submarines on patrol and they sank well over 300,000 tons. The Japanese merchant fleet had now fallen to half the size it had been at the beginning of the war. A great deal of shipping was thrown away in trying to reinforce the Philippine Islands, where aircraft destroyed very nearly as much as the submarines. Most of the losses were incurred in the South China Sea and round Formosa, where the wolf packs now had a complete superiority over the Japanese convoy system and, when they made contact, were able to sink two-thirds and sometimes even three-quarters of each convoy. From May to December some sixty wolf packs, of an average of three submarines each, had put to sea, but over the whole period half the submarines were still working independently. In October and November, in the area of greatest sinkings in the South China Sea, these independent submarines sank nearly as much as the wolf packs.

In November Guam was opened as an advanced base, which enabled submarines of the central Pacific force to average twenty-seven days in the operational areas instead of twenty-three days. With the narrowing of the Japanese perimeter by the advance of the American forces, shipping was virtually confined to Japanese waters and to the East China and Yellow Seas: after the capture of the Philippines, the operations of the central Pacific submarines were concentrated off Japan itself. Merchant ship losses fell off in December because there were so few Japanese ships left, but the *Flasher*, working in a pack with *Hawkbill* and *Becuna*, sank four tankers and two destroyers of 42,868 tons in the South China Sea, moving into first place in the tonnage stakes.

During the year nineteen American submarines had been lost. Of these, six were due to accidents of some sort and were nothing to do with the Japanese. *Tang* and *Tullibee* were sunk by their own circling torpedoes; *Seawolf* was lost through a mistake in identity by American anti-submarine forces; *Darter* was stranded and *Robalo* had a battery explosion. Six, and possibly two more, were sunk by Japanese air and surface anti-submarine forces, and mines probably claimed five. The average exchange rate for the year was forty-two merchant ships sunk for every U.S. submarine destroyed by the Japanese. No less than forty-one Japanese anti-submarine vessels were sunk during the year and the success of the American submarines was largely due to this mastery of the convoy escorts.

During 1944 the American submarines sank over five hundred ships of two and a half million tons. They had, however, been unable to exceed an average of one and a half ships each month for every submarine in the operational area, one attack in three proving successful. This was the same as in 1943 and the higher sinkings were due to the greater number of submarines operating. By the end of the year the Americans had 156 submarines working from bases closer to their areas than before, and so less time was wasted on passage. Although the American submarines were sinking less than the Germans at the height of the Battle of

220

the Atlantic, the Japanese mercantile marine was only a quarter of the size of the British, and so the losses were proportionally more effective.

Another million and a half tons of Japanese shipping were sunk by other forces, mostly carrier-borne and shore-based aircraft, and they had only two and three-quarter million tons left at the end of the year (see p. 226; fig. 23). As 3 million tons of shipping were required for Japanese civil needs alone, it was obvious that the end was near. The Japanese were very short of food; industry was running down and unable to produce the aircraft and munitions required because it could not get the raw materials; the operations of the armed forces were severely restricted by lack of oil; and there was insufficient iron to replace ships at more than a quarter of the rate at which they were being lost.

Whilst the American submarines were winning in the Pacific, ample numbers of British submarines had arrived to work in the Malacca Straits. Large targets were, however, scarce and only twenty-four ships of 48,000 tons were sunk during 1944. Much of their work was done with the gun, which they used to destroy a large number of small native craft working for the Japanese. They also laid twenty small minefields which claimed four victims. During the year they lost only two submarines and succeeded in sinking four small escort vessels.

By September 1944 there were twenty-six British submarines based at Trincomalee, in Ceylon, and this was more than could be profitably employed in the Malacca Straits. One flotilla was therefore sent to Western Australia to join the Americans at Fremantle. The British submarines were slower, of shorter endurance, without a good surface radar set and inferior to the American submarines for open sea work in the Pacific. On the other hand, their small size allowed them to work in shallow and confined waters and it was hoped that they would be of value in the final stage of the war.

In 1945 the sinkings by American submarines were under half a million tons, whereas aircraft and an intensive air minelaying

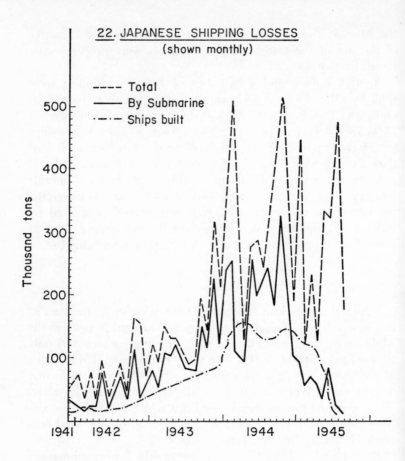

22. JAPANESE SHIPPING LOSSES
(shown monthly)

---- Total
—— By Submarine
·—·— Ships built

campaign in Japanese waters sank three times as much. From January onwards, traffic was progressively halted : not only were the Japanese very short of ships and escorts, but they had almost run out of fuel for them. The re-occupation of the Philippines made air operations over the South China Sea possible and this, combined with the work of the submarines, effectively cut communications with the south. Early in the year 'Loughlin's Loopers' were on patrol in the Formosa area when a convoy of seven tankers and five freighters with eight escorts left Japan for Singapore. They lost four ships in the Formosa Strait to 'Loughlin's Loopers' and the convoy put into Takao. Here it was attacked by U.S. carrier-borne aircraft, losing two more tankers and two freighters. Soon after sailing again, the convoy was diverted into

Hong Kong where it lost several more ships and escorts to air attack. The convoy, now reduced to two ships and four escorts, pressed on to the south, but one of the ships broke down. It was attacked again by a submarine off the coast of Malaya and an escort was hit and a single tanker with three escorts was all that reached Singapore. American air and submarine forces were able by now practically to deny the sea to the Japanese altogether.

The last cargo of oil got through to Japan from the south in March and the convoy route was stopped altogether during the month. Traffic routes were progressively abandoned until, by May, they were confined to the Yellow Sea, the Sea of Japan and the Inland Sea itself. In June in an attempt to stop even this traffic, nine submarines, using a new mine detector, penetrated through the barrier into the Sea of Japan and sank twenty-eight ships for the loss of one boat.

In the whole of 1945, the Americans lost eight submarines and the fate of two of these is unknown. The others fell to Japanese air and surface anti-submarine forces. Against this, thirty-nine new boats joined the Pacific fleet during the year. American submarines kept up their offensive against escorts and sank thirty-nine more frigates and submarine chasers, as well as two destroyers and a torpedo boat.

In 1945 the Americans had roughly the same number of submarines at sea as in 1944, but their rate of sinking fell to just over half a ship a month for every submarine on patrol. This was because targets were so scarce, which was an indication of the degree of control the Americans had established over the sea. During 1945 it had been the business of aircraft, which could attack ships in harbour and in shallow or landlocked waters, to finish the campaign. Well before the atomic bombs fell on Hiroshima and Nagasaki, Japan was hopelessly defeated by the cutting of her sea communications. Almost the whole Japanese merchant fleet was at the bottom of the sea. She had lost touch with her remaining outlying possessions, industry was at a standstill and her capacity to wage war had been drained away.

The Americans had used 288 individual submarines in the Pacific, but their highest operational strength at any one time did not exceed 156. In 1945 the British had thirty operational submarines in the Far East, but the Dutch strength was never higher than fifteen and the average more like half a dozen. Although conceived and trained entirely to attack warships, in which they were outstandingly successful, the U.S. submarine force gained an even greater victory in an unrestricted campaign against commerce after the German model. The main weapon of the American submarines was the torpedo, fired without warning, which sank over a thousand ships. Another seven hundred small vessels were sunk with the gun, but the mine laid by submarines was a comparatively unimportant weapon, causing under a dozen casualties.

The total number of ships and tonnages sunk by various types of ships and aircraft is shown in the table below. It can be seen that submarines sank well over half of the Japanese shipping casualties. Indeed, in the first two years of the campaign, they accounted for three-quarters of the Japanese shipping losses and, by the end of 1944, roughly two-thirds. Aircraft, which were their greatest rivals as commerce destroyers, did best right at the end of the war, after the victory had been won and in what can be described as the 'mopping up' phase. The total number of casualties inflicted by the British and Dutch submarines were some forty ships of 140,000 tons, which represented 2 per cent of the sinkings by submarines in the Pacific.

Agency	Number of ships sunk (excluding small craft)	Tonnage
Submarines	1,150	4,861,000
Carrier-borne aircraft	359	1,453,000
Shore-based aircraft	390	1,293,000
Mines	210	818,000
Marine casualties	116	353,000
Ships	16	86,000
Unknown	16	33,000

During the Second World War, the German U-boat campaign in the Atlantic and all other areas sank $14\frac{1}{2}$ million tons of shipping, or three times as much as the Americans in the Pacific. In their peak month of November 1942, they sank 106 ships of 636,000 tons, or nearly twice as much as the Americans in their peak month in October 1944, which was 68 ships of 328,000 tons. But such comparisons, although obviously of interest, are liable to be misleading. The Japanese shipping target was very much smaller: there were twice as many German U-boats at the end of the war as American submarines, and the German campaign lasted six years instead of under four years. On the other hand, the Germans had lost 250 U-boats by the time they were defeated in May 1943, whereas the Americans only lost 52 altogether. At the end, the German exchange rate had fallen to under one merchant ship sunk for every U-boat destroyed, whereas the American exchange rate in 1944 was forty-two merchant ships sunk for every submarine destroyed; and this is the key to their success.

It would be quite a false conclusion to assume that the American victory was due solely to the poor anti-submarine performance of the Japanese. Most of their escorts had Asdics, although they were only beginning to fit radar and search receivers in ships and aircraft by the autumn of 1944. They lacked tactical persistence, but they fought hard to defend their convoys. Their countermeasures were probably a good deal better than the German or Italian anti-submarine measures in the Mediterranean, and as good as the British in the early years of the Second World War. Although slow in starting a convoy system, it was in full operation in 1944, in which year they were defeated. Furthermore they used air escort of convoys extensively and they replaced over 3 million tons of shipping by new construction. They employed over 150 escorts which, when compared to the amount of shipping to be escorted, was relatively as large a force as the British had in the Atlantic.

The true reason for the victory of the American submarine campaign was their technical superiority over the Japanese. The splendid design and efficiency of the American submarine was of great importance, in spite of the poor performance of their torpedoes in the first eighteen months. Paramount, however, was their equipment with radar, an advantage which the German U-boats not only lacked but had to fight against from 1941 onwards. The American submarines, with their high speed and heavier torpedo armament and working in wolf packs, were superior to the German U-boats as commerce destroyers and this was a more important reason for their success than the inferior Japanese anti-submarine measures.

The superiority of the American submarines showed itself by their victory over the Japanese escorts. The American submarines sank six times as many anti-submarine vessels as the escorts sank submarines; in an action between a Japanese escort group round a convoy and a pack of American submarines, the submarines generally won. Obviously, if a convoy system is to succeed, the reverse must be the case and this is the essential difference between the German and American campaigns. The passive advantage of convoy was, furthermore, reduced in the Far East. The

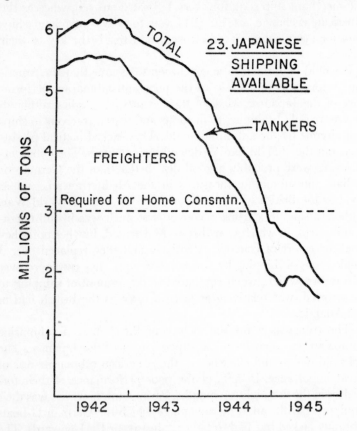

convoys were certainly harder to find than single ships, but were much more easily detected than in the Battle of the Atlantic. Radar virtually turned night into day for the American submarines, but night remained night for the Japanese. Geography also favoured the submarines: the operational area was smaller than in the Atlantic and there were a number of defiles through which shipping was forced to pass, which made dispersion difficult. The American submarines in wolf packs were therefore able

226

to intercept a higher proportion of the traffic than the Germans in the Atlantic.

In the Pacific, for the first time in history, a campaign of attrition, directed against commerce, succeeded. In the German U-boat campaigns in both world wars, the submarines had been defeated in the end and, indeed, no *guerre de course* had ever been decisive in the past. The campaign in the Pacific is of extreme interest, as it is the only example of the final phase : it illustrates that, once shipping losses pass a certain point, the total tonnage falls catastrophically; this, in its turn, reacts on the replacement programme and in a very short time the end is in sight. It shows how near Great Britain came to defeat in both world wars.

The campaign was also unique in that the *guerre de course* had been employed by the stronger sea power. In the past it had always been the weapon of the weaker navy. It can be argued that it was used only in areas where the Americans did not control the sea, which is true. Nevertheless, this was so because they could not intervene in any other way. Shore-based aircraft were out of range and carrier-borne air attacks, although possible, could be only raids or forays. It was only submarines that were capable of the sustained effort in enemy waters that was essential.

The American submarine campaign against commerce was probably the most important single factor in the defeat of Japan and at least of equal value to the great carrier and amphibious drive across the Pacific. Furthermore, it achieved its results with a comparatively small effort. At the end of the war the submarines constituted only 2 per cent of the American forces in the Pacific, and this effort was considerably less than the Germans put into the U-boats. The Americans won in the Pacific by waging an unrestricted campaign against sea communications, which weakened Japan to an extent which enabled an amphibious drive supported by carrier-borne air power to succeed. The campaign gave final proof that a *guerre de course* can win against a power dependent on the sea and that the submarine can be a decisive weapon of war in the hands of the stronger naval power as well as the weaker.

XIII

The German Development of the U-Boat 1943-45

In May 1943, when the German U-boats were withdrawn from the Atlantic, it was obvious to Admiral Doenitz that they could not win the war. The types then in service were quite unable to face the radar which had been fitted extensively in both ships and aircraft. They could not continue their wolf pack tactics on the surface and they saw no other way to defeat the convoy system. Moreover, the output of the American shipyards was now so great that the U-boats would have to sink more than twice the tonnage that they had destroyed in the record-breaking year of 1942. To clinch the matter, U-boats were being sunk at such a rate that their numbers were more likely to contract than expand.

What had happened was that the U-boat had been driven from the surface of the sea. The measures that had done this were not truly anti-submarine in character : they were directed against U-boats on the surface and had stopped the U-boats from operating as submersible torpedo boats. The only true anti-submarine measure capable of destroying a submerged U-boat was still the Asdic and its partner, the depth charge. Although fitted in many more ships and better maintained and operated than before, this combination had not improved technically very much since the beginning of the war. The obvious way for the U-boats to regain their effectiveness was, therefore, to return to their true element and work submerged all the time. If they could increase their mobility substantially when submerged, then they would be able not only to operate in face of radar but again to concentrate against the convoys. Moreover, they would have a greater chance to shake off escorts fitted with Asdics, which had a comparatively short detection range.

Not only were these ideas sound in theory but there were developments which indicated that there was a distinct possibility that they could be put into practice. Since 1937 a German scientist and engineer, Dr. H. Walther, had been working on a new

228

system for the submerged propulsion of submarines. This new system used Ingolin, which is a form of highly concentrated hydrogen peroxide. A small experimental boat had already run some preliminary trials and an 'Atlantic' type had been authorized. This system offered an enormous increase in mobility submerged, so making a 'true' submarine possible.

Ingolin is a liquid which is not only the most compact way to carry oxygen, which it gives up on being passed over a catalyst, but is a fuel, as this process involves the generation of heat. The oxygen, when released from the Ingolin, is burnt with a sulphur-free fuel, more water is injected generating more steam which is then passed through turbines to drive the submarine. The exhaust, composed of steam and carbon dioxide, the one condensing and the other dissolving in the sea, leaves no track. Ingolin, however, had the disadvantage that it was dangerous to handle and about ten times as expensive as oil fuel.

Preliminary designs showed that it would be possible to carry enough Ingolin to give some thirty-five times the energy that could be stored in an electric battery. This would propel a totally submerged submarine at 25 knots for three hours or more, and at lower speeds for very much longer. Such a submarine would not only have a greater submerged speed than the present type of U-boat had on the surface, but it would be for long enough to allow a pack to concentrate against a convoy without surfacing. Subsequently it would be able to withdraw at a speed at which few escorts could follow and be almost immune to counter attack. These boats, therefore, offered an opportunity to regain the initiative in the Atlantic and achieve sinking rates which would compete even with the American shipbuilding programme. In July 1943, therefore, Admiral Doenitz proposed that they should be mass-produced at once. Dr. Walther was, however, by no means ready and he feared that the boats could not become available for operations until 1946 at the earliest.

Germany was already on the defensive everywhere, and by 1946 the Allies would probably have invaded Europe and the end would have been in sight. The Walther submarine could not, therefore, be produced in quantity in time to win the war. The problem was to try to restore the technical initiative in the Battle of the Atlantic much earlier. The German submarine designers pointed out that with complete re-design they could substantially improve the submerged performance of a U-boat with the con-

229

ventional diesel and electric propulsion systems. The submarine, since the early years of the century, had given priority to surface performance and it had become, in fact, a torpedo boat which had the property of disappearing : once dived, it was therefore extremely slow, with a short endurance. If absolute priority were to be given to submerged performance at the expense of surface characteristics, a substantial improvement could be expected. The new type was to have a new form of streamlined hull of over double the tonnage and was to carry twice the normal weight of battery, which was to be of a new design with a higher capacity. The price of these advances was that they would have to sacrifice speed and seakeeping qualities on the surface. It was expected that a submerged speed of 18 knots for over an hour could be obtained, and 8 knots for the best part of twenty-four hours. This performance, although nowhere near that of the Walther boat, was a great advance over the present U-boats, whose maximum speed submerged was only 8 knots for one hour. It should make it possible to concentrate and attack slow convoys, whose speed was not expected to increase in the intervening period, without surfacing. Even if they could not claim to be able to run away from escorts, they would be almost impossible to damage with the slow-sinking depth charge when going at their full speed.

What was important was that these boats could be produced much more quickly than the Walther type, as they involved no new principles and were only a re-arrangement of well-tried existing systems. They would give a breathing-space until the revolutionary new Walther submarines could be brought into service. A smaller version for use in the Mediterranean and North Sea, but with a lesser performance all round, was also designed. These new boats were designated the types XXI and XXIII and a building programme was approved in July 1943. The first type XXI was to be completed in the spring of 1944. It was hoped, without waiting for a prototype to do trials and using a new prefabrication system, to mass-produce forty boats a month by the autumn of 1944.

German policy was now, therefore, to go all out for the Walther submarine but, as this would take a long time, to produce the types

XXI and XXIII as an interim measure. So much for new construction, but there was also the problem of what to do with the existing four hundred U-boats in the intervening period. To continue operations against Atlantic convoys was bound to bring very heavy casualties without much to show for it. To withdraw from the fight altogether would release huge naval and air forces for other purposes, and this would probably lead to the stepping-up of the bombing of Germany and the more rapid provision of amphibious forces for the invasion of Europe. Furthermore, if the Allies were able to discontinue the convoy system, this would increase the carrying power of their merchant fleets. It would, in any case, be disastrous, especially to morale, to withdraw the U-boats from operations altogether : it was essential also to keep in touch with enemy anti-submarine developments and to train crews for the new types which had been laid down. The Germans decided, therefore, to continue the struggle, even if it did mean heavy casualties, and the building of the 250 old-fashioned U-boats already under construction was stepped up to a rate of thirty boats a month.

It was still expected that a considerable tonnage of Allied and neutral shipping could be sunk by exploiting the distant areas and the weakest points of the convoy system. The four hundred-odd U-boats of the older types struggled on for the remaining two years of the war and succeeded in sinking another 337 ships of 1,860,000 tons. This was, however, less than half the size of the British shipbuilding programme, without including American construction which was seven or eight times as much. The Allied merchant fleets, therefore, steadily increased in size, whilst the Germans lost another 534 U-boats which was over twice as many as had been destroyed up to the time of their defeat in the Atlantic in May 1943. This was a heavy price to pay and one and a half U-boats were destroyed for each merchant ship they managed to sink. The strategic and economic aspects of this period, however, are not really significant. It is in the technical struggle to improve the operational efficiency of the older U-boats that the greater interest lies.

In the middle of 1943, Allied aircraft began to use the new ten-centimetre radar sets which the German search receivers could not pick up : casualties in the Bay of Biscay, therefore, began to rise. The U-boats had already been ordered to stay submerged as much as possible but this increased the time on passage and it

231

was taking as long as ten days to get out into the Atlantic. In May 1943, *U441* was converted to a trap for aircraft by arming her with two four-barrelled 20-mm and one 37-mm anti-aircraft guns. She was intended to patrol the Bay in the hope that the cumbersome anti-submarine aircraft would attack her and be shot down in the process. On 24 May she succeeded in destroying a Sunderland flying-boat, but she was damaged too and had to return to base. Nevertheless her success stimulated the fitting of anti-aircraft guns to the standard operational U-boats, in the hope that they would be able to shoot their way out of the Bay on the surface.

In June, the U-boats found that it was three times as safe to cross the Bay in groups so as to obtain mutual support. The inherent flexibility and mobility of aircraft was, however, soon used to shadow the groups until reinforcements arrived, and then make a co-ordinated attack. In an action between five U-boats and four aircraft in June, two of the U-boats were damaged and had to return to base. In this month also, British surface anti-submarine groups were sent to the approaches to the Bay to co-operate with the aircraft and break up the U-boat formations. At the end of July a group of three U-boats was wiped out by four aircraft assisted by a surface support group. During July and the first few days of August, eighty-six U-boats had attempted to cross the Bay and they succeeded in shooting down fourteen aircraft. Nevertheless, twenty U-boats were sunk and seven others were damaged and had to turn back and, early in August, they abandoned the policy of fighting their way out on the surface. This failure was a forgone conclusion: a submarine that fights with anti-aircraft guns loses its greatest asset of invisibility and such a policy is bound to fail in the end. Anti-aircraft guns were, however, retained in U-boats to be used on occasions when it was essential to stay on the surface.

The U-boats now put their faith in a new search receiver which was expected to be available at the end of August, and until then all sailings were suspended. It was hoped that it would be able to pick up the new enemy radar but, of course, however good the new search receiver proved to be, the U-boats would still be forced to dive on the approach of an aircraft. An efficient search receiver would certainly decrease losses but it would not entirely restore surface mobility.

At the end of August another new device with which to counter attack escorts was expected to be in service. This was the long-awaited acoustic homing torpedo. Attack on escort vessels with the ordinary straight-running torpedo had, of course, always been possible. Indeed, in the four years up to the introduction of the homing torpedo, forty-two anti-submarine vessels had been sunk in this way. Such targets were, however, small, of shallow draught and able to take rapid avoiding action, and a miss generally resulted in a dangerous counter attack with depth charges. The acoustic homing torpedo, which was attracted by the noise of the escort's propellers, was expected to make a hit certain on these difficult targets, even if avoiding action was attempted.

In September, with all three of these new devices, the U-boats felt able to return to the attack on Atlantic convoys. With the new search receivers they should be warned of the approach of radar-fitted ships and aircraft; with a heavy anti-aircraft armament it should be possible to hold off aircraft whilst they used their surface mobility, and with acoustic torpedoes they should be able to protect themselves against attack by Asdic-fitted escorts. In a period of five days in September, nineteen U-boats attacked convoys ONS18 and ON202 and succeeded in sinking three escorts and damaging another. Nevertheless, only six merchant ships were sunk for the loss of three U-boats destroyed and three more damaged.

The acoustic torpedo came as no surprise to the British Admiralty : they had, in fact, been expecting it for some time and had already devised a counter measure. This was a simple device towed astern of escorts which made a loud noise and decoyed the torpedoes away from the ship. The 'foxer', as it was called, was at once distributed and, for the rest of the war, the German results against escorts were little higher than they had been before the introduction of the acoustic torpedo. This weapon was, therefore, defeated very quickly by the British and is a good example of the value of technical initiative.

The Germans tried a number of other devices to restore the efficiency of the U-boats. They fitted some anti-aircraft radar sets, but these were not very efficient and, in any case, they were rightly afraid that the British would home on to them. They tried an anti-radar coating and also an anti-Asdic coating for the U-boats, but again without much success. Finally they produced a decoy on which they hoped the Asdic-fitted escorts would direct their attacks instead of on the U-boats. In general the British were able to compete with all these measures and hold their technical lead.

The Germans continued to suffer losses from aircraft and wrongly attributed this to a defect in their new search receivers, believing that the British aircraft could home on to them. They therefore stopped using these instruments and wasted much time trying to remedy this non-existent trouble. The U-boats were soon decisively defeated in their renewed attacks on convoys. In October, eighteen U-boats attacked SC143 which had twelve escorts which included a support group. They succeeded in sinking only one escort and one merchant ship for the loss of three U-boats. In a battle around ON206 and ONS20, six U-boats were lost and only one merchant ship was sunk. The campaign of the U-boats in distant waters was eventually defeated by the extension of convoy and the United States Escort Carrier groups in the central Atlantic, whose aircraft sank several U-tankers and made it very difficult to fuel.

In the middle of 1943 the Germans had started work on a more fundamental solution of their difficulties. They decided to develop a breathing-tube or schnorkel so that they could use their diesel engines submerged. With this schnorkel they would be able to recharge their batteries without surfacing or, alternatively, make a steady submerged passage at about 5 knots. This device took some time to perfect and it was not ready for fitting until the spring of 1944.

The schnorkel proved a great advance and the casualties from air attacks were soon more than halved. On 1 June the Germans decided that schnorkel was essential for operations and that they would not use U-boats without it in the Atlantic again. The schnorkel was a very small radar target compared with a U-boat on the surface and was seldom detected. Aircraft were, therefore, deprived of their best detecting device. The schnorkel itself was much larger, however, than a periscope and it was liable to emit smoke, so the U-boats could still be sighted and attacked by aircraft. The price of the greater safety conferred by the schnorkel was a considerable loss of mobility : time on passage was more than doubled and it was seldom possible to concentrate against convoys.

The schnorkel made it possible for the U-boats to operate again in coastal waters and the last phase of the German U-boat campaign took this form. In spite of radar fitted in ships, in aircraft and ashore, the U-boats patrolled in the Channel, the Irish Sea and off the east coasts of Great Britain. In these confined waters it was easier to locate targets and their low mobility was not such a great disadvantage. In March 1945, the escort vessels were having difficulty because wrecks and tiderips in coastal waters gave false echoes and confused their Asdics; radar seldom picked up a U-boat at all. Aircraft, the winners of the 1943 campaign in the Battle of the Atlantic, were reduced to the limited role of preventing the U-boats from surfacing : as a U-boat killer they had lost their potency. Furthermore, the German U-boats worked independently and so hardly used their radio at all. The Admiralty tracking-room had, therefore, very little material on which to work, so there was little intelligence of U-boat movements. The Allies had cause for worry but the U-boats had their troubles too. Aircraft made it hazardous for them to use their schnorkels and recharge their batteries. Having lost their surface mobility they had also lost their protection against Asdics, so the escorts, in spite of their difficulties, continued to take a heavy toll. Although Asdics had not been improved to any extent, anti-submarine weapons had taken a large step forward. In a depth charge attack contact had always been lost before the ship ran over the top of the submarine, so the pattern had to be dropped blind. In the new system, the charges were thrown ahead whilst the ship was still in contact, and the new projectiles sank faster, making it harder for the U-boat to evade the attack. The Allies concentrated the formidable force of 426 escorts and 420 anti-submarine aircraft in these confined waters and they sank twenty-nine U-boats. The inshore campaign was, therefore, decisively defeated by April 1945.

On 4 May 1945 the U-boats were ordered to cease operations, and the second attempt in thirty years to disrupt British seaborne trade finally came to an end. One hundred and fifty-six U-boats surrendered to the Allies and 221 scuttled themselves. The surrender came just as the new types XXI and XXIII were becoming available in quantity. A few type XXIII had, in fact, been operational since February : *U2336* penetrated the Firth of Forth and sank two ships off May Island and, out of the six patrols made by them altogether, all returned safely. On 30 April the first type XXI, *U2311*, sailed from Bergen for operations, but the end came before she could achieve anything. She easily evaded a British hunting group by using her submerged speed, and claims to have made an undetected dummy attack, after the cessation of hostilities, on an escorted British cruiser. The completion of these boats had been much delayed by the bombing of Germany, and their trials and working up by the mining of the Baltic by British aircraft. Nevertheless, they completed 181 of the new types before the end of the war and were producing them at the rate of twenty-six a month.

The type XXI (see p. 238; fig. 24) proved a very considerable technical success and were an immense advance on the schnorkel-fitted types VII and IX. They made over 17 knots submerged on trials and had an endurance of sixty hours at 6 knots. They had a much improved schnorkel, better hydrophones and could dive deeper than the older types. Furthermore, the type XXI proved very nearly silent at $5\frac{1}{2}$ knots and it could fire its torpedoes, whilst dived deep, with the aid of hydrophones. They had a remarkable strategic endurance and could patrol for three weeks off Capetown from Germany and return without refuelling.

It is difficult to speculate on what the final result would have been in a contest between a large number of type XXI U-boats and the highly efficient British anti-submarine forces which existed at the end of the war. Casualties from aircraft would probably have continued to be low and their high underwater speed would have helped them to evade anti-submarine patrols. They would, therefore, have been able to operate close in to the British Isles without heavy casualties. In coastal waters they should have been able to find the convoys without surfacing and close them to effective range. They had six torpedo tubes and rapid reloading gear, and expected to be able to keep up with a convoy submerged while they discharged three salvos in quick succession. They could in this way have been expected to do four times as much damage to a convoy as a schnorkelling type VII or IX. After an attack they had a very good chance to shake off asdic-fitted vessels by using their high speed submerged. The British Admiralty were right to be apprehensive, but whether the type XXI could have raised the merchant ship casualties sufficiently to compete with the gigantic American shipbuilding programme must remain an open question.

*   *   *

236

The Germans had found it possible to order a hundred of an operational type of Walther submarine (see p. 238; fig. 24) in the spring of 1944, but by the end of the war they were still very much in the trial stage and only four small Walther boats had been completed. The operational Walther boats would have been able to do far better than the type XXI. Their speed would have made it possible to close any convoy even from right astern. The type XXVI, as the operational Walther boat was called, was to have had ten torpedo tubes and it would have been able to discharge all of them in a single attack on a convoy. Subsequently the type XXVI could withdraw at a speed at which most escorts would not be able to follow at all, and even the fastest would fall astern in rough weather. The type XXVI could, in any case, go faster than escorts could operate their Asdics or have any chance of success with even the new ahead-thrown weapons. The Walther boat, however, had a limitation and that was its short endurance on Ingolin, the stowage of which would be insufficient to take them to their patrol area : they had therefore to carry diesel and electric propulsion systems to give them strategic mobility. The Walther boat had, therefore, three systems of propulsion; well over half the submarine was taken up with machinery and its schnorkelling performance was inferior to the type XXI and no better than the type VII. It was only a 'true' submarine when using Ingolin and on passage it would be as slow and as vulnerable as the older boats. Nevertheless the Walther submarine, which was well on the way to becoming a practicable warship, promised to compete with most of the existing anti-submarine measures. Nothing came to light in immediate post-war research to provide a counter to their threat to convoys. Working in the approaches to the British Isles, they would have stood a good chance of competing with even the American shipbuilding programme.

In this last chapter dealing with the Second World War, it is appropriate to sum up the effect of the submarine on sea power. It varied widely from the outstanding success of the Americans in the Pacific to the comparative ineffectiveness of the Italians in the Mediterranean. It was again as a commerce raider that it achieved its best results but, whereas the Americans won their

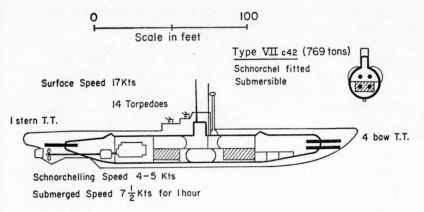

Scale in feet

0 — 100

Type VII c42 (769 tons)
Schnorchel fitted
Submersible

Surface Speed 17 Kts

14 Torpedoes

I stern T.T.

4 bow T.T.

Schnorchelling Speed 4−5 Kts
Submerged Speed 7½ Kts for I hour

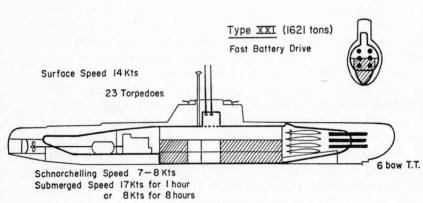

Type XXI (1621 tons)

Fast Battery Drive

Surface Speed 14 Kts

23 Torpedoes

6 bow T.T.

Schnorchelling Speed 7−8 Kts
Submerged Speed 17 Kts for I hour
or 8 Kts for 8 hours

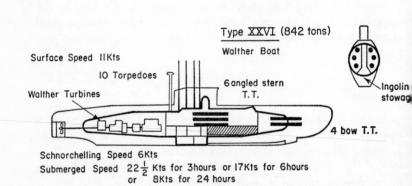

Type XXVI (842 tons)

Walther Boat

Surface Speed II Kts

10 Torpedoes

6 angled stern T.T.

Walther Turbines

Ingolin stowage

4 bow T.T.

Schnorchelling Speed 6 Kts
Submerged Speed 22½ Kts for 3 hours or 17 Kts for 6 hours
or 8 Kts for 24 hours

24. GERMAN U−BOAT DEVELOPMENT

campaign in the Far East, the Germans were defeated in the Atlantic. This was in spite of the fact that the Germans put four times the effort into the campaign that they had in the First World War and actually sank a greater tonnage. The reasons why the Americans won and the Germans failed have already been discussed and will not all be repeated. Convoy was again the basic strategy that defeated the U-boats, but it did not save the Japanese. Convoy always proved better than independent sailing but, unless the escorts could win the battles round them, the strategy would fail. This was the difference between the campaigns in the Atlantic and the Pacific and it was technical superiority, especially in radar and radio warfare, which was the common factor in the victories of the British anti-submarine forces and the American submarines. The American victory in the Pacific proved that the *guerre de course* could be decisive but, even if it had not, the German campaign came so near to winning, and needed such a huge effort to defeat it, that it again showed itself to be a potentially decisive weapon of sea power.

As a warship used for military purposes, the submarine enhanced its reputation during the Second World War. Submarines were able to compete in areas completely dominated by enemy air power as well as by superior surface forces. The submarine showed itself to be a flexible weapon able to carry out many functions, such as reconnaissance, minelaying, store-carrying and making small landings, in areas dominated by the enemy air and surface forces and which could not have been done in any other way. Submarines were often drawn into military operations, such as the many attempts to counter amphibious attacks, and were used in co-operation with surface fleets. But the submarine of the Second World War was not very mobile and, although it often proved useful, it was not in these ways that it achieved its most important results in the military sphere.

The Americans, who used their submarines mainly as commerce raiders, won an outstanding victory against warships and sank a third of the Japanese Navy. The Germans, also deployed mainly against commerce, sank more British warships than all the other types of ship and aircraft put together. The British in the Mediterranean, working like commerce raiders but against the supply line of an army, exercised an important effect which was military in character. All these results were achieved by using

239

submarines over a long period as weapons of attrition in enemy waters where the enemy had to use the sea. It was when the submarine was used in this way that it proved of most value against warships as well as against commerce.

Few will question that, both as a commerce raider and against warships, the submarine had a greater effect on sea power than in the First World War. Aircraft, operated from aircraft carriers or from ashore, became the new arbiters of sea power. Submarines undoubtedly came next and exercised a greater influence than battlefleets, although in a very different way and for different reasons than their protagonists at the turn of the century thought that they would. Although the U-boats in the Battle of the Atlantic were defeated and it could be held that the American submarines would not have succeeded against British anti-submarine measures, the German development of the submarine in the last two years of the war rendered such questions academic. When the war ended, the whole issue was back in the melting-pot. The lessons of history learnt in two world wars were unlikely to help in the future. The submarine seemed to be entering a new era in which it was likely to be again in the ascendancy.

XIV

Development Since the Second World War

At the end of the war, it was clear that naval warfare, and so the composition of fleets, was going to change radically. The eclipse of the battleship and its replacement by carrier-borne aircraft had hardly been digested when atomic weapons presaged a revolution in the nature of war itself. Early thought was directed to the investigation of the effect of atom bombs on maritime warfare waged in the conventional manner. It was thought that they would exert their greatest effect by the destruction of dockyards and ports and everything upon which a navy or merchant fleet depended: ships at sea were not believed to be sufficiently important to warrant the expenditure of so scarce and expensive a weapon. If, however, nuclear weapons came to be used at sea their effect could probably be limited by a greater dispersion of fleets or convoys. In the period immediately following the war, therefore, when no potential adversary possessed nuclear weapons, the study of naval warfare at sea continued with little alteration.

The British realized that it was only the surface pack tactics of the German U-boats that they had defeated in the Battle of the Atlantic and that they were far from any effective countermeasure to the highspeed true submarine of the future. They were as anxious as they had been after the First World War to find an answer, and anti-submarine matters were given the highest priority. Although British submarines had done very well in the war and had achieved substantial results, it was realized that they had not had the stiff opposition that the U-boats had encountered in the Atlantic. At the same time, British anti-submarine circles tended to blame the submarine branch for failing to predict the German night surface pack tactics which had so nearly proved fatal. Moreover they had given no warning of the German technical developments such as the schnorkel or high submerged speed. To compete with these surprises and to give the anti-submarine forces some training to meet the type XXI, a few S-boats had had to be disarmed and streamlined to give the best underwater speed, which was only 12 knots: other submarines had to be fitted with dummy schnorkels.

It would be quite wrong to blame the British submarine service entirely for these failures: they were busy fighting a different kind of opposition which needed different measures to compete with it. Nevertheless, the British Navy were determined to be better warned of what to expect in the future. Their policy for submarines became now, first and foremost, to ensure that their anti-submarine measures had the most modern opposition against which to develop counter measures. British submarines were, therefore, not simply to be 'clockwork mice' on which the ships could practise using their Asdics, as in the past, but were to keep in the lead in submarine development and tactics. Although this was a similar policy to that of 1901, when the British first adopted the submarine, the emphasis on modernity and taking the lead in their development was much stronger and this was obviously very acceptable to the submarine branch. The policy also fitted in with those who saw that, with the tremendous power of nuclear weapons against ships, it was probable that in the distant future the submarine would be better able to compete than anything else.

At the end of the war the British scrapped forty-five old and worn-out submarines and cancelled another fifty which were building, leaving a fleet of just under a hundred. They decided to complete sixteen of the A class which had been designed for the Pacific and were submersibles with a high surface speed. These boats were a great improvement on the older British types, but it was clear that they could not be more than a stop-gap until something like the German type XXI could replace them. A type XXI German U-boat, *U2518*, was put into commission for experiments and proper schnorkels, or snorts as they were called, were fitted to the whole British submarine fleet during the next few years. On completion of trials with *U2518*, it was decided to lengthen a number of the T class to obtain a similar performance and later to lay down a new British class based on the type XXI. Both these types were given radar which could be used with a periscopic aerial from submerged and so it was hoped to combine the submerged mobility of the type XXI with the detection equipment which had proved so successful for finding targets in the Pacific.

One of the small Walther boats, *U1407*, fell intact into British hands and they decided to refit her and run trials. At the same time, two larger submarines driven by hydrogen peroxide, but of a British design, were authorized. The *Explorer* and *Excalibur*, as they were named, were unarmed experimental vehicles and it was not intended to produce an operational type driven by hydrogen peroxide until their trials were complete. The experiments were thorough but took a long time. The *Meteorite*, as *U1407* was renamed, ran trials in 1949, but the *Explorer* was not accepted for service until ten years after the war.

British post-war submarine design, although the techniques and methods of construction were their own, was therefore based almost entirely on German ideas. Concern about how to counter the submarine of the future was so great that attack on enemy submarines was also made the primary operational task of British submarines. British submarines had sunk forty German, Italian and Japanese U-boats during the war and had done this as a sideline. The vast majority were sunk whilst they were on the surface, and this was unlikely to occur in the future, but two U-boats sunk at the end of the war had been submerged and schnorkelling at the time. It was confidently believed that the submarine had a future in this role, especially if it gave its whole attention to it, and that it would be an important addition to the British anti-submarine armoury. The necessary characteristics were worked into the converted T class and this new function was kept well in mind during the design of the new 'Porpoise' type. Both were given much improved acoustic detection gear and the new boats were designed to be very silent. The original intention was to use these submarines offensively against enemy submarines, as it was in enemy waters that most of the U-boats had been destroyed by Allied submarines during the war.

At the end of the war, the Americans scrapped over seventy of their more elderly submarines and cancelled another ninety-two of those building, leaving just under two hundred of the fleet type. They ran trials with German U-boats, notably *U2351*, which was another type XXI. In the same way, but independently of the British, the Americans produced what was known as a 'Guppy' conversion of the fleet type submarine to improve its underwater speed, and subsequently built the new 'Tang' class which was the American version of the type XXI. Although they fitted a number of their fleet submarines with 'snorkel', as they spelt it, they did not fit their whole fleet and did not make any large-scale experiments with hydrogen peroxide. They converted some of their submarines to carry troops and cargo and others to what they called 'killer' submarines or anti-submarine submarines. But here their policy was different from the British, as they intended to use them in co-operation with other anti-submarine forces in their own waters.

The American post-war navy was based on the aircraft carrier whose aircraft were armed with the atomic bomb. They conceived the new strategy of commanding the sea by a massive nuclear attack on the enemy air and naval bases, and the function of all other units of the fleet was to protect the carriers whilst they launched their strikes. Two altogether new types of submarines were converted from the fleet type to co-operate in this general strategy. In carrier operations it had been found necessary to push the radar screen well out in specially fitted destroyers or pickets. This proved dangerous and a large number of picket destroyers was sunk in the Pacific towards the end of the war. It was believed that submarines, which would be able to dive before they could be attacked by aircraft, would be more suitable for this task, especially when the opposition was strong. The first of these new submarine conversions was therefore designed to act as a radar picket. The second new type of conversion was to take part in the nuclear strike itself and were the first submarines to be armed with missiles. The 'Regulus' missile was similar to the German V1, but with a nuclear warhead. It was designed to attack shore targets several hundred miles inland. The original arrangement was primitive by modern standards: the submarine carried only one of these missiles in a hangar and had to surface to launch it. Nevertheless the importance of the submarine as a warship was immensely enhanced by this development. The best that any submarine had been able to do in the past was to sink ships, whereas the missile submarine could destroy land targets, such as a complete naval base.

The Russians ended the war with between one and two hundred submarines and in the post-war years built up their numbers steadily until by 1950 they had about three hundred and fifty. Several of the type XXI had been handed over to Russia, and this large building programme was embarked upon with full knowledge of the latest German developments. Coupled with the political break between the East and the West, it seriously alarmed the British and Americans who were well aware that the Germans had started the war with a fraction of this number of submarines.

The existence of this modern submarine fleet, nearly as large as the Germans had possessed at the end of the war, was taken as a threat to sea communications in general and as showing an intention to renew the Battle of the Atlantic. The function of the Russian Navy was, however, still primarily the defence of the homeland and it is doubtful if this programme was intended for anything but defence, or, at most, an attack on the communications of the American Army in Europe. Many of the Russian submarines were of a small coastal type, and they were split into four separate fleets in the Far North, the Baltic, the Black Sea and the Far East. It seems more likely that they had decided to extend their defence to seawards to try to keep the American aircraft carriers at a distance, and it was this role which stimulated the building of so large a number of submarines. This expansion of the Russian submarine fleet gave impetus to the policy of allotting an anti-submarine role to British and American submarines.

The American development in the immediate post-war years, when they visualized using the submarine for many purposes, was original and prolific. But all these advances were to be dwarfed by their decision to develop nuclear power to propel submarines. The nuclear submarine uses a reactor to produce heat from which steam is generated to drive turbines. No contact with the atmosphere is necessary and there is no exhaust. This source of energy promised not only to give a completely submerged submarine an unlimited endurance but to give it at high speed. If the old-fashioned U-boat's overall submerged performance is represented by m, then the type XXI would be 10m., the Walther boat 40m. and the nuclear submarine 5,000m. The advent of nuclear power for submarines was, therefore, an immense advance, probably as great as the step from T.N.T. to nuclear explosives.

Oddly enough, nuclear power has not proved a very great advance for propelling ships. It does not at present show any improvement over conventional machinery in its power-weight ratio or any saving in the space it occupies: moreover, it is far more expensive. To a ship, therefore, it does not promise any great increase in speed. It offers almost unlimited endurance, but this is at a price that is uneconomical for merchant ships and of marginal military value for surface warships. In a submerged submarine, because of the laws governing hull resistance and wave-making, it is possible to reach the same speed as a surface vessel of the same tonnage with roughly half the power. In a submarine, therefore, nuclear power does offer a considerable increase in speed, and the endurance, because it is attainable totally submerged, is a gigantic improvement. Thus it is in the submarine that nuclear power offers the most spectacular results. As a warship, the development of the submarine takes a huge step forward, whilst that of the surface ship remains practically stationary.

The Americans completed their first nuclear submarine, the *Nautilus*, in 1954 and she proved a complete success. She was a large boat of 3,180 tons with a speed in excess of 20 knots and was armed with some twenty conventional torpedoes. The *Nautilus* was followed by a number of the Skate class which were similar but smaller. In 1956 they laid down the *Triton*, a nuclear-propelled radar picket submarine of 5,500 tons which also had a high surface speed, and the *Halibut* which was able to carry several Regulus missiles but still had to surface to fire them. A little later they designed the *Tullibee*, a nuclear-propelled 'killer' submarine of more moderate dimensions.. The introduction of nuclear power did not, therefore, alter the roles of their submarines, but it enormously improved their capacity to carry them out.

Whilst they were building the *Nautilus*, the Americans laid down an experimental submarine called the *Albacore*. Her purpose was hydrodynamic research and she was only driven by electric batteries. She confirmed that the short, fat, streamlined shape with a single screw was the best. Thereafter, nuclear submarines were built to this hull form, resulting in a considerable increase of speed in the Skipjack class. The Americans now stopped the construction of conventional submarines altogether and by 1960 had fifteen nuclear boats with another fourteen building.

Probably the most important asset that nuclear power gives to a submarine is that, as it needs no contact with the atmosphere, it allows it to remain totally submerged permanently whilst at sea. Air purification equipment for the crew makes this perfectly possible for months on end. It never needs to surface or to use a snort and so it has become the 'true' submarine. The great ad-

H.M.S. *Walrus*, diesel-electric propulsion (fast battery drive)

H.M.S. *Excalibur*, hydrogen peroxide propulsion

H.M.S. *Dreadnought*, nuclear propulsion

The Seaborne Deterrent—a Polaris submarine on patrol

U.S.S. *George Washington*—the first Polaris submarine

A Polaris missile
fired by a
submerged
submarine

POLARIS
*Official U.S.
Navy
photographs*

vantage of this is, of course, that it has completely countered radar as a method of detection. By relying on its own acoustic detecting devices, a nuclear submarine can operate without raising anything above the surface at all. Nevertheless it can gain operational advantages by using a periscope, search receiver, or even radar, and it will have to raise an aerial to transmit on radio. The raising of anything above the surface may result in the submarine's detection by radar, but the use of any of these devices would be intermittent and present a very small target.

Nuclear power does not, however, give any immunity against detection by sonar or Asdics and the range of these devices may be assumed to be greater than in the last war. The fact that it is a true submarine is of no assistance against these active acoustic detectors and it can still be found when totally submerged. It can, however, always hear Asdic-fitted ships approaching at a greater range than that at which they can gain contact and, with its high speed, has an excellent chance to evade them. The nuclear submarine can also out-distance homing torpedoes and all but the fastest ships and its speed has made it almost impossible to destroy with depth charges or even more modern fast-sinking projectiles.

The speed of the nuclear submarine is not, in fact, much higher than can be obtained with hydrogen peroxide, but, of course, it can use high speed for very much longer. Nevertheless, it is considerably faster than diesel-propelled submarines used to be on the surface and is not far short of the speed of a fast frigate or destroyer. The average speed of merchant ships has increased by a few knots in the last twenty years, but the speed of the nuclear submarine gives it a greater margin over them than a surfaced submarine had in the Second World War. Its capacity to overtake or intercept merchant ships or convoys is therefore improved. When it is forced to reveal its presence by making an attack, the nuclear submarine can clear the area at high speed and ships or aircraft which arrive, even a short time afterwards, will have little chance to find it. Finally, the speed of the nuclear submarine on passage can be faster than before, resulting in a longer time in the operational area and a possibility of redeployment, such as in fleet operations or to oppose amphibious attacks, of an entirely different order from the past.

High speed is liable to make a noise and this opens up the possibility of passive acoustic counter measures which could make it dangerous for the nuclear submarine to use its mobility. The success that various nations have had in silencing nuclear submarines is not, of course, published and will vary according to the amount of research they had put into it. Immense strides were made in silencing submarines in the Second World War and there does not seem to be any fundamental reason why passive acoustic detectors should unduly handicap the nuclear submarine.

The endurance conferred by nuclear power is for practical purposes unlimited and high speed can be used without decreasing the radius of action. The endurance is, in fact, greater than the largest conventionally-propelled ship afloat and this was emphasized in 1960, when the U.S.S. *Triton* circumnavigated the globe totally submerged. The nuclear submarine can, therefore, cruise to any part of the world without intermediate bases, supply ships or U-tankers, and can, if it wishes, do so at high speed. High speed does ultimately decrease the life of the reactor, but this is measured in years and is of financial rather than strategic interest. Patrols of two months at sea totally submerged are already made as a matter of routine and this can undoubtedly be exceeded substantially.

A unique advantage of the nuclear submarine is that it can dive under the polar ice cap and so can operate where ships cannot go at all. The U.S.S. *Nautilus* successfully made the voyage from Hawaii to Great Britain via the Pole in 1958. The route over the Pole is, in fact, the shortest way from Europe to the Pacific. A nuclear submarine could spend a month actually on patrol off Singapore from the United Kingdom through the Arctic without exceeding two months at sea. The north polar regions are directly between Russia and North America and this area is bound to be of some strategic interest in the future. Against this, the nuclear submarine is somewhat limited in shallow water, where it cannot develop its full performance. So there are large areas of sea which are too shallow for it to dive at all and others where it will not be able to go very fast. Nevertheless, it is still a true submarine in shallow water and is far better than an old-fashioned conventional boat would be in similar circumstances. In general, however, nuclear submarines may be expected to operate in waters of over a hundred fathoms.

Although at intervals nuclear power plants require considerable refitting in a dockyard, they have shown themselves to be very reliable for long periods and less dependent on depot ships than diesel electric machinery. In war, therefore, nuclear submarines can be expected to spend a greater proportion of their time at sea, using relief crews if necessary. Nuclear submarines are undoubtedly expensive to build but, by spending a greater proportion of their life at sea, by taking less time on passage and proving very much more effective when on patrol, they represent far better value for money.

The British experiments with hydrogen peroxide were expensive but were eventually successful. The *Explorer* was not accepted for service until after the nuclear-propelled *Nautilus* in 1956; she was faster and made over 25 knots but did not hold this lead for long and the whole project was completely overtaken by nuclear power. In retrospect it seems odd that so much effort was spent when nuclear power, in which the British led the world, was just round the corner. The explanation appears to be that fissionable material was not expected to be available after the claims of nuclear weapons had been met. With the appointment of Admiral Mountbatten as First Sea Lord in 1955, the policy was changed, and the first British nuclear submarine, the *Dreadnought*, was authorized. In 1959, in order to bring her into service earlier, a complete American propulsion plant was purchased. *Dreadnought* was built primarily to help develop counter measures to the nuclear submarine and was, like the *Nautilus*, armed only with torpedoes. She was of similar hull form to the *Skipjack* and embodied new equipment for attacking other submarines, so also continuing the British post-war role of the submarine unchanged. It had not, however, escaped the notice of the British that the submarine now had the speed and endurance to escort a fleet or convoy.

The British continued to build the conventional Porpoise type, of which an increasing proportion of their submarine strength was composed. Total numbers had fallen to forty-three by 1960, but all were then modernized and capable of anti-submarine duties.

The Russians continued to expand their conventional submarine fleet and by the late nineteen-fifties its strength had risen to 475 vessels. The majority of the new boats were between 1,000 and 2,000 tons and so of medium or long range and they built no more of the very small defensive types. Russian submarines were often sighted making long voyages across the oceans of the world and it was obvious that they intended to implement a more offensive strategy than in the past. By 1958 they had built a nuclear-propelled ice-breaker and it could only be a matter of time before they, too, possessed nuclear submarines.

Hardly had the trials of the *Nautilus* been completed than the United States conceived a role for submarines which was more important than any they had ever had before. The explosion of a nuclear weapon by Soviet Russia in 1953 altered the whole strategic situation. From the west holding a position of absolute power it became one in which mutual extermination became a possibility. The antagonists were leading up to a position in which they would be able to destroy each other completely with inter-continental ballistic missiles against which there was no known defence. If attacked, it would be essential to retaliate in a matter of minutes to prevent one's own missiles from being destroyed on the ground. Apart from the appalling danger of a mistake, the situation made a nuclear war quite likely, as the enemy might really believe that he could win by a so-called 'pre-emptive' attack. It became essential to find a 'second-strike' weapon that would be certain to survive the first attack and still be available to retaliate.

If missiles could be launched from nuclear submarines at sea, it would provide an excellent second-strike delivery system. It would be well-nigh impossible to find them before they fired and they could be kept on station continuously. A submarine-launched missile would be smaller and cheaper than the inter-continental ballistic missile, as it could be carried close to the target. It would not draw attack on to its own homeland and would be strategic-ally mobile. Furthermore it would pose a harder problem for any anti-missile system that might be developed, because of its short time of flight and uncertain starting point. Retaliation with it would be certain and inevitable and it would be difficult to think of any possible counter measure, except, as an American scientist once suggested, draining the sea. There were two other possible second-strike systems: a mobile land-based inter-continental missile and an air-launched version. The United States decided to adopt a policy of diversification of their deterrent forces which entailed the production of all three systems.

The *Polaris* system, as the missile fired from a submarine was called, was developed in the astonishingly short period of five years, and the first three submarines were laid down early in 1958. The *George Washington*, the prototype, launched a missile from submerged in July 1960 and thereafter a gradually increasing force of Polaris submarines began to patrol continuously in peacetime.

The Polaris submarines carry sixteen missiles each and therefore have the power to destroy about a dozen cities. The missiles now have a range of 1,500 miles and this will eventually be increased to 2,500 miles, which is sufficient to reach anywhere within the Soviet Union from the sea. The submarines have double crews and spend two months at sea, totally submerged all the time, followed by a month in harbour. Three operational Polaris submarines should, therefore, be able to keep two at sea continuously, but more than three would be needed to allow for dockyard refits and unexpected defects.

The Polaris system was an entirely new role not only for the submarine but also for naval forces in general. Although it is the technical successor to the Regulus missile-firing submarine, its strategic purpose is much more profound. It is to be instantly ready in peacetime to launch missiles in retaliation for a nuclear attack, with the aim of preventing, by its presence and readiness, such a catastrophe from ever occurring. If Polaris ever has to be used, therefore, it has failed.

In 1958, the Russians began to convert some of their larger conventional submarines to carry ballistic missiles. The first boats had only two missiles and these were probably an adaptation of an existing land-based weapon with a range of under 400 miles : moreover they probably had to surface to launch them. After making a number of these conversions, they laid down a new type of submarine, still conventionally propelled, but carrying three missiles. Their intention was almost certainly to bombard the shore in the same way as Polaris, but their aim was not so much to diversify their means of delivery as to make up for the fact that their inter-continental ballistic missiles could not, at that time, reach the United States. The Russians do not seem to keep a force of ballistic missile submarines at sea continuously, and so they cannot intend them to act as a deterrent. Their purpose seemed initially, therefore, to be simply to extend the range of their nuclear weapons.

To the British it was apparent that, even if they could protect the sites of their new 'Blue Streak' inter-continental missiles by placing them underground, in an attack on them the near misses would practically destroy the country. It was obvious that they must, as the Americans, go for some second-strike system instead. After considerable thought they chose the airborne system called Skybolt, for which they hoped to employ the existing V bomber force. The Skybolt project, however, promised to be so expensive that it was discontinued and, as in a small country such as the United Kingdom the mobile land-based missile called Minuteman would suffer from the same disadvantage as Blue Streak, they somewhat reluctantly adopted Polaris in 1963. The submarines and nuclear warheads were to be of a British design, but the missiles were to be purchased from the U.S.A.

The British reluctance to adopt Polaris was partly because they had not the financial resources to diversify their deterrent and could afford only one system. Polaris submarines did not promise to be cheap and the British took some time studying alternatives, such as a conventional submarine or a disguised merchantman. The disguised merchantman was, however, a fundamentally unsound way to mount the deterrent, as the ships would inevitably become known and could be followed and sunk one by one: the only way this process could be halted would be to start a nuclear war and this would be the negation of a deterrent policy. A conventional submarine would scarcely have been cheaper, as many more would be required to keep the same number of missiles at sea. Intensive anti-submarine operations might, in any case, find them, with the same consequences as for the disguised merchantmen.

In 1963, shortly after they had exploded their first atomic weapon, the French announced their intention to provide an independent nuclear *'force de frappe'*. It was to consist of between three and five Polaris-type submarines. The French design of nuclear submarine has not yet, however, been fully developed but the first has been laid down and experiments with missiles are being made in a conventional boat.

The Soviet Union developed nuclear-propelled submarines during the early nineteen-sixties and soon produced a ballistic missile version. At the same time they continued to build conventional types and developed what was clearly a tactical missile to be used at sea against ships in place of the torpedo. This development was in line with the general Soviet policy of re-arming their fleet with missiles. These weapons are carried by both nuclear and conventionally propelled boats but it is not known whether they have nuclear warheads, whether they are ballistic or of the cruise type (see Note 29) and whether they have to surface to launch them. Although therefore these Russian tactical missiles may not, at first, prove to be immune from counter measures, they are bound to represent a great increase in the effectiveness of the submarine especially when combined with nuclear power.

Thirty navies of the world now have some 760 submarines between them : three-quarters of these, however, belong to the U.S.A., the U.S.S.R. and Great Britain. Of all these underwater fleets, that of the United States is incomparably the most powerful. With forty-one Polaris submarines built and completing, they will be able to keep some 320 missiles instantly ready at sea with the power to destroy every city of over 100,000 inhabitants in Russia twice over. The United States has another twenty nuclear 'attack' submarines with nineteen more building and 134 conventionals of various types, only about forty of which are, however, modern operational boats. Such a force would be capable of interdicting surface operations close to the Russian coast and substantially decreasing the effectiveness of the Russian submarine fleet.

Russia, with 425 submarines, has numerically by far the largest underwater fleet. Although sixty-five of these are armed with strategic ballistic missiles, the total number they can carry is just over 200, all of which are of the short-range type, and less than half are in nuclear submarines. Allowing for a proportion of these boats being under repair at the critical time and for casualties among the conventional boats, this still gives them the power to destroy all the major cities of the NATO alliance in Europe or the coastal areas of the United States far enough inland to include well over half the population. It is, indeed, fortunate for the West that their deterrent policy gives them a complete defence against this menace. Of the remaining Russian submarine fleet, twelve are nuclear-propelled; seventy are large boats of very long endurance : 250 are of medium size and only twenty-five are now of the small coastal type. Of these probably less than a quarter have the new tactical missile as yet, but this powerful force forms the principal oceanic strength of the Russian Navy and could be used against commerce or to defend the homeland against the approach of carrier or amphibious forces with an excellent chance to succeed.

Great Britain has the third largest submarine fleet (see Note 30) and expects to replace her strategic bombers with a Polaris force of four submarines in 1970. Its deterrent value will be the threat of destruction of about a quarter of the large cities of the U.S.S.R. Of her remaining force of about forty submarines, only three are, as yet, nuclear-propelled. Over half of the conventionals are, however, of post-war construction and the rest have been modernized so that they constitute an important element of her anti-submarine forces.

France expects to have her Polaris force operational by 1972 with about the same deterrent value as the British. Communist China, as well as having the fourth largest number of submarines, has two conventionally propelled ballistic missile boats of Russian design capable of launching a total of six missiles. Of the remaining underwater fleets, those of Germany and Sweden are numerically next in size but are both composed of small submarines for use in the Baltic. The Netherlands, although they have at present only five conventional boats, have announced their intention of building a nuclear submarine. The other twenty underwater fleets are small and many are composed of obsolete submarines.

The influence of the submarine as an instrument of sea power is now greater than ever before. In the twenty years following the Second World War, it has developed at a pace which has left the counter measures far behind. Anti-submarine measures have certainly not stood still and may have kept pace with the conventionals of the type XXI variety. This has, however, only been done by resorting to great complexity and expense and the high quality of equipment which is essential would make it difficult to produce anti-submarine forces in sufficient quantity to be effective even against modern conventionals. Against nuclear submarines the latest anti-submarine measures have little hope at all. Above all the strategic missile-firing submarines, apart from being the most powerful warships the world has ever known, have a function which is more important than a navy has ever had before, and have broadened the limits of sea power itself.

XV

The Submarine and the Future

The prediction of the nature of war, and the part that various weapons or ships will play in it, has always been a risky business. Many have tried, but the majority have been proved wrong in the event. Even the highly-qualified naval and scientific staffs of the Defence Ministries, who spend all their time studying the problem and who have available accurate and up-to-date information, are often wrong too. The complete failure of all but a few, notably Sir Arthur Conan Doyle, to predict the German U-boat campaign against commerce before the First World War is an outstanding example; the belief, held in the Royal Navy before the Second World War, that the Asdic was the answer to the submarine and that U-boats were no longer an important factor in naval warfare, is another.

The study of the past gives only a part of the guide to what will happen in the future. It is unlikely to give direct lessons which can be followed in this swiftly moving scientific age. If its study leads to the fighting of the last war over again, it will undoubtedly mislead us. Nevertheless a study of history is important; it will certainly show how difficult it is to predict the nature of war but will, if it is properly interpreted, contribute a great deal.

A study of the changes in science and technology and of modern weapons and what they hope to achieve is obviously necessary, but, however important we may think science is, a study of it in isolation will not tell us what is going to happen or even the nature of a future conflict. War, after all, is not a science any more than it is an art. It is a conflict and is fought by men whose reactions, politics and aims influence matters fundamentally. We cannot assume even that the enemy's reactions to any particular situation will be the same as our own or, because something is possible, that it will be put into practice by either side. The course and nature of a war will be greatly influenced by the efficiency that weapons achieve, not in theory but in practice, and the numbers with which various countries think fit to supply themselves.

The professionals rely to a great extent on war games, on trials and on live exercises with ships and aircraft. Here the amateur is at a great disadvantage as the results of such activities are not available to him. The interpretation of the results is in any case an expert business and needs to be analysed with great care, using the modern techniques of operational research. Nevertheless, to think that these activities can give the full answer, either, is illusory. To believe that trials and exercises are like war is self-deception. The lack of real danger, the difficulty of imposing casualties, the need for peacetime safety restrictions, all distort the results. Furthermore the exercises seldom last long enough and are too concentrated to give a true picture of war.

The lessons of the past and how the submarine was used form nine-tenths of this book but cannot give more than some guidance for the future. Yet a discussion of the effect of possible advances in the submarine on naval warfare follows naturally from a study of the tactics and policies of the past. It can be said with confidence that naval warfare in the future will be different and so a wide discussion of the subject is bound to contribute something.

In any study of the future of the submarine in war, it is essential to know whether any new detecting device is likely to become available. The whole key to the operation of the submarine is still that it should remain invisible and undetected. With the rapid advance of science, it is often believed that some new detection system is only a matter of time. It would be rash to assert that there will never be a solution but, in spite of an immense expenditure on research in the last twenty years, acoustic methods such as sonar and Asdics are still the only ones that promise any success. But these, in spite of substantial improvement, cannot hope to be revolutionary. Indeed the submarine has almost certainly developed faster than they have and the sonar of today is probably of less use against a nuclear submarine than the early Asdics were against the U-boats in 1939.

There is nothing in sight, therefore, at present to challenge the Polaris submarine which will almost certainly be able to remain invisible, especially as it does not have to reveal its position at any time before it launches its missiles. Polaris seems likely to have a considerable life before it. Sea power based on the combination of nuclear power with nuclear weapons in a submarine should, by a policy of deterrence, provide a complete defence against nuclear attack and should remain a safeguard against an all-out nuclear war for many years to come. It will exert an influence which has no geographical boundaries and will undoubtedly be paramount in the military sphere.

It is, of course, just possible that an all-out nuclear war might start by miscalculation or mistake. If it did, then all would probably be over before sea power, with its blockades and campaigns of attrition, could take effect. Nuclear submarines would, however, probably be the only important warships to survive the holocaust. If for some reason, which is at present difficult to visualize, the struggle continued, then, with their unlimited endurance and independence of bases, they would be more likely to be of use than any other kind of warship.

The present situation in which there is nuclear stalemate and so great stability with what is believed to be little chance of a major war, is a very happy one. If it could be certain that this will persist in the future, Polaris would be all that is necessary to preserve the peace and few other naval forces, except for fighting minor wars, would be required. But history here sounds a warning; it is very difficult to predict the future nature of war and other possibilities must be considered.

There are many who think that the consequences of an all-out nuclear attack are so suicidal that it would never be used, except to retaliate on an enemy who had already launched such an attack. As the order to bomb Moscow cannot be given without the order to bomb Washington or vice versa, there is much sense in this view. If this is accepted, then the all-out nuclear attack cannot be used to stave off defeat in a conventional campaign, which may have started as a limited war. Therefore, if a country such as Great Britain loses command of the sea in such a situation, she cannot regain it by unleashing Polaris on the enemy. This would be like saying: 'If you continue to starve me, I will commit suicide'.

The only valid defence is to regain command of the sea in the conventional manner and herein lies the justification for other instruments of sea power. Whether anyone believes that this theory is likely or not, it must surely be accepted that it is an alternative possibility to the more usual view of the future which it would be foolhardy to neglect. The deterrent may, therefore, only deter all-out nuclear war and not an all-out conventional maritime attack. If this is so, then the danger of defeat by loss of command of the sea is greater than in the past, and this fact is not altered because the more rapid fate of atomization is always there. In this case a conventional war at sea, thought by many to be out of the question, could certainly happen and should at least be studied.

In a new Battle of the Atlantic in which the enemy had nuclear submarines, there can be little doubt that the anti-submarine measures would have the greatest difficulty in competing, and the submarines would be able to do practically as they pleased. They would, as in the past, have to be able to find the convoys and have the capacity to sink enough shipping to be decisive. They would probably be able to operate in the focal areas in packs, and, with their improved hydrophones and high submerged speed, should be able to concentrate against many more convoys than the German U-boats in 1943. They would certainly be able to do so if they had the co-operation of high-flying jet aircraft with powerful radar sets, which, with flight refuelling, could operate over the whole Atlantic.

Nuclear submarines are, however, still armed only with some twenty torpedoes and their effectiveness would depend on what kind of torpedoes these were. Torpedoes of greater speed and range with homing, pattern-running and guidance systems, and so with a much greater chance of hitting, are becoming available. With such weapons a nuclear submarine should be able to sink something like fifteen ships a month, or three times that which was sunk by the U-boats of the last war in their hey-day. As they could return to base and reload far more quickly, a force of thirty of them could sink some fifty million tons of shipping a year. If counter measures proved better than estimated and they sank only a third of this tonnage, it would still be greater than the American shipbuilding effort at its height in the last war. If these figures mean anything, then the nuclear submarine using only the torpedo is surely a warship of such power and mobility that it can deny the sea to commerce. Its effect would be as decisive as a battlefleet exercising command of the sea in the past, and it would, with little doubt, be the dominating maritime weapon.

British nuclear submarines are generally referred to as 'hunter-killers' for use against other submarines and, although the subject of such operations is rightly shrouded in mystery, it can be assumed that they have a considerable capability for attacking and destroying their own kind. Indeed, efficiency in this role has been given as a justification for building this type. It may well be that the nuclear submarine, like the battleship of the past, will prove to be the only answer to its own kind. (See Note 30.)

In a conventional maritime conflict, its character would change radically if tactical nuclear weapons came to be used at sea. Many hold that their use would quickly and inevitably escalate into all-out nuclear war. It would again be a mistake to be dogmatic: escalation might result, but on the other hand it probably would not. Is it really possible that one side would say: 'You have used a nuclear depth charge, so I will unleash unlimited nuclear war on you' and in parenthesis: 'On me as well'? Escalation is very unlikely to start by mistake, as nuclear weapons used at sea could hardly be taken as the start of an all-out nuclear attack. Even if one side was afraid of escalation and decided not to use nuclear weapons at sea, they would be caught at a fatal disadvantage if they were not prepared and the other side resorted to them. Naval forces of the future will therefore always have to be in an anti-nuclear posture and be ready with nuclear weapons, whether they intend to use them at the outset or not. Therefore, in a conventional war at sea in the future, the use of tactical nuclear weapons must be taken as a distinct possibility.

Russian submarines are known to be armed already with tactical missiles which may have nuclear heads. It is only a matter of time before these are of the ballistic type, which have a very short time of flight and are unlikely to be countered and certainly cannot be avoided. They can already be fired from a greater range than the torpedo and this can still further be extended, with the assistance of satellites or aircraft, to find the target. It will then be possible to fire from such a range that prior detection of the submarine is very unlikely, and the first that a task force or convoy will know of an attack is the explosion of the nuclear weapon. The combination of the reconnaissance satellite, the immense mobility of the nuclear submarine and the surprise and lethality of the tactical ballistic missile with a nuclear head make the future of any task force or convoy in this kind of warfare seem bleak.

Convoys and task forces can, of course, use a more dispersed formation to prevent too many ships from being sunk by one explosion. The use of a number of thermo-nuclear weapons exploded deep in the ocean will, however, sink ships over such a wide area that it is likely to destroy or cripple most of them. If convoys are not used, then the ships can be picked off one by one by torpedo and the result is likely to be the same.

The power of aircraft over the submersible in the past has been progressively reduced as it developed into the 'true' submarine. It is now only a matter of time before surface-to-air guided weapons are adapted for submarines and they acquire the power to shoot aircraft down. The slow anti-submarine aircraft and the helicopter would be very vulnerable to a simple short-range missile launched from a submerged submarine. Apart from Doenitz's short-lived arming of U-boats with anti-aircraft guns, submarines have not in the past been able to do more than evade aircraft and play a passive part. In the future, far from the submarine living in fear of aircraft, it is likely to be the other way round, and aircraft flying over the sea will never be sure that a guided weapon is not about to be launched at them from an undetected submarine.

Nuclear depth charges could, of course, be used against submarines and would be lethal at a considerable distance. The problem of detection of the nuclear submarine is, however, the crux of the matter. If it cannot be found, it cannot be attacked. Submarines which allowed themselves to be detected could indeed be rapidly disposed of, but there is no doubt that the balance of the advantage, if tactical nuclear weapons were used at sea, would rest with the submarine, and the survival of the surface warship cannot but be in question. Whether the conventional war at sea in which tactical nuclear missiles are used is considered possible or not, if it did happen the nuclear submarine is likely to dominate it. Not only would it be able to break up the convoy system, so its effectiveness against commerce would be increased, but it would have the power to destroy any task force afloat.

Although the potency of the submarine would be reduced if tactical nuclear weapons were not used, when armed with missiles even without nuclear warheads it would still probably be the master of the aircraft and probably also of the surface ship. It would operate with confidence in the knowledge that, if tactical nuclear weapons came to be used, its power would be increased. There will clearly be the possibility of more limited conflicts when nuclear weapons are not even threatened, and where ships will be able to operate and perform many tasks for which a submarine is unsuited. But even then, if the command of the sea itself is in question, the nuclear submarine would be the warship which would dominate the situation.

These predictions are, of course, opinions which are fallible and which history shows are often wrong. A study of the past, however, helps to formulate them and to see what the effect of new developments is likely to be. The historical study of the turning-point of naval warfare and the reasons why the galley was replaced by the galleon, the ship of the line by the steam ironclad and the battleship by carrier-borne aircraft is very relevant. It is difficult to escape the conclusion that another such turning-point has been reached.

The aircraft carrier will be necessary for some years to come to fill the gap until the nuclear submarine has developed from what the United States call the 'Attack' type, and the British the 'Hunter-killer', into the missile-carrying capital ship of the future. Thereafter the carrier may have a role as an auxiliary in limited wars for supporting the army, provided there is no threat of nuclear weapons, but will not be able to command even the surface of the sea as it did in the Second World War.

During the first twenty years of its existence the submarine developed from being an insignificant harbour defence vessel into a potentially decisive weapon of sea power when used against commerce. In the last twenty years it has gone far towards becoming the capital ship capable of commanding the sea and is capable of defending its homeland against nuclear attack by a policy of deterrence. In the future it is likely to be not only the dominating weapon of sea power but the means by which sea power itself will exercise a far greater influence than in the past.

Bibliography

Aspinall-Oglander, Brig.-Gen. C. F. *Military Operations—Gallipoli,* vols. 1 and 2. London : Heinemann 1929-32.

Bacon, Admiral Sir Reginald. *From 1900 Onwards.* London : H.M. Stationery Office and Longmans, Green 1935.

Belot, Raymond de. *The Struggle for the Mediterranean 1939-45.* Trans. by James A. Field, Jr. Princeton : Princeton University Press 1951.

Blackburn, J. A. and Watkins, Kenneth, *The British Submarine in Being.* London : John Hogg 1928.

Bragadin, Marc Antonio. *The Italian Navy in World War II.* Trans. by Gale Hoffman. Annapolis : United States Naval Institute 1957.

Brassey's Naval Annual. 1888-1949. London : William Clowes.

Brassey's Annual. 1950-65. London : William Clowes.

Burgoyne, Alan H. *Submarine Navigation,* vols. 1 and 2. London : Grant Richards 1903.

Busch, Harald. *U-Boats at War.* Trans. by L. R. P. Wilson. London : Putnam 1955.

Churchill, Winston S. *The World Crisis, 1911-19.* 6 vols. London : Thornton Butterworth 1923-31.

Churchill, Winston S. *The Second World War,* vols. 1-6. London : Cassell 1948-54.

Ciano's Diary. Ed. by Malcolm Muggeridge. London : Heinemann 1947.

Corbett, Sir Julian S. *Naval Operations,* vols. 1-3. London : Longmans, Green 1920-23.

Creswell, John. *Sea Warfare 1939-45.* Longmans 1950.

Derry, T. K. *The Campaign in Norway.* London : H.M. Stationery Office 1952.

Doenitz, Admiral. *Memoirs.* Trans. by R. H. Stevens. London : Weidenfeld and Nicolson 1959.

Edwards, Kenneth. *We Dive at Dawn.* London 1939.

Encyclopaedia Britannica. 23 vols. London : William Benton 1963.

'Etienne'. *The Diary of a U-Boat Commander.* London : Hutchinson 1920.

Fayle, C. Ernest. *Seaborne Trade,* vols. 1-3. London : John Murray 1923.

Field, Colonel Cyril. *The Story of the Submarine.* London : Sampson, Low 1908.

Fisher, Admiral of the Fleet Lord. *Memoirs* and *Records*. London : Hodder and Stoughton 1919.

Fyfe, Herbert C. *Submarine Warfare*. London : Grant Richards 1902.

Gibson, R. H. and Prendergast, Maurice. *The German Submarine War 1914-1918*. London : Constable 1931.

Grenfell, Russell. *Main Fleet to Singapore*. London : Faber 1951.

Hashimoto, Mochitsura. *Sunk, the Story of the Japanese Submarine Fleet 1942-45*. Trans. by E. J. M. Cole Grave. London : Cassell 1954.

Jane's Fighting Ships. 1900-1966. Sampson Low, Marston.

Jellicoe, Admiral of the Fleet Viscount. *The Crisis of the Naval War*. London : Cassell 1920.

Jellicoe, Admiral of the Fleet the Earl. *The Submarine Peril*. London : Cassell 1934.

Jones, H. A. *The War in the Air*, vols. 1-6. Oxford : The Clarendon Press 1928-37.

Kemp, Lieut.-Com. P. K. *H.M. Submarines*. London : Herbert Jenkins 1952.

Kemp, Lieut.-Com. P. K. *The Papers of Admiral Sir John Fisher*, vol. 2. Navy Records Society vol. 106. London 1964.

Keyes, Admiral of the Fleet Sir Roger. *Naval Memoirs*, vols. 1 and 2. London : Thornton Butterworth 1934-5.

Lipscomb, Commander F. W. *The British Submarine*. London : Adam and Charles Black 1954.

Lockwood, Charles A. *Sink 'Em All*. New York : E. P. Dutton 1951.

Macintyre, Donald. *The Battle of the Atlantic*. London : B. T. Batsford 1961.

Mahan, Captain A. T. *The Influence of Sea Power upon History*. London : Sampson Low, Marston, Searle and Rivington.

Ministry of Information. *His Majesty's Submarines*. London : H.M. Stationery Office 1945.

Morison, Samuel E. *History of the United States Naval Operations in World War II*. 15 vols. London : Oxford University Press 1948-62.

Newbolt, Henry. *Submarine and Anti-submarine*. London : Longmans, Green 1918.

Newbolt, Henry. *Naval Operations*, vols. 4 and 5. London : Longmans, Green 1928-31.

Olson, Mancur, Jr. *The Economics of the Wartime Shortage: A History of British Food Supplies in the Napoleonic Wars and in World Wars I and II*. North Carolina : Duke University Press.

Playfair, Major-General I. S. O. *The Mediterranean and Middle East*, vols 1-3. London : H.M. Stationery Office 1954-60.

Raeder, Grand Admiral. *Struggle for the Sea*. Trans. by Edward Fitzgerald. London : William Kimber 1959.

Raleigh, Walter. *The War in the Air*, vol. 1. Oxford : The Clarendon Press 1922.

Roscoe, Theodore. *United States Submarine Operations in World War II*. Annapolis : U.S. Naval Institute 1949.

Roskill, Captain S. W. *The War at Sea 1939-45*. 3 vols. London : H.M. Stationery Office 1954-61.

Sanders, Liman von. *Five Years in Turkey*. Annapolis : U.S. Naval Institute 1927.

Scheer, Admiral. *Germany's High Seas Fleet in the World War*. London : Cassell 1920.

Sims, Rear Admiral William S. and Hendrick, B. J. *The Victory at Sea*. Murray 1920.

Sueter, Commander Murray F. *The Evolution of the Submarine Boat, Mine and Torpedo*. Portsmouth : J. Griffin 1907.

Thomas, Lowell. *Raiders of the Deep*. London : Heinemann 1929.

Tirpitz, Grand Admiral von. *My Memoirs*, vols. 1 and 2. Hurst and Blackett.

Wemyss, Admiral of the Fleet Lord Wester. *The Navy in the Dardanelles Campaign*. London : Hodder and Stoughton.

Woodburn Kirby, Major-General S. *The War against Japan*, vols. 1-3. London : H.M. Stationery Office 1957-61.

Notes

1.   Known collectively as 'Davids'.

2.   This, in fact, was Lamm's system. The latent heat of the steam was conserved by the use of a large hot water reservoir.

3.   The strategy of the *guerre de course* was not, of course, new. It had been used since the earliest times. For those who have not heard the term before, it is a strategy of attacking the enemy's trade directly by using cruisers, privateers or, in modern times, submarines without gaining command of the sea by defeating or neutralizing the enemy fleet.

4.   One of these attacks was not, somewhat unfairly, allowed by the umpire.

5.   *Nautilus,* although of pre-war design, was not completed until 1917, and was by then overtaken by the later fleet submarines of the K class.

6.   The 'exchange rate' is a useful 'barometer' to show how a campaign against commerce is progressing. It is, for a given period, the number of merchant ships sunk divided by the number of raiders (surface or submarine) destroyed. It ranges from a value of over a hundred, in which case the campaign is doing very well indeed, to under one, when a campaign has generally been defeated. A figure of ten is tough going and twenty-five satisfactory for the corsairs.

7.   The political restrictions in the various phases that follow are complicated, as are the masses of figures which are essential if an analysis of a submarine campaign against shipping is to be more than cursory. It will be necessary for the reader to consult the diagrams and graphs frequently. These are referred to when first needed, but, to avoid overcomplicating the text, not every time they should be consulted.

8.   *Nautilus* and *Swordfish.*

9.   The number of ships sunk per month seems to vary considerably between sources. This is because they emanate sometimes from Allied and sometimes from German records. They may include British, Allied or neutral losses or any combination of them. Furthermore they sometimes only list ships of over 1,000 or 500 tons. In this book the figures quoted are those that best illustrate the point being made, but are generally the gross totals.

10.   This diagram has been plotted from the official list of losses published by H.M. Government. The plan will be found to differ from that published in the official history (*Naval Operations—Newbolt*) the source of which is not known.

11.   The 'rate of sinking' is the second 'barometer' which shows the progress or otherwise of a campaign of attrition against commerce. It is the number of ships sunk in a month divided by the average number of submarines actually on patrol in their operational areas at any one time. It does not, of course, depend only on the efficiency of the submarines, but on the volume of trade available to be attacked. In general, however, a figure of five is extremely good, whilst a figure of under one is poor.

12.   The 3,000 voyages took place in May, June and July, when the convoy system had just begun. The 2,000 casualties were the total for the first six months of the unrestricted campaign from February to July 1917.

13.   Tonnages quoted are the total of British, Allied and neutral ships sunk.

14.   The author is well aware of the high authorities who have denied that convoy is a defensive measure. They include Admirals Sims and Jellicoe and the official naval historian of the Second World War. Nevertheless, if words mean anything, convoy must surely be considered a defensive strategy. The assertion to the contrary stems from a desire to reconcile the undoubted success of convoy with the Principles of War. Such an assertion, however, creates a dogma which is liable to confuse rather than clarify the study of war. The fact that convoy is defensive, however, does not mean that it is necessarily less desirable than an offensive strategy as might be assumed from the Principles of War : indeed the lessons of the two world wars show that against the U-boats the contrary was the case. This was because, in the particular circumstances, a defensive strategy could be made effective and an offensive one could not.

15.   During the period 1914-20, the American submarine force was nearly trebled. Most of the new boats were of the patrol type, of which they had a further thirty-eight building. In the same period the French underwater fleet's strength slightly declined although the average size increased and half of their boats were now ocean-going. The Japanese expanded from fifteen small coastal submarines to a force of twenty-six, some of which were large. The Italian submarine force was still composed of coastal boats.

16.   This development is fully covered in Chapter XIII.

268

17.   These were not suicide weapons, but slow torpedoes with two divers sitting astride and guiding them to the target. The explosive head would then be fixed to the target's bottom : a time fuse set and the crew would escape on the torpedo. They were called 'Chariots' by the British.

18.   Surface Motor Torpedo Boats.

19.   *Cairo* was, in fact, finally despatched by British forces after being torpedoed by *Axum*.

20.   These are nominal tonnages by which the types were originally known. The actual tonnages were about half as much again.

21.   HX and SC convoys were homeward-bound convoys from Halifax, Nova Scotia, to the United Kingdom. SC were slower than HX.

22.   OB convoys were outward-bound from Liverpool by the north-western approaches across the Atlantic.

23.   HG convoys were homeward-bound from Gibraltar to the United Kingdom.

24.   According to German accounts.

25.   ON convoys were outward-bound from the United Kingdom to Halifax. ONS convoys were the same but slower. These convoys had replaced the former OB convoys.

26.   Sonar is the American equivalent to the British Asdic.

27.   In fact oil tankers were also above destroyers.

28.   The actual sinkings are shown in the following table :—

Type of Ship Sunk	Casualties caused by			
	Submarines	Surface Ships	Aircraft	Other Causes
Aircraft Carriers	7	$\frac{1}{4}$	$4\frac{3}{4}$	–
Battleships	1	2	1	–
Cruisers	$10\frac{1}{2}$	2	$8\frac{1}{2}$	–
Destroyers	$29\frac{1}{2}$	$8\frac{1}{2}$	23	2

29.   Missiles which fly like an aircraft such as the German V1

30.   Submarines in the Royal Navy have recently been categorized according to their military characteristics as follows :—
  (a) Fleet Ballistic Missile Submarines (the four Polaris submarines of the Resolution class).
  (b) Fleet Submarines (the nuclear-propelled submarines *Dreadnought*, *Valiant* and *Warspite*).
  (c) Patrol submarines (all the conventionally propelled submarines of the Oberon, Porpoise and converted T and A classes).

INDEX

A class submarines, British 19, 22, 242
Abolition policy for submarines, British 110, 115, 116, 122, 161
Aboukir, H.M.S. sunk 27-28
Abruzzi, Italian cruiser, damaged 144
Admiralty, British 9, 17, 18, 40, 41, 64, 67, 69, 74, 75, 76, 83, 165, 171, 233, 236
Admiralty, U-boat tracking room 172-3, **235**
Adriatic, U-boats built for 31, 38; U-boat bases 55; evacuation of 100, 101
AE.2, Australian submarine 36, 37
Afrika Korps, German 140, 145
Agano, Japanese cruiser 201
Ahead thrown weapons 235, 237
Aigrette, French submersible 17
Aircraft in anti-submarine operations 83, 169, 173-4, 235, 259; British submarines sunk by 84
Aircraft carriers 262
Air reconnaissance for submarines 141-2
Airships in anti-submarine operations 53
Air striking forces in the Mediterranean 141, 143, 146, 149, 152
Akitsuki, Japanese destroyer 203
Alagi, Italian submarine 150
Albacore, U.S. submarine 198, 202; U.S. Experimental submarine 246
Alexander the Great 1
Alexandria, British submarines based at 139, 146, 147
Algiers, British submarines based at 152-3, 155
Alten Fjord, attack on 130
American submarine policy, early 5, 8, 12, 16, 21; between the wars 110, 113-4, 123; recent 243-4, 245-6
American submarines, construction in World War II 193, 212, 214, 217. Development between the wars 113-4, 120. Losses in World War II 202, 212, 216, 220. Operations in World War II, Aleutians 198, 199, 211; against Japanese submarines 205-6; Japanese waters 210; North African landings 152; Pacific 191-227, 237—effect of 194-5, 196, 200, 209; South East Asia 194, 209, 210; Solomons 198, 200, 211. Strength, in 1900 15; between the wars 116, 123; in World War II, Pacific 192, 211, 214, 217, 219, 220, 223, Atlantic 193; after World War II 243, 246, 253. Successes in the Pacific in World War II 198, 199, 200, 204, 207-8, 211, 214-5, 217-221; comparison with other forces 224; comparison with German U-boats 224-5. Tactics 214
America, United States of, in World War I, army 87, 93, 96, 101-2, 106; British submarines built in 31; declares war 89; effect of entry into war 105-6; loss of citizens in *Lusitania* 49; opposition to German U-boat campaign 54, 56, 58, 66, 86-7. Neutrality operations in World War II 175
Anglo-German Naval Agreement 118, 121
Anti-submarine barriers 47, 53, 66
Anti-submarine forces, British, in Battle of the Atlantic 165, 171, 173, 180, 182
Anti-submarine measures, against U-boats in World War I 30, 46, 47, 48, 53, 55, 57, 59, 64-6, 88, 95, 99; in the Mediterranean 58. Against U-boats in World

War II 169, 174, 178, 180, 183, 188-9. Japanese in World War II 211-12, 215-6, 217, 225. Latest 254-5
Aoba, Japanese cruiser 203
Arabic, S.S., sunk 52
Archangel 35
Archerfish, U.S. submarine 204
Archimedes 1
Argonaut, U.S. submarine 117, 199, 202
Ark Royal, H.M.S. 145, 165
Armando Diaz, Italian cruiser 141
Armistice after World War I 97, 108
Asdics, British 111-2, 119-122; in World War II 125-6, 163, 166-7, 171, 189, 228, 233, 235, 237; since World War II 242, 247, 256-7. German 146. Italian 139, 146-7, 155-6. Japanese 225
Ash (Campbell and Ash), submarine inventors 9
Ashigara, Japanese cruiser 206
Atago, Japanese cruiser 203
Athenia, S.S., sinking of 164, 188
Atlantic, Battle of 130, 131, 134-5, 162-190; Prime Minister's directive on 171
Attack type submarine 262
Attendolo, Italian cruiser 149
Attrition, policy of 25, 29, 41, 82
Aube, Admiral 11
Audacity, H.M.S. 174
Australia, traffic to 63
Austrian Fleet 31
Austrian submarines 31
Auxiliary patrol 47-8, 53, 57, 88
Avenger, H.M.S. 134
Axis shipping in the Mediterranean 160-1
Axis supply lines to Africa, attacks on 138-141, 143-147, 149-151, 158-160
Axis supply line to Tunisia, attack on 152
Axum, Italian submarine 150

B class submarines, British 19, 22
B.1, British submarine 18
B.11, British submarine 35-6
Bagnolini, Italian submarine 138
Baker, submarine inventor 12
Baltic 26, 33
Banda Nere, Italian cruiser 147
Barb, U.S. submarine 204
Barham, H.M.S. 125, 145
Batfish, U.S. submarine 206
Bauer, submarine inventor 4, 7, 9
Bay of Biscay, offensive by aircraft against U-boats 183, 185, 231-2
Beachy Head, Battle of 110
Beatty, Admiral 41, 75
Becuna, U.S. submarine 220
Beilul, Italian submarine 138
Beirut, British submarines based at 149, 153
Bergall, U.S. submarine 203
Besugo, U.S. submarine 203
Bismark, German battleship 130-1
Blackfish, U.S. submarine 203
Bliss, U.S. transport 132
Blue Streak, British Missile 252
Blyth, British submarines based at 40, 67, 69, 74, 124-5
Bolzano, Italian cruiser 144, 149
Bream, U.S. submarine 203
Breslau, German cruiser 35, 37
Brest-Litovsk, Treaty of 35
Brisbane, U.S. submarines based at 200

271

British Battle Cruiser Fleet 69, 82
British Blockade of Germany in World War I 43-45, 56, 64, 87, 92
British Expeditionary Force 24, 27, 102
British Mediterranean Fleet 138
British submarines, World War I, construction 31, 83. Losses, accident 84; Baltic 35; Dardanelles 37; North Sea 33, 73, 80; by own forces 77, 84; by U-boats 77, 84. Operations, Baltic 33-35, 40; Dardanelles 35-38; North Sea 26-27, 31-33, 40-41, 67-8, 72-3, 77, 80; with the Fleet 73-5; against the U-boats 30-1, 52-3, 64, 67. 75-7, 80-1, 83, 88-9, 99; role in 1916 75-6. Strength at the armistice 108. Successes, North Sea 26, 33, 73, 80; against U-boats 30, 77, 109; Dardanelles 36, 37; Baltic 33, 44. Tactics against U-boats 76-7. Early Years, commercial building 17; building programme 19; strength in 1914 23. Between the wars, development 108-114, 116, 119, 120; strength 108, 115, 122-3. World War II, operations in Home Waters 124-5, 128; losses 124, 127, 131; strength 125; successes 125-6, 131; against U-boats 130. Operations in the Mediterranean 138-155; losses 139-140, 144, 146-7, 151, 153, 155; strength 138-40, 144, 147-9, 151-3, 155, 158, 160-1; successes 139-41, 143-4, 147, 150-1, 153, 155; tactics 155-6. Operations in the Norwegian Campaign 125-128. Operations in the Pacific 193-5, 201, 206, 223-4; losses 221; Malacca Straits 195, 201, 204, 221; successes 201, 221. Post World War II, development 241-3, 249, 252; strength 242, 249, 253-4
British Submarine Policy, before World War I 3, 4, 8-10, 17-18; between the wars 111; post World War II 242-3, 249
Bronzo, Italian submarine 150
Bruges, German U-boats based at 29, 52
Bulgaria 56
Bulges, anti-torpedo 111
Burma, sea communications of Japanese army in 201, 204
Burroughs, Admiral 150
Bushnell, submarine inventor 2, 4, 7, 9

C class submarines, British 19-20, 30, 35, 62, 76
Cairo, H.M.S. 150
Calabria, Battle of 138
Calypso, H.M.S. 138
Campbell (and Ash), submarine inventors 9
Canada, air bases in 173
Canada, British submarines built in 31
Canadian Escort Groups 173
Capelle, Admiral von 62, 104
Cape of Good Hope, traffic diverted round 63
Capponi, Italian submarine 141
Carden, Admiral 36
Cattaro, Allied submarines patrol off 31
Cavalla, U.S. submarine 202
Cavite, U.S. submarine base 194
Ceramic, British troopship 134
Cero, U.S. submarine 215
Cervera, Admiral 11
Channel, hunting flotillas in 64; submarines used against U-boats in 76
Charles Martel, French battleship 16
Charleston, submarine attack off 5; submersibles found at 7
Charr, U.S. submarine 205
Chesapeake Bay, proposed defence by submarines 16
Chester, U.S. cruiser 199
Chuyo, Japanese escort carrier 200
Civil countermeasures to the U-boat 188
Clyde, British submarine 127

Coastal Command, Royal Air Force 124, 167, 169, 172-4, 180
Coastal submarines 20, 23, 41
Cobalto, Italian submarine 149-50
Colombo, British and Netherlands submarines based at 195
Commerce raiding by ships 24
Communist China, submarines 254
Competition for submarine design, U.S.A. 12; France 13
Conan Doyle, Sir Arthur 256
Confederate States, submarine policy 5, 7
Conte Rosse, Italian troopship 140
Conventional war at sea 258-9, 260
Convoy in World War I, formation of 90; extension of 93, 97. System 90, 93-5, 104; attacks on 98-9. Between the wars, German plans to attack 121. In World War II, convoy system 163-4, 167, 171, 173, 175, 182, 185, 188-90, 228, 231, 234, 239, 261. Convoys formed on U.S. Coast 178-9; Italian, in Mediterranean 142; Japanese in Pacific 211, 215-220, 222-3, 225-6. Post World War II, possible escort by nuclear submarines 249; in the future 259-61. Individual convoys, HG Note 23; HG76, 174; HX Note 21; HX79, 168; HX112, 172; HX129, 173; HX150, 175; HX217, 180; HX229, 182; HX233, 183; HX239, 183; OB Note 22; OB293, 172; ON Note 25; ON116, 182; ON202, 233; ON206, 234; ONS Note 25; ONS5, 183; ONS18, 233; ONS20, 234; ONS165, 182; SC Note 21; SC7, 168; SC32, 174; SC94, 180; SC104, 180; SC107, 180; SC122, 182; SC130, 183; SC143, 234; SL125, 132; TM1, 182
Coronel, Battle of 28
Courageous, H.M.S. 165
Cressy, H.M.S., sunk by *U9* 27-28
Cruiser submarines 112, 114, 115
Cuttlefish, U.S. submarine 196

D class submarines, British 19, 22
D1, British submarine 19, 20
D3, British submarine 40
Dace, U.S. submarine 203
Dagabur, Italian submarine 150
Dardenelles, Campaign, submarines in 35-40, 83-4, 131
Darter, U.S. submarine 203, 220
Darwin, U.S. submarines based at 194
Decoys as an anti-submarine measure in World War I 30, 53, 65
Decoys in World War II 233
Delaware Bay, proposed defence by submarines 16
Denmark 60
Depth Charges 59, 65, 99, 112, 119
Dessie, Italian submarine 150
Detecting Devices, new 257
Deterrent Policy 258-9, 262
Deutschland, German commercial submarine 62
Deutschland, German pocket battleship 124, 165
Devonport, submarines stationed at 19
Dewey, Admiral 11
Diamante, Italian submarine 139
Doenitz, Captain, later Admiral 121, 169, 170, 174, 176, 177, 181, 183, 185, 213, 228, 229, 261
Dogger Bank 72
Dogger Bank Action 26, 31
Dover 41
Dover Straits, 24, 29, 88, 166; barrage 47, 53, 60, 64, 88, 96, 98, 100; defence by submarines 19; minefield 30; U-boats, use of 47, 52, 55, 59, 63, 101
Down the throat shot, U.S. submarine tactic 201-2, 216
Dreadnought, British nuclear submarine 249

272

274

275

276

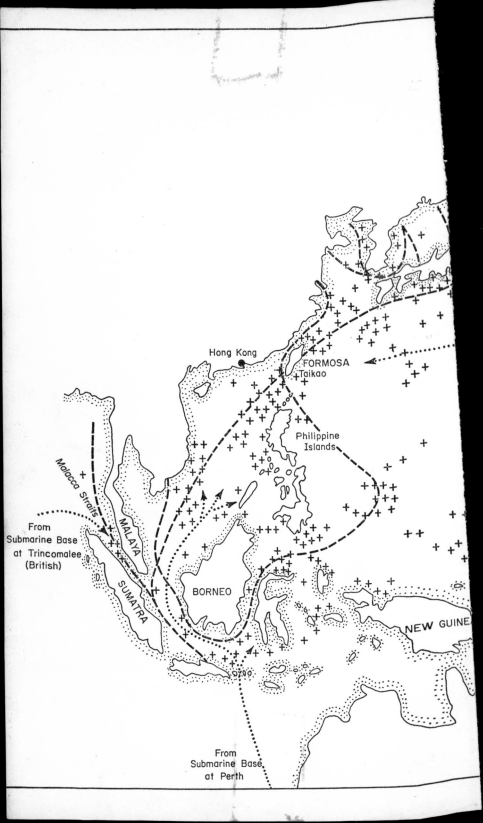